Baseball Research Journal

Volume 47, Number 2

Fall 2018

Published by the Society for American Baseball Research

THE BASEBALL RESEARCH JOURNAL, Volume 47, Number 2

Editor: Cecilia M. Tan
Design and Production: Lisa Hochstein
Cover Design: Lisa Hochstein
Fact Checker: Clifford Blau
Copyeditor: King Kaufman
Proofreader: Keith DeCandido

Front cover photo: Courtesy of Keith Allison

Published by:
Society for American Baseball Research, Inc.
Cronkite School at ASU
555 N. Central Ave. #416
Phoenix, AZ 85004

Phone: (602) 496–1460
Web: www.sabr.org
Twitter: @sabr
Facebook: Society for American Baseball Research

Contents

Note from the Editor

Why do you love baseball? Many of us caught the baseball bug from a parent or other adult when we were young. Baseball hooks our emotions when we're impressionable, engages our civic pride and maybe even patriotism, and stirs our excitement. Baseball is parent-approved fun, but it also provides lessons in disappointment. There are a million reasons to be into baseball, which is part of its strength and its appeal.

But lately I've come to realize that there's one reason some people are into baseball that doesn't make sense to me. I always thought the goal of baseball was to win the game. When people resisted the sabermetric revolution, I thought of it as differing opinions on how to win the game, some based on "traditional wisdom," some on data and observation. I hadn't realized how much of the fight was, at a deep level, about American ideals of masculinity. One example: swinging the bat was considered manly, taking a walk was not. It has taken decades for the walk to be destigmatized. It boils down to some people being more interested in baseball players performing their masculinity than performing the winning actions of the sport.

The sabermetric revolution may have won, but the attitude that performing masculinity is baseball's central function persists. I know because women in baseball continue to meet resistance. There are still people against girls in Little League, despite the fact that the court ruling allowing girls into Little League dates back to 1974. In 2014, the year of Mo'ne Davis and Emma March, *The New York Times* declared in a wishful-thinking headline that girls in the Little League World Series were "A Novelty No Longer."[1] Tell that to the huge total of 18 girls who had appeared in the tournament by that date—out of over 5,000 players.[2] There are still too many leagues where having a girl on a team is treated as the exception, not the rule.[3] That won't change while some people still believe that if a girl steps on the same field with the boys, the boys are somehow "brought down." The poor boys get told that they're no good, second class, or "sissies" if a girl pitcher strikes them out. Those are not what I consider good ol' American values!

These folks truly believe that female baseball players ruin the sport. I'm here to assure you neither the biological sexes of the players nor their performed gender roles are what make baseball great. The only thing that's ruined when women walk on the field is the notion that baseball should be the ultimate expression of American maleness.

This attitude also keeps women out of umpiring and creates a second-class status for softball—a place to shunt female ballplayers where they "belong." Sexism in sports is not new, but not every country has this particular nonsensical divide. In Australia, women and men play both softball and baseball. They're a former British colony, too. How did the United States end up like this? SABR's historians can offer a clue. Former Congressman Mark Souder's article in 2017's *The National Pastime* showed me how baseball teams were synonymous with institutions of government post-Civil War, a literal part of the fabric of the rebuilt nation.[4]

(continued)

Back in the day, the Supreme Court and the US Congress used to be all-male American institutions. Like major league baseball, they were also all-white. As we know, that didn't last. I don't think the male "ownership" of American baseball can last, either, not when Japan has a women's pro baseball league.[5] Not when independent teams like the Sonoma Stompers keep thinking outside the box.[6] Did you know that the United States has a national women's baseball team? Did you know they compete with international women's teams who are much better supported by their nations? Did you know Team USA took gold in the 2015 Pan American Games? And this past August, the US women made it to the bronze medal round of the Women's Baseball World Cup, despite barely ever practicing together. Historians take note: in the wake of recent pioneers like Ila Borders, Robin Wallace, and Justine Siegal, history is being made right now by American women like Marti Sementelli, Malaika Underwood, and Stacy Piagno, and their accomplishments deserve to be recognized and recorded.

If you want to know more, SABR has a committee devoted to women in baseball, and you don't even have to be a woman to join it. Of course, you don't have to be part of a SABR committee to research a topic. And just in case you don't know, the *Baseball Research Journal* is open to submissions all year round.

— Cecilia M. Tan
Publications Director

Notes

1. Mike Tierney, "A Novelty No Longer," *The New York Times*, August 13, 2014. Accessed October 8, 2018. https://www.nytimes.com/2014/08/14/sports/girls-in-little-league-world-series-become-less-of-a-novelty.html.
2. "The 18 Girls Who Have Made Little League Baseball World Series History," LittleLeague.org, February 4, 2015. Accessed October 8, 2018. https://www.littleleague.org/news/18-girls-made-little-league-baseball-world-series-history/.
3. Howard Megdal, "If She's Playing Baseball, She Must Be Badass," Fansided, May 31, 2018. Accessed October 8, 2018. https://fansided.com/2018/05/31/little-league-co-ed-girls-baseball/.
4. Mark Souder, "Captain John Wildey, Tammany Hall, and the Rise of Professional Baseball," *The National Pastime*: 2017. Accessible online at https://sabr.org/research/captain-john-wildey-tammany-hall-and-rise-professional-baseball.
5. Jessica Luther, "What Does Japan Know About Women's Baseball That The US Doesn't?" Huffington Post, August 25, 2018. Accessed October 8, 2018. https://www.huffingtonpost.com/entry/japanese-women-baseball_us_5b804007e4b0cd327dfc774b.
6. Chris Arnold, "2 Women Play for Sonoma Stompers Baseball Team," NPR.org, Jul 1, 2016. Accessed October 8, 2018. https://www.npr.org/sections/thetwo-way/2016/07/01/484316791/two-women-play-for-sonoma-stompers-baseball-team.

WAR and the World Series

Is WAR an Indicator of World Series Success?

Ryan Borgemenke

INTRODUCTION

The statistic Wins Above Replacement, or WAR, is an increasingly popular method of quickly determining a player's worth, and by extension, the value of an entire team. Baseball is unlike most sports in that there are a multitude of statistics to describe a player, but WAR eloquently summarizes a player in one number. Rather than looking at the batting average, OBP, and SLG to make a judgment, one can instead look at the WAR value of a player for any given season and compare the value with the ranges listed on Baseball-Reference.com, which states a value of 8+ is MVP quality, 5+ is All-Star quality, 2+ is starter quality, 0–2 is a reserve-quality player, and 0 is replacement level. Mike Trout, for example, regarded as one of the best players in the majors, has not finished a full season with a WAR value less than 7.6; he has justifiably finished first or second in the league MVP voting in all but one of the six seasons he has played.

The actual WAR calculation is fairly complex, but is based on the number of runs, and thus wins, a player contributes to his team. There is no set formula for how WAR is calculated, so values will inevitably differ between sources. The values used in for this study were taken from Baseball-Reference.com, which calculates WAR with different formulas for batters and pitchers. For batters, the WAR calculation has six parameters: batting runs, baserunning runs, runs added or lost due to grounding into double plays in double-play situations, fielding runs, positional adjustment runs, and replacement level runs (based on playing time). The park a batter plays in is accounted for in the batting runs calculation. To increase the number of runs, batters can collect more extra-base hits per plate appearance, advance more on the basepath without getting thrown out, ground into fewer double plays, increase the number of defensive runs saved, or play a position such as catcher or shortstop, where the average offensive numbers aren't as good. The replacement level of runs for batters corresponds to 20.5 over the course of 600 plate appearances, meaning if an average starter is replaced with a replacement player, there would be a 20-run difference between those players.

For pitchers, the WAR calculation is based on the number of runs allowed by a pitcher compared to the league average pitcher (adjusting for quality of opposition), parks pitched in, and quality of fielding behind the pitcher. The replacement level runs for pitchers is a multiple of 20.5 and based on the number of outs pitched. After the total runs a player accumulated is found, it is converted to wins. The number of runs per win is calculated based on the league average number of runs per game that year. The player's calculated runs total is then divided by the runs/win value, resulting in the player's WAR.

Replacement level is set at a winning percentage of 29.4, and with 30 teams, there are approximately 1,000 Wins Above Replacement combined for both leagues in a 162-game season. WAR is a cumulative, or "counting" stat, like home runs, so the total WAR available in a 154-game season, or in seasons with fewer major-league teams, was lower. In 2017, to account for quality disparities between leagues, approximately 525 Wins Above Replacement were assigned to the American League and 475 to the National League. Those proportions vary each year; more wins were assigned to the National League between 1942 and 1968 because of the league's perceived higher comparative quality, primarily due to postwar integration.

According to Baseball-Reference.com, although WAR is a statistic assigned to an individual, each player's WAR value can be added together for a team total. In fact, adding 48 (the number of wins a replacement team would achieve, which is found by multiplying .294 and 162) to a team's total WAR value will closely match the team's actual wins for the season. But does a higher WAR, a value based on regular-season statistics, correlate with a higher winning percentage in the World Series? Can WAR be used to describe teams that play in the World Series? Also, using a historical approach, were there decades in which teams with lower WAR values than their opponent won more frequently?

METHODOLOGY AND RESULTS

WAR values for pitching and batting categories of every team that played in the World Series since 1903 were compiled. However, only values since the live-ball era began in 1920 were considered because of the rule changes implemented that year. WAR values for the pitching and batting categories were added together for a team total WAR value category and the difference between the winner's and loser's total WAR value for each World Series was found. If the difference was positive, the winner had a higher total WAR value, and if the difference was negative, the loser had a higher total WAR value. The minimum, maximum, and average for the pitching, batting, and total categories were found to describe all World Series winners and losers. The results and the respective teams for each value are found in Table 1. The 2017 American League, National League, and MLB averages for each category are also listed for comparison.

The winning percentage of the team with the higher WAR value, or "Favored Team," was calculated for all World Series since the live-ball era began. This was accomplished by counting the total number of times the "Favored Team" won and dividing by the total number of World Series played. Although 97 World Series have been played since 1920, the 1959 World Series was excluded from the calculation because both teams had an equal total WAR value, leaving 96 World Series to consider. The results are found in Table 2.

In a similar way, the "Favored Team" winning percentage for each decade was calculated by counting the number of times the winner had a higher total WAR value than the loser and dividing by the number of World Series played in the corresponding decade. As stated before, the teams in the 1959 World Series had an equal total WAR value, so this series was excluded from its corresponding decade. Likewise, there was no World Series played in 1994. The results are found in Table 3.

Table 1. World Series winners and losers WAR values with AL, NL, and MLB averages

Winning Team	Batting WAR (Team)	Pitching WAR (Team)	Total WAR (Team)
Minimum	13.6 (1985 Kansas City Royals)	5.8 (1952 New York Yankees)	30.4 (2006 St. Louis Cardinals)
Maximum	48.0 (1927 New York Yankees)	30.8 (2007 Boston Red Sox)	68.1 (1927 New York Yankees)
Average	29.7	17.3	47.0

Losing Team	Batting WAR (Team)	Pitching WAR (Team)	Total WAR (Team)
Minimum	10.1 (1944 St. Louis Browns)	4.5 (1960 New York Yankees)	30.3 (1944 St. Louis Browns)
Maximum	43.9 (1969 Baltimore Orioles)	30.8 (1991 Atlanta Braves)	61.8 (1969 Baltimore Orioles)
Average	28.0	17.6	45.6

	Batting WAR	Pitching WAR	Total WAR
2017 AL Team Average	21.1	14.3	35.4
2017 NL Team Average	18.1	13.0	31.1
2017 MLB Team Average	19.6	13.7	33.3

Table 2. Overall winning percentage for the "Favored Team" since the live-ball era began

Number of World Series	"Favored Team" Wins	"Favored Team" Losses	"Favored Team" Winning %
96	55	41	.573

Table 3. "Favored Team" World Series winning percentage by decade

Years	"Favored Team" Winning %
1920–29	.600
1930–39	.700
1940–49	.500
1950–58	.222
1960–69	.700
1970–79	.700
1980–89	.500
1990–93, 1995–99	.556
2000–09	.700
2010–17	.500

Next, World Series match-ups were examined based on WAR values. The largest WAR difference between teams that resulted in a "Favored Team" win and loss were found. The largest WAR difference with a "Favored Team" win is a match-up in which the "Favored Team" had the most value over their opponent ever and won. The largest WAR difference with a "Favored Team" loss is the largest upset by an underdog where their opponent had the most value over them and lost. The smallest WAR difference is a match-up where the teams were most evenly matched. The maximum both teams total WAR is where two "extremely valuable" teams played each other and the minimum both teams total WAR is the "least valuable" match-up of any World Series in a non-strike year. The 1981 season was shortened by about a third because of a strike, so the totals for WAR, a counting stat, were drastically lower that year. These values and the corresponding years and teams are listed in Table 4.

World Series match-ups were further examined by comparing the WAR difference between teams and "Favored Team" winning percentage. Using the total WAR difference between teams for each year calculated earlier, all values were made positive to examine the WAR difference magnitude of each match-up. The match-ups were then sorted into WAR difference ranges in increments of one, starting with a difference range between 0.0 and 0.99 (excluding any year with a difference of 0.0) and increasing to the highest WAR difference range between 28.0 and 28.99. The ranges with no World Series with a WAR difference value that included them were excluded. Likewise, to ensure a large enough sample size for each range, any range that contained fewer than five series was excluded. The "Favored Team" winning percentage for each WAR difference range was found by counting the number of times the "Favored Team" won and dividing by the number of series that fell into the corresponding range. The results are found in Table 5.

The WAR difference between teams and "Favored Team" winning percentage found in Table 5 were then plotted against each other. Because it's not possible to plot the WAR difference range itself, the average of all total WAR values falling into each range was used instead. A linear trendline was then added and the results are found in Figure 1 (next page).

Table 4. WAR differences between teams and maximum and minimum combined team WAR

	WAR Value	Year	Winning Team	Losing Team
Largest WAR Difference with "Favored Team" Win	28.7	1944	St. Louis Cardinals	St. Louis Browns
Largest WAR Difference with "Favored Team" Loss	-20.6	1969	New York Mets	Baltimore Orioles
Smallest WAR Difference	0.0	1959	Los Angeles Dodgers	Chicago White Sox
Maximum Both Teams Total WAR	112.1	1927	New York Yankees	Pittsburgh Pirates
Minimum Both Teams Total WAR	70.5	1987	Minnesota Twins	St. Louis Cardinals

Table 5. WAR difference and "Favored Team" winning percentage

War Difference Range	Number of World Series	"Favored Team" Wins	"Favored Team" Losses	"Favored Team" Winning %
1.0–1.99	7	4	3	.571
3.0–3.99	10	6	4	.600
4.0–4.99	11	8	3	.727
5.0–5.99	7	3	4	.429
6.0–6.99	5	3	2	.600
7.0–7.99	8	3	5	.375
8.0–8.99	6	2	4	.333
11.0–11.99	6	4	2	.667
Total World Series	60			

Figure 1. WAR difference vs "Favored Team" winning percentage

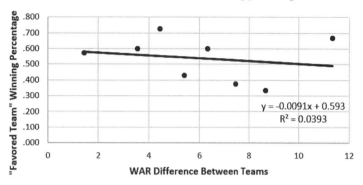

Total WAR values for all teams playing in the World Series since the live-ball era began were then examined. The total WAR values between the winning and losing teams were compared using a Student's t-test. Alpha, or the significance level, was set at 0.05 and it was assumed the total WAR values for both the winning and losing teams had similar variance. The results are found in Table 6.

Table 6. Total WAR value Student's t-test comparison

	Winning Team	Losing Team
Average Total WAR Value	47.0	45.6
Standard Deviation	7.1	5.8
Number of Observations	97	97
P(T<=t) two-tail		0.141

DISCUSSION

WAR was used to describe the average team playing in the World Series by averaging the batting, pitching, and total categories of every winning and losing team since 1920. Comparing WAR values found in Table 1, the average winner of the World Series (with a WAR value of 47.0) has a team total WAR value 13.7 higher than the 2017 MLB team average (33.3). More specifically, the average team would need to add the value of an equivalent MVP batter, with a WAR of 10.0, along with a quality starting pitcher, with a WAR of 3.7, to achieve the same value of a World Series winner. The calculated team total WAR values are logical, because after adding 48 to the total WAR value, the average World Series winner will achieve an estimated 95 wins in the regular season and the MLB average team will achieve 81 wins. It should also be noted that the American League has a higher team average total WAR than the National League because of how WAR is distributed, as described earlier. On average, the World Series winner slightly edges out the loser with a WAR of about 1.4 higher, although the p-value from the two-tailed Student's t-test in Table 6 is greater than alpha (0.05), meaning the WAR difference between

teams isn't statistically significant and opponents are evenly matched.

A historical approach was used to analyze WAR values of teams in the World Series as well as match-ups. Looking at the WAR values for pitching, batting, and total categories in Table 1, the team with the lowest total WAR of any World Series winner (30.4, which is less than the 2017 MLB team average) was the St. Louis Cardinals in 2006. This was also the team with the lowest regular-season winning percentage to win a World Series.

The team with the highest total WAR of any World Series winner (68.1, which is more than double the 2017 MLB team average) was the New York Yankees in 1927, which is generally regarded as one of the best teams ever.

Examining World Series match-ups based on WAR in Table 4, the largest upset, where the team with a much lower WAR value than their opponent won a World Series, occurred in 1969, when the "Miracle Mets" defeated the mighty Baltimore Orioles. The World Series with the highest combined WAR for both teams was in 1927, when the New York Yankees defeated the Pittsburgh Pirates, and the lowest combined WAR for both teams in a non-strike year was in 1987, when the Minnesota Twins defeated the St. Louis Cardinals. Because the team total WAR value appears to match with actual winning percentage and general opinion of how teams are regarded historically, it can be used as a benchmark indicator of how good a team is. At the same time, this study also challenges the similar observations and judgments of one team in particular: the New York Yankees.

Examining Table 3, the "Favored Team" winning percentage in each decade remained close to the average of 57.3 found in Table 2, except between 1950 and 1958. The 1950s was a decade primarily dominated by the Yankees; they would appear in the World Series eight times and win six. However successful, according to the WAR values in each match-up, they were the underdog every year they won (1950–53, 1956, 1958) as well as the two times they lost (1955 and 1957). This demonstrates one of the limitations of WAR: Although it does a good job estimating a player's and team's worth, there are many other intangible factors that make a winning ballclub, a couple of which include club morale and luck. Longtime Yankees manager Casey Stengel described Yogi Berra as "my man," because he was confident in his catcher's ability to hit and handle pitchers. Was Stengel's managerial skill or Berra's presence the difference that led to so many victories? Another idiosyncrasy of the 1950s, as mentioned earlier, was that 1959 was the only year in which the opponent's team total WAR values were equal. Although equal statistically by WAR, the Los Angeles Dodgers would defeat the Chicago White Sox in 6 games.

Total WAR difference between teams was also compared against winning percentage using the methodology described above. Initially, it was hypothesized that a higher WAR difference would correlate to a higher winning percentage because the "Favored Team" would have a WAR value that was increasingly more than their opponent. However, the linear trendline in Figure 1 has a negative slope and the corresponding coefficient of determination (0.0393) is very low, meaning only about 3.9 percent of the variance in the data was caused by the linear relationship. Therefore, there is no correlation between WAR difference and winning percentage, although teams with a higher team total WAR win about 57.3 percent of the time, as found in Table 2.

In the future, more work can be done to attempt a better correlation model when graphing the WAR difference and "Favored Team" winning percentage. This could be done by increasing the number of ranges used by decreasing the WAR difference increments to a value less than one. Although 97 World Series have been played since the live-ball era began, only 96 of the data were usable and even fewer (60) could be used for the model used in this study to ensure the winning percentages for each range had averaged out to equilibrium. The main limitation with the current model is lack of sample size, which would only become more problematic if the range increments were decreased. Future work can also be done by increasing the scope and examining WAR difference between the World Series winner and the average team that made the playoffs that same year. It would be especially interesting to compare WAR values between eras of playoff expansion.

CONCLUSION

WAR can be used to describe the average team playing in the World Series, with the average winner having a team total WAR value of 47.0, or 13.7 above the 2017 MLB team average. Through historical analysis, WAR as a statistic and its values appear to be validated when comparing team total WAR values with actual winning percentage and general opinion. WAR values also don't vary much between decades, with the 1950s being the exception. Although the WAR value analysis for each World Series shows that teams with a higher WAR value win about 57.3 percent of the time, there is no correlation between the WAR difference between teams and winning percentage, leaving postseason outcomes subject to intangible factors. ∎

Sources

The author used Baseball-Reference.com for all statistical values and World Series match-up information. WAR values are accurate as of July 1, 2018.

The Specialized Bullpen

History, Analysis, and Strategic Models for Success

Dr. John Daniels, Sara Andrasik, and David Hooley

A great deal of attention has been given to the baseball closer, particularly since the save was officially recognized in 1969. But the modern bullpen is now multidimensional, complete with analytics and new algorithms, and this should give a manager more weapons with a late-game lead. This paper discusses the evolution of the specialized bullpen, how it has affected baseball, and how much the specialized bullpen contributes to a significant playoff run. This research should reinforce some accepted baseball adages and provide some examples that less is sometimes more.

INTRODUCTION

Pitch counts are now an integral part of the game. No more "Iron Man" Joe McGinnity pitching both games of a doubleheader. Arms are now too expensive—some would argue too fragile—to be taxed to any extremes. Pitchers, of course, want to stay in as long as possible. But the complete game is now the exception and the modern bullpen is an integral part of strategy.

In well over a century of professional baseball, the strategic bullpen was born and has evolved, mutated, and been continuously refined by innovative managers. The bullpen is the home of the relief specialist. The origins of the term "bullpen" are debated, but it has always been the area where the relief pitchers get to sit. Until 1889, the rules stated that no player substitution was allowed except for injury or sickness. An ineffective starting pitcher would simply change positions with another player on the field. The replacement was known as a "change" pitcher. After 1889, a player substitution could occur at any time and the bullpen was officially born.

Since starters were regarded as the team's best pitchers, the first relief pitchers were often the starters, who might pitch a few innings between scheduled appearances. Today, this is rarely seen except during the postseason. It was more common in the early years of the bullpen. In the 1920s and '30s, Hall of Fame starters Waite Hoyt, Dizzy Dean, Carl Hubbell, and Lefty Grove each led the league in saves once

though no one knew it until the metric was invented decades later.

As time wore on, the use of the bullpen as a home for individual specialists began to emerge. Although subject to debate, one of the first recognized relief specialists was Firpo Marberry. His relief work for the Washington Nationals and Detroit Tigers in 1923–36 included 20 saves in a season (awarded retroactively), more than 50 relief appearances in a season twice, and 365 relief appearances. The leagues took notice and other specialists like Johnny Murphy, Joe Page, Hoyt Wilhelm, and Elroy Face made important contributions.

By the 1970s, the "fireman" was an accepted role on a team. Some were heavily relied on, like Mike Marshall, with his 106 games and 208⅓ innings pitched for the Los Angeles Dodgers in 1974. Sparky Lyle, Bruce Sutter, Rollie Fingers, Dennis Eckersley, Trevor Hoffman, and Mariano Rivera come to mind. Some firemen—or closers, as they came to be called—were one-year wonders (Willie Hernandez in 1984), while others enjoyed long and successful careers and made it or will make it to Cooperstown as relief pitchers.

As closers evolved into one-inning specialists, the set-up man also emerged as a part of the specialized bullpen. Certainly not as glamorous as closers, set-up men were often future closers who pitched the seventh or eighth inning. It's hard to pin down the precise beginnings of set-up man use, but it's worth noting the New York Yankees bullpen of 1996, when Rivera would often pitch the seventh and eighth innings and closer John Wetteland would pitch the ninth. Broadcaster Tim McCarver said that the Yankees played "six-inning games" that year. In other words, if the Yankees had the lead after six innings, the Rivera-Wetteland combination almost assured a win. And indeed, when Rivera entered games in the seventh inning, the Yanks went 18–2. When he entered in the eighth, they went 14–6.

The emergence of analytics has resulted in even more bullpen specialists. The lefty-on-lefty matchup has been around for years. This was analytics in its infancy, since it was relatively easy to split a batter's performance against left- and right-handed pitchers. The situational lefty could exploit the weakness of most left-handed batters against left-handed pitchers. But today's analytics are so detailed that a manager can try to dial up a strikeout, double play, or any other desired outcome. A pitcher who gets a ground ball at an opportune time can save an inning. Obviously, managers are dealing with tendencies and probabilities, but if the information is available, nobody wishes to be second-guessed by the media or fans.

RESEARCH QUESTIONS

Using Retrosheet, SAS, and R statistical software, 136,395 game outcomes from 1921 through 2016 were examined. All of these games involve a starting pitcher leaving a game, but in line for a win (five innings pitched with a lead of one run or more). Using available data and 1945 and 1990 as arbitrary cutoff dates, 15,897 of the games were in 1921–45 (Pre-closer Era), 63,030 of the games in 1946–90 (Closer Era), and the remaining 57,468 games in 1991–2016 (Specialized Bullpen Era). The research questions posed are as follows:

1. Looking at the different eras, what influence does innings pitched by a starter and his run differential have on the odds of winning a game?

2. Looking at the different eras, given that a starting pitcher leaves the game in line for a win, what is the probability of a team getting the win, accounting for innings pitched and run differential?

3. Have these probabilities changed to any degree across these three eras? Has the specialized bullpen helped to increase the likelihood of a team keeping its lead and winning?

4. Has the specialized bullpen diminished the late rally?

5. Based on these results, are there any general strategies that can be suggested regarding the use of the specialized bullpen?

RESULTS
Research Questions 1, 2 and 3: Did We Win?
Utilizing logistic regression, analytic models for the three eras (Pre-closer, Closer, Specialized Bullpen) were created. Let Y = 1 represent the team ahead winning the game (assuming a starter goes five innings with a lead) and Y = 0 indicating a team loss. These

models are used to understand the influence of important variables, specifically innings pitched by the starter and run differential at the time of starter exit. The models are also used to predict the probability of winning a game. A detailed explanation of logistic regression is beyond the scope of this paper, but the Appendix contains additional details of logistic regression, the models created, and how they are interpreted.

Table 1 summarizes the influence of the variables in the logistic regression model.

Table 1. Increase in odds of winning the game

Bullpen Era	Innings Pitched	Run Differential
Pre-closer (1921–45)	127%	96.5%
Closer (1946–90)	93%	97.2%
Specialized Bullpen (1991–2016)	61%	98.7%

These models are quite insightful since:

1. For the Pre-closer Era, it appears that innings pitched has a slightly stronger influence on the odds of winning over run differential (127 percent versus 96.5). This would seem to support the theory that these starting pitchers, even tired ones, might have a better chance of winning the game than a Pre-closer Era reliever. Remember, in this era, relievers were considered pitchers not quite good enough to be starters. Relievers had not begun to specialize.

2. For the Closer Era, innings pitched (93 percent) and run differential (97.2 percent) odds were much closer. The emergence of the closer meant it was not as critical for the starter to pitch a complete game.

3. For the Specialized Bullpen, run differential (98.7 percent) is now significantly more important than innings pitched (61 percent). This result is a reflection of the strategy of the era. Having a specialized bullpen means that, if you are ahead, your best relievers will probably be put in the game. If you are losing, the manager would probably be less likely to bring in these pitchers.

Now, again using these models, Tables 2, 3, and 4 are used to estimate the probability of a team getting a win. The number of innings the starter pitched and the run differential were used as inputs for each model. These estimates are the predictions of the logistic models already used and discussed in the Appendix.

Table 2 shows the percentage of games won for the Pre-closer bullpen:

Table 2. Win percentage matrix, Pre-closer Era

Innings Pitched by Starter	Run Differential for Team Ahead				
	1	2	3	4	5
5	37.6	54.2	69.9	82.1	90.0
6	57.7	72.9	84.1	91.2	95.3
7	75.6	85.9	92.3	95.9	97.9
8	87.5	93.2	96.4	98.2	99.1
9	94.1	96.9	98.4	99.2	99.6

In examining Table 2, it is intuitively obvious that the percentage of wins increases with both increasing run differential and starter innings pitched. Also note that in the Pre-closer Era, a one-run lead in the eighth inning is better than a two-run lead in the seventh inning and so forth. This reinforces the notion that in the Pre-closer era, an extra inning from the starter is more valuable than an extra run. Again, in the Pre-closer Era, relievers had not begun to specialize. A relief pitcher was considered inferior to a starter but was brought in when the starter was no longer effective.

Now, Table 3 has the same variables, but for the Closer Era.

Table 3. Win percentage matrix, Closer Era

Innings Pitched by Starter	Run Differential for Team Ahead				
	1	2	3	4	5
5	46.2	62.9	77.0	86.8	92.8
6	62.3	76.6	86.6	92.7	96.2
7	76.2	86.3	92.6	96.1	98.0
8	86.0	92.4	96.0	97.9	98.9
9	92.2	95.9	97.9	98.9	99.4

In Table 3, similar results can be seen as in Table 2. What is interesting in Table 3 is that the relative influence of run differential and innings pitched has changed. Now, generally speaking, an extra run lead is slightly more valuable than an extra inning from the starter. One could speculate on this change, but the importance of that extra run may have to do with the increasing quality of relief pitching. As competent relievers replaced lesser starters in bullpens, pulling the starting pitcher no longer meant a probable dropoff in effectiveness. That extra run became more critical because it was less likely that the lead would be blown by the bullpen.

Finally, Table 4 is for the Specialized Bullpen Era.

Table 4. Win percentage matrix, Specialized Bullpen Era

Innings Pitched by Starter	Run Differential for Team Ahead				
	1	2	3	4	5
5	54.9	70.8	82.8	90.5	95.0
6	66.3	79.6	88.6	93.9	96.8
7	76.0	86.3	92.6	96.1	98.0
8	83.6	91.0	95.3	97.6	98.8
9	89.1	94.2	97.0	98.5	99.2

In Table 4, the importance of that extra insurance run is very clear. A two-run lead in the seventh inning is even more important than a one-run lead in the eighth inning and so on. Again, with relief pitchers less likely to blow the lead than they had been in the Pre-closer Era, the probability that a lead in the seventh or eighth inning will result in a win grows.

RESEARCH QUESTION 4: RALLY TIME

An entire volume of books could be devoted to stories of baseball superstitions, rally rituals, etc. In the era of the specialized bullpen, has the hope of a rally been dimmed? In other words, teams are now facing fresh flamethrowers in the late innings instead of tired starters. Has this situation diminished the late rally?

The following table indicates the game result by inning and run differential for the team in the lead. In these examples, it does not matter how long the starter pitches. Are teams able to hold onto a one-, two-, or three-run lead in the last three innings? Table 5 shows the percentage of time the team with the lead won the game in the Pre-closer Era.

Table 5. Percentage of wins with the lead Pre-closer Era

Inning	Run Differential		
	1	2	3
7	70.0	81.9	90.6
8	75.2	86.9	93.5
9	84.2	92.6	96.8

Now for the Closer Era in Table 6:

Table 6. Percentage of wins with the lead, Closer Era

Inning	Run Differential		
	1	2	3
7	71.2	83.6	91.3
8	76.7	88.4	94.5
9	85.9	93.7	97.6

Now for the Specialized Bullpen Era in Table 7:

Firpo Marberry was one of the first relief specialists in the 1920s and '30s. He was retroactively awarded "saves" after the stat was invented.

Table 7. Percentage of wins with the lead, Specialized Bullpen Era

Inning	Run Differential		
	1	2	3
7	71.1	83.3	91.1
8	76.4	88.3	94.5
9	85.8	94.1	97.7

When these tables are compared to Pete Palmer's empirical data (Palmer, 2018) the logistic models compare quite well. For example, Palmer's mean win probabilities in the ninth inning for one-, two-, and three-run leads are 85.7, 93.8, and 97.4 percent respectively. This logistic model, seen here in the last row of Table 7, is slightly more optimistic, by about 0.1 – 0.3 percent. Not much difference.

In comparing the individual cells of Table 5 (Pre-closer) with Table 7 (Specialized Bullpen), notice that the Specialized Bullpen percentages are only slightly better per cell, with a maximum increase of 1.6 percentage points (ninth-inning, one-run lead). At best, this is about 2.6 extra wins per year. The percentages here are irrespective of how far a starter pitches into a game. It is simply a comparison of overall pitching staff performance in the two eras. In theory, in the era of specialized bullpens, we might expect the values in Table 7 to increase significantly, but the effect is modest.

Also, to support the premise that the rally is not dead, here are some results. Table 8 represents the probability of blowing the lead and the probability of winning the game after blowing the lead, given a one-, two-, or three-run lead in the seventh inning.

Table 8. Holding the lead

	Pre-closer	Closer	Specialized Bullpen
Prob (blowing the lead)	.280	.275	.260
Prob (winning the game after blowing the lead)	.273	.284	.270

Here, we can see that fewer leads were being blown (.28 down to .26) in the Specialized Bullpen Era. This would be about three games per season. In addition, teams are rallying from a blown lead at almost the same rate (.273 versus .270). This difference is less than one game per season. So, as can be seen, things have not really changed all that much. The game finds a way to balance itself out. The rally is still alive and well.

RESEARCH QUESTION 5: WHAT SHOULD WE DO?

This quote is attributed to Tommy Lasorda, although others have said it in different ways:

> No matter how good you are, you're going to lose one-third of your games. No matter how bad you are, you're going to win one-third of your games. It's the other third that makes the difference.

Although the numbers do show a slight pitching advantage for the Specialized Bullpen, perhaps 2–3 wins per season, does this guarantee team success on the playing field? The bullpen is only one facet of a team, and this should be examined within the context of the playoffs and World Series.

In 2017, the American League playoff teams in order of seeding were the Indians, Astros, Red Sox, Yankees, and Twins. In the National League: the Dodgers, Nationals, Cubs, Diamondbacks, and Rockies. The Rockies and the White Sox (non-playoff team) appeared to have good bullpens but struggled to win as many games as the other teams. The White Sox lost 95 games, although they were better than their competitors at protecting a lead (when they occasionally had one). Now, from the chicken-or-egg perspective, do good bullpens help a team win or do good teams (capable of come-from-behind wins) make a bullpen look better? Probably a little of both. It's a somewhat symbiotic relationship, which somewhat diminishes the bullpen's importance on an elite hitting team.

Of the playoff teams, the Diamondbacks, Dodgers, and Indians appeared to be best at holding a late lead. As you may recall, the Astros defeated the Dodgers in a seven-game World Series. The overall team comparisons are not as easy here, due to the DH, but Houston was first in runs scored, in the AL and all of baseball, while LA was 12th overall and 6th in the National League. On paper, the Astros had the stronger offense and the Dodgers had the stronger pitching, but Houston lost the DH for four games.

The point isn't that good hitting beats good pitching, which would be a revelation and historically incorrect. The point is that the bullpen is only one piece of a team's makeup, along with starting pitching, hitting, fielding, and intangibles. In 2017, the apparent better bullpen did not win the World Series. Now, this is not always true, but the argument is that teams seem to spend a lot of roster spots and money on something that does not appear to make any more difference, perhaps less, than good hitters, good starters, and good fielding.

As Fran Zimniuch wrote in his 2009 book, *Fireman:*

> The challenge in the dugout is not limited to having enough position players. Even with a 12- or 13-man pitching staff, a manager's hands are often tied by his pitchers' specialized roles. With some relievers unable to throw more than one inning, managers sometimes run out of available pitchers and find themselves in a predicament on the mound.

This is an expensive predicament. As pointed out by Bill Felber in *The Book on the Book* in 2005:

> In 2004, Major League teams committed $283.6 million to the care and feeding of their collective bullpens. That's $9.45 million per team.

It also represents 14 percent of the 2004 payroll—for players who might play, perhaps, a few times per week, often for only a few innings. Is this the best investment strategy? If we assume 90 player innings per team game in the American League and 81 in the National, and the bullpen pitches 3.5 innings per game (the MLB average in 2017), that represents roughly 4 percent of player innings being used up by 14 percent or more of the payroll.

Now, recalling what Tommy Lasorda said, and not taking the math too literally, every team will win about 60 games and lose about 60 games. The remaining 42 games determine who makes the playoffs and who finishes in last place. Win about 30 of those 42 special games (71.4 percent) and you have 92 wins and will probably be in the playoffs. So, in theory, there are going to be some pivotal games during the year that will define the team's season—which ones are only

Mike Marshall appeared in 106 games with 208 ⅓ innings pitched for the Los Angeles Dodgers in 1974.

known in hindsight. Strategically, when the game's outcome is in doubt, a good team should win around 70 percent of the time.

Using this 70 percent figure, recall the information provided in Table 4. With a one-run lead, getting the starter past the sixth inning is the point at which you can theoretically win around 70 percent of the time. The longer the starter is able to continue, assuming he is still getting outs, the better your chances of winning. With a two-run lead, a starter can begin to lose effectiveness as early as the sixth inning, get relief help, and still maintain the 70 percent probability. Usually, managers rely on pitch counts and sometimes their own senses to determine bullpen strategy. If the starter can get through seven innings with a one-run lead, then the set-up man and closer can get the team a win 71.1 percent of the time. If this were to happen, assuming the team has the lead in the late innings, then this team will most likely be in the playoffs. But is this always the best approach? Are pitch counts the best determining factor in replacing a starter?

In *The Book on the Book*, Felber also shows that late in the game a tiring starter is often more effective than the relief pitcher. He shows that, on average, a starter who had faced 28 batters retired 72.3 percent of the hitters he faced after that, while set-up men and closers facing one to three men retired 70.4 percent and 71.4 percent respectively. Felber also found that, generally speaking, good starters began to decline around pitch 115. Most managers are more conservative than this (100 pitches seems to be the magic number). If a batter sees an average of about four pitches (in 2017 it was 3.87 per plate appearance), this is an additional three to four batters, or an extra inning of work.

Another argument against keeping a starter later in the game is the chance of injury over the course of a long season. No manager wants to explain why the ace of the staff will be unavailable for the postseason, especially if the easy excuse is an overworked pitcher. But Felber argues that injury can be as much the fault of *underuse* as overuse. Today's starters pitch far fewer innings than their predecessors, yet the trend of pitchers on the disabled list is on an upward trend (2.5 percent in 1948 versus 18 percent in 1998 and 21 percent in 2017). Perhaps sports medicine can diagnose injuries better, perhaps guaranteed contracts reduce the fear of communicating minor injuries, or perhaps expensive starters are just coddled more.

Unfortunately, today's bullpen approach seems almost programmed and mechanical. Everyone has a specific job to do. One of the downsides of the specialized bullpen is that it is hierarchal in nature and simulates, to some degree, an assembly line at a factory. Felber uses that metaphor in *The Book on the Book*:

> To be fully functional, a hierarchical system requires that virtually every reliever be as competent as the closer—otherwise, the prospect increases that the car breaks down before it ever gets to the closer's station on the assembly line of victory.

A counterproposal to the assembly-line mentality may be advanced informatics. Perhaps a particular batter has had little success against a certain pitcher. In a key situation, this pitcher might be better suited for the task than the set-up man or closer. Certainly, over time, the set-up man and closer are probably the team's two best relief pitchers, but they are not going to be lights out every night. Of course, they might not even be available due to previous workloads. Small sample sizes are problematic too, but a manager should manage and not always execute a computer algorithm.

STRATEGIES FOR SUCCESS

Based on this research, what advice could be given to both managers and general managers?

A. Most teams do not have both an elite set-up man and closer. Forget about pitch counts and trust your instincts. Let the starter go as long as he can. What is so special about 100 pitches? Every pitcher is different in regard to mechanics, stamina, etc. In past eras, assessing a starter was an important job for the manager, pitching coach, and catcher. Today, managers follow a script so as not to be second guessed.

B. If a team has an elite set-up man and closer, then the situational bullpen can be an effective strategy. The problem is most teams do not have this luxury. This again suggests letting the starter pitch a bit longer, or letting the best relievers pitch a bit longer. Why can't a closer pitch more than one inning, it the situation presents itself? Is the marginal wear and tear on an arm that significant? Is throwing 30 pitches riskier than 15 pitches? This should be investigated. A pitcher has to get up, warm up, and pitch anyway. How is an extra 15–20 pitches going to make that much difference?

FINAL WORDS

In reference to the research questions previously asked, here is a brief summary of the results:

1. In the Pre-closer Era, innings pitched by a starter was more important than run differential. In the Situational Bullpen Era, this relationship is reversed. Today, a two-run lead in the eighth inning is slightly better than a one-run lead in the ninth inning and so forth. This might be due to the instability of a new pitcher late in a game.

2. The specialized bullpen has been shown to be a more effective strategy, but marginally so. On average, perhaps two to three wins per season. Not every team has an elite set-up man and closer, and one must question the merits of this investment for teams lacking such pitching.

3. The rally is still alive. Batters may be facing more pitchers, who throw harder late in the game, but batters are stronger and faster too. The game has a way of balancing itself out, no matter the changes to the rules or strategy.

4. The specialized bullpen, like pitching, hitting, and fielding, is only one part of team success. Bullpen is a subset of pitching, and its influence on winning is arguably the weakest of the components. A weak bullpen can cost you a game, but a strong bullpen does not guarantee a World Series ring. You still need the lead late in the game, or the bullpen is irrelevant.

5. Bullpen strategy is programmed and pitch counts may not always be the best way to manage a game. A starter should be evaluated on more than just number of pitches. There are certainly other factors, equally important, that should be considered.

As the game continues to evolve, one must wonder what the future of the specialized bullpen will be. Perhaps, someday, we may regularly have nine pitchers appearing in a game, each a one-inning specialist. Don't laugh. In his day, Iron Man McGinnity would have sneered at the idea of a closer. ■

Appendix

Logistic regression is a technique to model probabilities using multiple linear regression. In this situation, $Y = 1$ is defined as winning the ballgame while $Y = 0$ is defined as losing. This particular model has an intercept and two slope parameters.

For example, in the Pre-closer model:

$$\frac{e^{(-5.27 + .82 * P + .68 * RunDiff)}}{1 + e^{(-5.27 + .82 * P + .68 * RunDiff)}}$$

Where 5.27 is the intercept and .82 and .68 are the respective slope estimates. In logistic regression models, the slopes are interpreted to show the change in the odds [Prob(win)/Prob(loss)]. For example, for the number of innings pitched by the starter (IP):

Odds Ratios: IP: $e^{.74}$ = 2.23 (each inning pitched increases the odds of winning 110% holding Run Diff constant)

Mathematically, it can be shown that each out (⅓ of an inning) increases the odds of winning 28%:

Run Diff: $e^{.69}$ = 1.97 (each additional run ahead increases the odds of winning 99% holding IP constant)

The probability of a win can be estimated by plugging in the IP and Run Diff into the logistic equation and the result will be a value between 0 and 1, representing the probability of a win.

To validate a logistic regression model, the residuals (Y minus predicted Y) versus the fits (predicted Y) are displayed on a plot with a localized regression line (lowess) included. If the lowess line is approximately horizontal, this indicates a valid logistic regression model. Here in Figure 1 is the residuals versus the fits for the Pre-closer model. The other models had similar results. ■

Figure 1. Fit Plot for Residuals

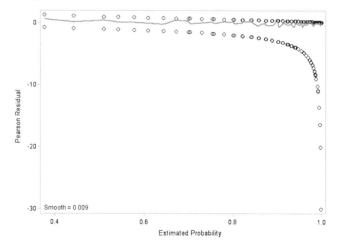

Sources

Bill Felber, *The Book on the Book*, 1st ed., (New York: Thomas Dunne Books, 2005).

Fran Zimniuch, *Fireman: The Evolution of the Closer in Baseball* (Chicago: Triumph Books, 2009).

Sean Lahman, Baseball Database, http://www.seanlahman.com/baseball-archive/statistics.

Pete Palmer, "Relief Pitching Strategy: Past, Present, and Future?" *Baseball Research Journal*, 47 (2018).

Offensive Explosion

Trends in Hitting Production in Major League Baseball

Laura Schreck and Eric Sickles

ABSTRACT

2014 was a record year for pitchers, but it was followed by an abrupt reversal in trends, with offensive numbers increasing steadily in 2015 and 2016, culminating in a record-setting year for hitters in 2017. This article explores similar offensive explosions throughout the history of major-league baseball in order to draw parallels to the current extraordinary increase in offense. Evidence of this increase is provided by analyzing the trends of 10 separate statistical categories, as well as the statistical trends of the top 40 hitters and 20 pitchers in the major leagues. This analysis and research provides the context for discussing possible reasons for such a profound offensive explosion. From steroid use to the changes in the manufacturing of the baseball itself, this article discusses the implications of a dramatically changing baseball landscape where offense reigns supreme.

INTRODUCTION

1968 was considered the Year of the Pitcher because of league-wide statistics for batting average, on-base percentage, home runs per game, earned-run average, walks and hits per inning pitched (WHIP), and bases on balls per game that had rarely been so low. Forty-six years later, the Year of the Pitcher moniker was revived by baseball pundits as offensive stats dropped to levels that hadn't been seen since the early '80s. The glaring difference between 1968 and 2014, however, is that the original Year of the Pitcher was intrinsically anomalous. In other words, there was no significant trend that would lead one to infer such a dramatically favorable year for pitchers. In 1969, statistics generally returned to a level more reflective of those from 1967 and before, though the causes of that may have been Major League Baseball lowering the mound height to the current 10 inches and the shrinking of the strike zone. On the other hand, there is clearly a pitcher-friendly trend in the years leading up to 2014 that hits its apex of pitcher dominance in that season. Indeed, data from the previous 10 years show a trend that favored pitchers in several different measures of pitcher efficiency—batting average, ERA, home runs allowed, WHIP, on base plus slugging percentage (OPS), bases on balls per game, and runs per game.

What can account for the trends that favored the pitcher up to 2014, and their abrupt reversal in 2015? Notably, Robert Manfred became commissioner in 2015 and baseballs manufactured by Rawlings for use in major-league games needed to be redesigned in order to accommodate his signature. This redesign was not intended to otherwise alter the ball, yet still, Manfred joked, "Actually, if there is a surge in offense, we'll all be happy."[1] Manfred's joke became reality in the 2015–17 seasons. As offensive records were being set in 2017, Houston Astros pitcher Justin Verlander said, "I know Mr. Manfred said the balls haven't changed, but I think there's enough information out there to say that's not true. Whether he has the say-so or not, I don't know."[2] A report on the 2015–17 home run surge released in May 2018 by a commitee formed by the comissioner said that "the increases in home runs are primarily due to better 'carry' for given launch conditions. ... Analysis shows that the better carry is not due to changes in temperature but rather to changes in the aerodynamic properties of the baseball itself, specifically to those properties affecting the drag."[3]

LITERATURE REVIEW

Despite Commissioner Manfred joking about a surge in offense, those marketing baseball may have had the goal of increasing offensive output since the game's infancy. In 1884, the Chicago White Stockings played at White Stocking Park, where the fences at the foul lines were just under 200 feet from home plate. As if playing in a park smaller than a standard Little League field wasn't enough to substantially increase power statistics, the organization made the decision to count balls hit over the fence that year as home runs rather than doubles, as it had in the past. This resulted in Chicago's season home run totals jumping from 13 to 142, which was only the most startling datum in the trend of home runs increasing across the major leagues to their nineteenth-century peak of 764 in 1890.[4]

Perhaps the most comprehensive research done on the topic of offensive potency in professional baseball was done by the late David Vincent in his book *Home Run: The Definitive History of Baseball's Ultimate Weapon*. Vincent outlines the effect of several rule changes in the 1920s that had an impact on offensive production. The nineteenth century ended with Roger Conner atop the career leaders in home runs with just 138. Even still, prior to 1920, league-wide home run production in the twentieth century had been significantly lower than home run production in the nineteenth. This led to three rule changes before the 1920 season that aimed to increase offensive production in order to balance out the dominance of "dead ball" pitching and fielding. The first of these was judging whether a home run was fair or foul not by where the ball landed, but by where it crossed over the fence. This revolutionary rule did not last long however: On June 25, 1920, with fewer than 60 games per team played, the rule was changed back to its 1919 version, thus returning the judgement of a home run by where it "disappears from view."[5] The rule would not return again to its present form until 1931.

The second rule change affected the way that walk-off home runs were scored. Previously, only the number of bases needed to score the winning run would be awarded. In other words, if the game was tied and a runner was on second base, a ball hit out of the park became a double, since, when the runner on second scored, the game ended.[6] This new rule allowed walk-off home runs to be scored as such. Interestingly, Babe Ruth is the only player who hit a would-be walk off home run prior to 1920, and also hit one in 1920.

The third and perhaps most hitter friendly rule change was the elimination of instances where a pitch's natural movement is altered by a foreign substance, such as spit or mud. This rule, after some adjustments over the next year, ended up allowing 17 pitchers to continue throwing spitballs for the rest of their careers.[7]

Though these rules have had long-term effects on the level of offensive production since their 1920s conception, one key change to the game of baseball was fundamental when looking to the cause of that decade's power boom: the baseball.

The live-ball era of baseball began in 1920, when baseball manufacturers began importing a higher quality wool from Australia, allowing the baseballs to be more tightly wound. This change in the manufacturing process made the balls more elastic and thus allowed them to travel farther. The new ball and rules resulted in the home run production rate more than doubling in just 10 years, from 630 in 1920 to 1,565 in 1930.[8]

Similar to 1920, there were also several preseason rule changes in 2015. However, where the 1920 changes, as well as the lowering of the mound in 1969, were specifically designed to increase offensive production, the 2015 changes were focused primarily on increasing the pace of play. The efforts to increase the pace of play included adding an in-stadium clock to limit the time of inning breaks and pitching changes (analogous to a play clock in football). Players would also allegedly be fined if they removed both feet from the batter's box during an at-bat, though little evidence can be found regarding how much, or how frequently, players have been fined for such offenses. A minor amendment to the existing instant replay rules was also added, stating that managers would no longer be required to leave the dugout in order to challenge a play. Less specific to pace of play alterations, Major League Baseball did increase the number of challengeable plays, as well as allowing managers to keep their challenges after every overturned call, rather than the pre-2015 version of the rule that allowed managers to only keep their challenge after one overturned call.[9]

The issue of a "live" or "juiced" ball was revived when the 1987 season yielded unprecedented production with the bats, earning it the nickname the "Rabbit Ball Year." The conspiracy of a juiced ball gained so much steam that MLB conducted internal tests to determine whether its baseballs had been tampered with in the hopes of increased offense output. Not surprisingly, despite the unusually high level of offense, MLB concluded that there was nothing unusual, or "juiced," about the baseballs.[10]

In the most recent examination of MLB's possible attempt to increase offense, Ben Lindbergh and Michel Lichtman in *The Ringer* note that offensive production increased intensely in the second half of the 2015 season. Strikingly similar to 1987, MLB conducted an internal investigation to determine if the baseball had indeed been made easier to launch. Again, similarly to 1987, the University of Massachusetts, Lowell, Baseball Research Center (BRC), carrying out research for MLB, determined that not only were the baseballs not juiced, but they were in fact 95 percent confident that the results were comparable to previous compliance data.[11]

Still another possible explanation for the increased number of home runs that many scholars point to is the style of hitting that's come into vogue, where emphasis is placed on fly balls. In theory, more fly balls would translate to more home runs given the fact that a ball must have a certain amount of loft to carry enough distance to get over the fence. This would explain the dramatic increase in home runs if more fly balls were in fact being hit. In reality, according to Fangraphs, 2015 actually saw a lower percentage of fly balls hit compared to 2014.

Further, Lindbergh and Lichtman note that in addition to the BRC and MLB's independent study in 2017, Washington State University conducted a study to determine if the coefficient of restitution (COR) measurements, essentially a measure of a baseball's bounciness, were truly different. The study found that Manfred's new baseball traveled, on average, an additional 7.1 feet.[12]

While the previous research has provided substantial explanation of previous instances when MLB has made efforts to increase offense, our own research hopes to shed light on the current rise in offense that has greatly affected the game of baseball.

METHOD

Using data on pitcher efficiency in 2004–17, we ran one-sample t-tests to determine the likelihood that the 2014 data represented an outstanding year for pitching. We examined four key statistics using one-sample t-tests for the 20 top performing pitchers and five key

statistics for the top 40 performing batters to see if the same trends held true for their performance as was generally seen in the major leagues. The significance of our results will be measured by "P-Values"; a value of p less than 0.05 ($p \leq 0.05$) typically indicates that the results are at least 95 percent significant, or unlikely to be due to chance. A P-Value of $p \leq 0.0001$ would mean the results of a t-test are 99.9999 percent significant, or highly unlikely to be due to chance fluctuations.

DATA

We gathered statistical data measuring league-wide pitcher performance between 2004 and 2017 in seven key areas—ERA, R/G, HR, WHIP, AVG, OPS, and BB/G—from Baseball-Reference.com. The league-wide data gathered begin in 2004 in order to capture statistics outside of the "Steroid Era" of the early- to mid-2000s which included offensive production that skyrocketed allegedly as a result of illegal use of performance enhancing drugs. Additional data examined included data from the top 20 pitchers and top 40 hitters of 2014 as determined by WAR, to determine whether trends for all players had an equal impact on the statistics of top performers, as well as the home run by pitch type data from Baseball Savant.

RESULTS

Figure 1. ERA, 2004–17
One-sample t-tests (p < 0.0001) indicated a significant difference in ERA in 2014 compared to the 2004–17 sample.

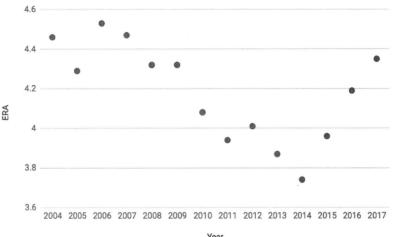

Figure 2. OPS, 2004–17
One-sample t-tests (p < 0.0001) indicated a significant difference in OPS in 2014 compared to the 2004–17 sample.

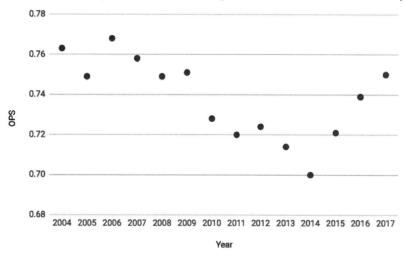

Figure 3. Home Runs, 2004–17
One-sample t-tests (p < 0.0001) indicated a significant difference in HR in 2014 compared to the 2004–17 sample.
A time series analysis shows significant difference in the trend of data between 2014 and 2015.

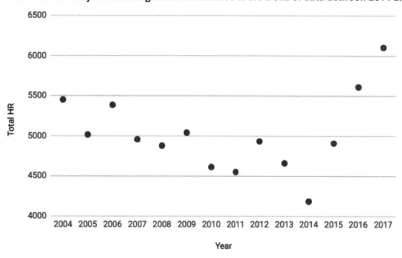

Figure 4. Runs/game, 2004–17
One-sample t-tests (p < 0.0001) indicated a significant difference in runs/game in 2014 compared to the 2004–17 sample.

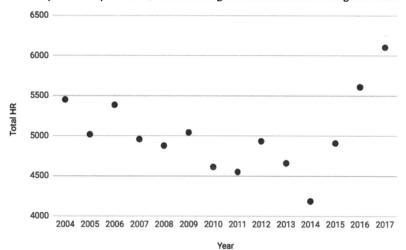

Figure 5. HR per hits allowed, 2004–17
One-sample t-tests (p < 0.0001) indicated a significant difference in HR/hit allowed in 2014 compared to the 2004–17 sample. Moreover, the graph shows the same trend of steady decrease between 2004 and 2014 with a reversal of this trend in 2015.

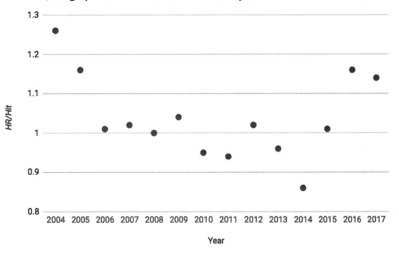

Figure 6. WHIP, 2004–17
 One-sample t-tests (p < 0.0001) indicated a significant difference in WHIP in 2014 compared to the 2004–17 sample.

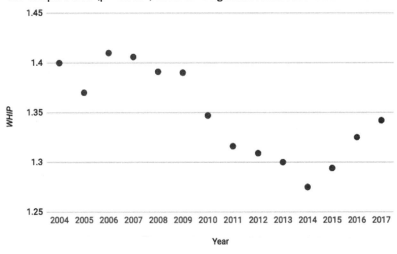

Figure 7. Bases on balls per game, 2004–17
One-sample t-tests (p < 0.0001) indicated a significant difference in BB in 2014 compared to the 2004–17 sample.

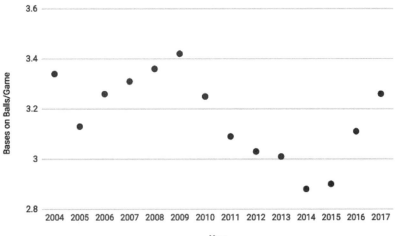

There are several factors to be considered that cannot account for either the anomaly of 2014 or the reversal of the trends favoring pitching in 2015.

The only ballpark to change its dimensions in 2015 was Citi Field in New York, which shortened the distance from home plate to the right field fence by 10 feet; while this did result in 38 additional home runs, it represents only 5 percent of the 723-home run increase in 2015 and the additional 701-home run increase in 2016. Admittedly, this change in dimensions was brought about due to analytics that suggested the shift would result in more home runs for the Mets.[13] While changing dimensions of ballparks to increase offensive production for the home team may be the next frontier in analytics, it cannot explain the offensive explosion of 2015. Likewise, Marlins Park in Miami was adjusted in the hopes of creating more offense in 2016, bringing in the center-field fence by 11 feet and lowering walls.[14] In 2017, the Atlanta Braves moved from Turner Field to the newly opened SunTrust Park, where the fences are 5 feet closer to home plate in left-center, 15 feet closer in right-center, and 5 feet closer in the right-field corner, with the decreased dimensions of right field compensated for by a wall that's 7½ feet taller.[15]

Some pundits have suggested that the increasing number of home runs in 2015, '16, and '17 can be attributed to hitters catching up to the increasing velocity of pitchers. To examine this theory, home runs as a percentage of pitch type are examined.

Table 1. HR as a percentage of pitch type, 2009–17

Year	Fastball HR	Slider HR	Changeup HR	Sinker HR	Curve Ball HR
2009	0.7653	0.6541	0.7571	0.6725	0.4845
2010	0.6828	0.6025	0.7132	0.6252	0.5350
2011	0.6745	0.6279	0.7089	0.6515	0.4152
2012	0.7422	0.6808	0.8068	0.6519	0.4978
2013	0.7017	0.6484	0.7273	0.5875	0.4682
2014	0.6217	0.5858	0.6736	0.5461	0.4827
2015	0.7483	0.6356	0.7391	0.6769	0.5548
2016	0.8325	0.7669	0.8583	0.7316	0.5887
2017	0.8908	0.8095	0.9129	0.8375	0.6235

In 2015, '16, and '17, there are increases in the percentage hit in every pitch type; the increase is not limited to fastballs. One-sample t-tests reveal that 2017 was a statistically significant anomalous year for every pitch type: fastball ($p < 0.0006$), slider ($p < 0.004$), changeup ($p < 0.0005$), sinker ($p < .0003$), and curveball ($p < 0.0011$).

Data regarding the percentage of home runs per fly ball thrown do not mirror the trends seen in the other data. The increase in 2015, '16, and '17 suggests that balls are traveling farther (see Figure 8).

Interestingly, the swinging strike percentage has also been trending upward every year since 2010 (see Figure 9), but the data do not follow the same trend, negating the possibility that batters began offering at more pitches since 2014. Likewise, strikeouts have increased steadily since 2005 (see Figure 10).

Figure 8. HR/Fly ball percentage, 2004–17

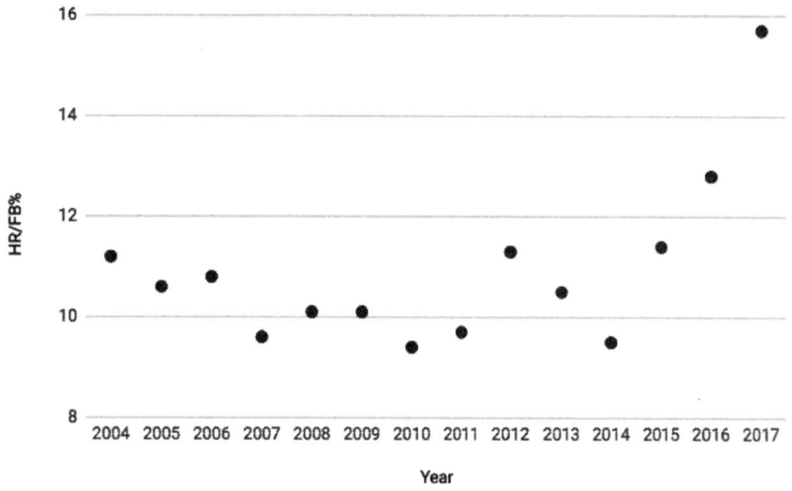

Figure 9. Swinging strike percentage, 2004–16

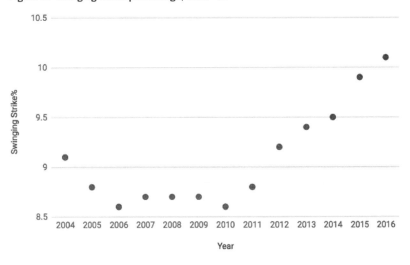

Figure 10. Strikeout percentage, 2004–17

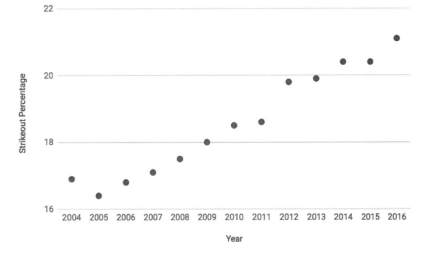

To examine whether the trends seen across all of major-league baseball hold true for the top performing pitchers, AVG, WHIP, ERA, and HR/9 data were collected for the top 20 pitchers of 2014 as determined by WAR values.

Table 2. Top 20 pitchers of 2014 performance, 2014–17

	AVG	WHIP	ERA	HR/9
2014	.229	1.09	2.77	.654
2015	.235	1.17	3.23	.904
2016	.238	1.18	3.56	1.075
2017	.232	1.17	3.66	1.132

These data reveal negligible increases in opponent AVG (and WHIP), suggesting consistency in these elite pitchers' effectiveness based on one-sample t-tests. However, there is a marked increase in ERA ($p < 0.0314$) and HR/9 ($p < 0.0305$) within this group of elite pitchers that is likely not due to chance fluctuations from one season to the next.

Similarly, to examine whether the trends seen across all of major-league baseball hold true for the top performing hitters, AVG, OBA, OPS, HR, and strikeout (SO) data were collected for the top 40 hitters of 2014 as determined by WAR values.

Table 3. Top 40 hitters of 2014–17

	AVG	OBA	OPS	HR	SO
2014	.291	.362	.833	20.10	106.38
2015	.275	.344	.797	18.45	93.38
2016	.270	.344	.792	20.63	104.35
2017	.267	.349	.792	19.45	90.58

Data from the hitters do not show the same trends as the data from the pitchers. In fact, they show slight decreases, which may well be due to chance, based on one-sample t-tests.

DISCUSSION

The data show a clear trend of increasing pitcher dominance between 2004 and 2014. This trend is abruptly reversed in 2015, most remarkably in the category of home runs.

Certain explanations can be dismissed based on the data available. The changing dimensions of the two ballparks, Citi Field and Marlins Park, and the Braves' move from Turner Field to SunTrust Park are not sufficient to explain the offensive increases of the past three seasons. This leads us to look to the plausible explanations based on previous increases in offense. Historically, home runs have increased for three reasons: rule change, use of steroids, and changes in the baseball itself.

There have been no rule changes in 2015–17 that would increase offense. The rule changes pertained to pace of play.

Major League Baseball only releases results results of failed steroid tests. Details of which players are tested and what the test specifically screens for are not released. Given the sudden improvement in hitting performance, performance enhancing substances as an explanation cannot be dismissed out of hand. Fewer players have been suspended for failed testing in 2015–17 than were suspended in 2012–14.[16] However, insufficient data are available to make any claims beyond commenting that this is a possible explanation for the significant increase in offense.

Measures of plate discipline—bases on balls, swinging strikes percentage, and strikeouts—do not suggest that there has been an increase in batters' skills in this area. In fact, swinging strike outs have been increasing steadily since 2010, suggesting that batters may be attempting an all-or-nothing approach; while this may be their intention, it seems to be a strategy that has been in place since 2010, a full five years before the reversal of trends in runs. If a strategy of swinging for the fences could account for the dramatic increase in home runs, one would expect to see runs increasing concurrently, rather than starting to pay dividends six years down the road. Given that plate discipline appears to be decreasing, the bases on balls coupled with increasing home runs and earned runs suggests that pitcher control is decreasing or that umpires may be calling the strike zone differently. Such a statistically significant shift in pitcher control is likely not due to an overall decrease in pitching

skill but may be due to an overall more cautious approach by pitchers—though if this is case, this approach is not successful at mitigating home runs. Home runs are up on every pitch type, so increased velocity is not a likely explanation.

The performance of the top 20 pitchers of 2014 is illuminating as to the changes that have occurred. Their opponent average and WHIP have remained steady, but there was been a statistically significant increase in their ERA and HR/9. They remain equally effective at keeping the ball out of play; the only difference is that the balls are flying out of the park. That is, they are traveling a greater distance. The Washington State University study that suggested that the new baseballs, on average, traveled an additional 7.1 feet could explain this phenomenon. Additionally, the top 40 hitters of 2014 actually show a non-significant decrease in performance between 2014 and 2017. This could be due to a decline in the performance of the top 40 hitters of 2014 as they aged, but given the consistency in the data from the top pitchers of 2014 over the following three seasons, it is the most valid comparison to measure against the ongoing performance of the same individual batters. This is particularly true given that the performance of pitchers over the course of time declines more precipitously than that of batters due to the wear and tear on pitchers' arms.

Given the shift in the numbers, it is not possible to ignore what the players, particularly the pitchers, are saying. Verlander, a Cy Young Award-winner, said, "So on one hand you can have somebody say, that manufactures the ball, they're not different. And on the other hand you can say that the people that have held a ball in their hand their entire life, saying it's different. You value one over the other. You take your pick."[17] While Rawlings did insist that it continues to manufacture the balls within the specified parameters, this does not preclude a shift in the average. That is to say it is possible for a ball to still fall within the acceptable parameters, but closer to one end of the spectrum such that it will travel farther. Indeed, the May 2018 report noted "a decrease in the ball's drag properties, which cause it to carry further than previously, given the same set of initial conditions—exit velocity, launch and spray angle, and spin."[18] These properties undeniably have an effect on home run production.

CONCLUSION

Having examined multiple possible explanations, we can conclude that the historical record offers the best potential explanations for what is clearly an offensive surge, with the increase in home runs being most notable. It is no secret that the commissioner of baseball has made increased offense a goal. The data support the proposition that offense has increased in ways not due to changes in rules or dimensions. This leaves the explanations of steroid usage or a change in the composition of the baseballs.

Ultimately, Major League Baseball can choose to make changes to promote offense in order to make the sport more marketable and appeal to a larger audience. In the past, these changes have been made with transparency. It is not necessarily wrong to alter the baseball to promote offense, but if such a change has occurred, there are significant implications for teams. Had teams been informed in advance of the changes in the ball, it could have affected choices they made in payroll allocations for pitching versus position players, draft strategies, and trade decisions. While all teams arguably were equally disadvantaged by this lack of information, it is undeniable that some teams do invest more in their pitching and thus will be more affected by the change, at least in the short term. The decision to make a change to the baseballs without transparency also alters the dynamic between Major League Baseball and the franchises and players, as it is now clear that there was an imbalance of information for teams and individuals hoping to compete.

To remain competitive moving forward, major-league franchises will need to change their approach in building a team. The balance of investment in hitting and pitching may shift. Alternately, teams built around pitching could consider alterations to their ballpark dimensions in order to offset the additional distance batted balls travel. Other changes that may affect the way a ballpark plays may also be considered. While opening or closing a roof is ostensibly a weather-based decision, it also alters how the ball carries in the park. Perhaps, if not forbidden by the rules, teams could consider putting in walls with adjustable height that could be set before the game based on the particular data of the pitchers scheduled to start—a shift of the park itself rather than the defense. Pitchers can continue to reject balls that feel as though they are wound more tightly by tossing them back. Teams may implement a humidor in their home park, though whether this would mitigate the changed aerodynamic properties of a baseball would remain to be seen.

Within games, the reality that the ball travels farther can change the way managers approach situations. Teams may want to try to hit the ball in the air. For example, rather than simply allowing the ball to be put in play, pitching for a ground ball may be a sound strategy. Defensive shifts, in addition to responding to a hitter's tendencies, may also be able to compensate and adjust for additional distance. The future success of teams may be affected by how they are either able to exploit or compensate for the change in the baseballs. ■

Notes

1. David Waldstein, "Rob Manfred puts his stamp on the game and an era," *The New York Times*, April 7, 2015. https://www.nytimes.com/2015/04/08/sports/baseball/a-signature-moment-as-a-new-baseball-season-begins.html.
2. Kevin Kernan, "Justin Verlander dumps fuel on Ball-gate: Can feel the difference," *New York Post*, October 29, 2017. https://nypost.com/2017/10/29/justin-verlander-dumps-fuel-on-ball-gate-can-feel-the-difference/.
3. Jim Albert et al., "Report of the Committee Studying Home Run Rates in Major League Baseball," Office of the Commissioner of Baseball, May 24, 2018. http://www.mlb.com/documents/7/9/4/278128794/Full_Report_of_the_Committee_Studying_Home_Run_Rates_in_Major_League_Baseball_052418.pdf.
4. Christopher D. Green, "Baseball's first power surge: Home runs in the late 19th-century major leagues," *Baseball Research Journal*, Fall 2011. http://sabr.org/research/baseball-s-first-power-surge-home-runs-late-19th-century-major-leagues.
5. David Vincent, *Home Run: The Definitive History of Baseballs Ultimate Weapon* (Washington: Potomac Books, 2008), 35.
6. Vincent, 38.
7. Herman Weiskopf, "The Infamous Spitter," *Sports Illustrated*, July 30, 1967. https://www.si.com/vault/1967/07/31/609382/the-infamous-spitter.
8. Vincent, *Home Run*, 42.
9. Major League Baseball, "MLBPA, MLB announce pace-of-game initiatives, game modifications," Press release, February 20, 2015. http://mlb.mlb.com/pa/releases/releases.jsp?content=022015.
10. Larry Granillo, "Living through the rabbit ball in 1987," *Sport Business Nation*, June 13, 2012. https://www.sbnation.com/2013/6/13/4426478/japan-juiced-baseball-power-mlb-1987-rabbit-ball.
11. Ben Lindbergh with Mitchell Lichtman, "The Juiced Ball Is Back," *The Ringer*, June 14, 2017, https://www.theringer.com/2017/6/14/16044264/2017-mlb-home-run-spike-juiced-ball-testing-reveal-155cd21108bc.
12. Lindbergh.
13. Tim Rohan, "Mets Bring in Fences, Again," *The New York Times*, November 18, 2014. https://www.nytimes.com/2014/11/19/sports/baseball/mets-fences-citi-field.html.
14. Joe Frisaro, "Marlins will lower and move in fences in 2016," MLB.com, October 7, 2015. https://www.mlb.com/news/c-153568328.
15. Alan Carpenter, "Atlanta Braves Reveal SunTrust Park Dimensions, New Wall," Tomahawk Take, March 10, 2016. https://tomahawktake.com/2016/03/10/atlanta-braves-reveal-suntrust-park-dimensions-new-wall.
16. Tom Verducci, "The numbers—and the truth—about baseball's PED problem and why it may never go away," *Sports Illustrated*, May 16, 2017. https://www.si.com/mlb/2017/05/16/ped-suspensions-home-run-rate.
17. Kernan, "Justin Verlander dumps fuel."
18. Jim Albert et al., "Executive Summary of the Report of the Committee Studying Home Run Rates in Major League Baseball," Office of the Commissioner of Baseball, May 24, 2018. http://www.mlb.com/documents/2/3/4/278129234/Executive_Summary_of_HR_Committee_Report_by_Dr_Leonard_Mlodinow_052418.pdf.

Home Runs and Strikeouts

Another Look

Douglas Jordan

INTRODUCTION

The 2017 MLB season set records for both home runs (6,105) and strikeouts (40,104). Conventional wisdom would suggest that this is not a coincidence. The argument is that players don't mind striking out more often if they also hit more home runs. The raw data for these two parameters are easily plotted over time to show periods of strong offense (the 1920s and late 1990s) or strong pitching (the 1960s, around 2010).[1] However, additional insight into the relationship between home runs and strikeouts can be gained by relating both home runs and strikeouts to at-bats. This can be done in aggregate for baseball as a whole, in aggregate for a single player's career, or for individual players for a single year. The purpose of this article is to examine the relationship between home runs and strikeouts, after both parameters are adjusted for at-bats. All the data used for the calculations in this article are from Baseball-Reference.com.

CHECKING THE CONVENTIONAL WISDOM

The conventional wisdom suggests that there should be a positive relationship between the number of home runs hit and the number of strikeouts. Therefore, strikeouts should increase as the number of home runs increases. Data for the 2017 season for all batters with more than 400 at-bats are used to test this hypothesis. The results are shown in Figure 1.

A least-squares regression of strikeouts against home runs shows that the relationship is characterized by the equation Strikeouts = 1.9 x Home Runs + 71.

The coefficient of 1.9 is statistically significant at the 1 percent level and the coefficient of determination (the R-squared value) is 0.33.

Similar results are found using 2016 data. These results support the conventional wisdom that there is a positive relationship between home runs and strikeouts.

ADJUSTING FOR AT-BATS

Additional insight into home runs and strikeouts over time can be gained by adjusting each of them by at-bats. This is done by dividing total at-bats by home runs and by strikeouts. For example, in 2017 major-league batters hit 6,105 home runs in 165,567 at-bats for an AB/HR variable of 27.1. There were 40,104 strikeouts, so the variable AB/K was 4.1. A plot of these variables starting in 1903 is shown in Figures 2 and 3. At-bats per home run are discussed first.

First, smaller numbers are better in Figure 2, since a smaller number means that it took fewer at-bats to produce a home run. Between 1903 and 1918, hitters had between 160 and 329 at-bats per home run. No wonder this is referred to as the Deadball Era. The figure stood at 286 in 1918 but declined precipitously over the next three years, as offense increased dramatically, to 91 in 1921. AB/HR continued to decline at a

Figure 1. SO Vs HR for players with >400 AB, 2017

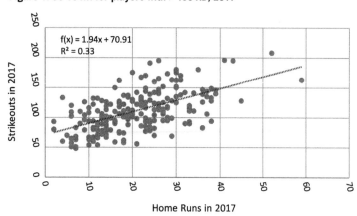

$f(x) = 1.94x + 70.91$
$R^2 = 0.33$

Home Runs in 2017

Figure 2. MLB, Total AB/Total HR: 1903–2017

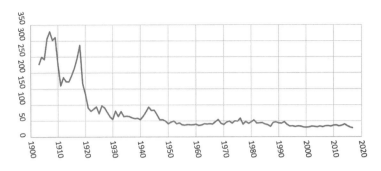

Figure 3. MLB, Total AB/Total SO: 1903–2017

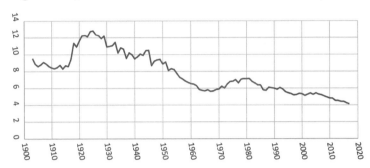

slower rate (with the exception of an uptick during the World War II years) until 1962, when it bottomed at 37. As pitching gained prominence during the 1960s, AB/HR increased to 59 in 1976. Since that year, AB/HR have declined by about half to 27 in 2017. But it should also be noted that, in spite of the record number of home runs hit in 2017, and the steady increase in home run totals over the past few years, the AB/HR number in 2017 (27) is not very much below the AB/HR figure of 29 in 2000, at the height of the steroid era.

The AB/K data are shown in Figure 3. In this case, however, smaller numbers indicate poorer performance, because it means that there were fewer at-bats between each strikeout. Not surprisingly, given the positive statistical relationship between home runs and strikeouts, the AB/K graph is similar to the AB/HR graph. AB/K peaked at 12.8 in 1925 and has declined since then to 4.1 AB/K in 2017. There was an increase between the mid-1960s and 1980, but with the exception of that time period, the trend has been downward. The 2017 number of 4.1 is surprisingly low. It means that about 25 percent of at-bats result in a strikeout. Clearly, there is little stigma attached to striking out in the modern game.

COMBINING AB/HR AND AB/K

The two parameters, AB/HR and AB/K, can be examined jointly in order to compare the effectiveness of power hitters. All other things being equal, since strikeouts are almost always a nonproductive at-bat, a slugger who strikes out less frequently is preferable to one who strikes out more frequently. Therefore, subtracting AB/K from AB/HR is a measure of the effectiveness of power hitters that includes an adjustment for how frequently they strike out. Let's call this measure HRKAB, which you're free to pronounce as either "her cab" or "home run cab." The lower the number, the better, since a smaller AB/HR figure means more frequent home runs and a higher AB/K figure means the hitter strikes out less frequently. The difference will get smaller as AB/HR decreases and AB/K increases.

The 2017 home run leader, Giancarlo Stanton, is used to demonstrate the calculations. Stanton had a historic 2017 campaign, hitting 59 home runs. He accomplished this feat in 597 at-bats while also striking out 163 times. Therefore, his AB/HR and AB/K numbers are 10.12 and 3.66 respectively. The difference between these numbers is his HRKAB, 6.46. This number means little by itself, but when compared to other power hitters, it gives a measure of the effectiveness of one power hitter compared to another. Table 1 compares Stanton's numbers to the 10 players with the next highest number of home runs in 2017.

The HRKAB numbers in Table 1 show that Stanton's 6.46 is better than all but one of the players who hit 38 or more home runs in 2017. J.D. Martinez had a better mark with 6.23. Given the historic nature of the numbers that Stanton put up, this shows that Martinez also had an excellent season even though he

Table 1. 2017 Season, HRKAB for the top 11 home run hitters

	At-bats	HR	AB/HR	K	AB/K	HRKAB
Giancarlo Stanton	597	59	10.12	163	3.66	6.46
Aaron Judge	542	52	10.42	208	2.61	7.82
J.D. Martinez	432	45	9.60	128	3.38	6.23
Khris Davis	566	43	13.16	195	2.90	10.26
Joey Gallo	449	41	10.95	196	2.29	8.66
Cody Bellinger	480	39	12.31	146	3.29	9.02
Nelson Cruz	556	39	14.26	140	3.97	10.28
Edwin Encarnacion	554	38	14.58	133	4.17	10.41
Logan Morrison	512	38	13.47	149	3.44	10.04
Mike Moustakas	555	38	14.61	94	5.90	8.70
Justin Smoak	560	38	14.74	128	4.38	10.36

trailed Stanton by 14 home runs. This is an example of the advantage of using HRKAB rather than just home runs as a measure of power hitter effectiveness. Martinez's total of 45 home runs is not that impressive by itself, but using HRKAB shows that his season was comparable to Stanton's.

Aaron Judge also had a historic season, setting a home run record for rookies. But his 208 strikeouts were the most in baseball, and his 2.6 AB/ K shows that he struck out more frequently than every third at-bat. In comparison, Mike Moustakas hit 38 home runs (14 fewer than Judge), but he struck out less than half as frequently as Judge, with an AB/K figure of 5.9. This gave Moustakas a HRKAB of 8.7, which is not too far above the 7.8 that Judge had. This is another illustration of why using HRKAB can yield greater insight than home run totals by themselves.

Table 1 shows the top 11 players in terms of home runs. It would appear that Khris Davis, with his 43 homers, is a much better power hitter than Michael Conforto (not shown in Table 1), who hit 27. However, HRKAB allows the two hitters to be compared on an apples-to-apples basis. In this case, Davis has a HRKAB figure of 10.26 while the same figure for Conforto is 10.51. So, despite the large difference in total home runs, Conforto is about as effective a hitter as Davis is.

Similarly, HRKAB can be used to identify effective power hitters even if they don't have impressive home run totals. This is easily done by ranking hitters in terms of HRKAB. Table 2 shows the top 10 list for 2017 among all players who hit at least 20 home runs.

The first thing to note about Table 2 is that there are four players in the top 10 who are not among the top 11 home run hitters shown in Table 1. Since HRKAB is a measure of power hitter effectiveness, it is not surprising that Mike Trout, Joey Votto, and Josh Donaldson appear on the list when ranked this way. All three are former MVPs who are considered among the best players in the game. Votto strikes out the least frequently, with a mark of 6.7 AB/K. Another excellent young player, Bryce Harper, is not shown in Table 2 simply because the list is only the top 10. Harper is number 12 at 10.24 HRKAB.

There is one big surprise at the top of the list. The player with at least 20 home runs with the best HRKAB figure is Matt Olson. Olson is not exactly a nationally known player. The 2017 season was his second year with the Oakland A's, and he only started playing regularly in

June. He had only 189 at-bats in 59 games, but his ratio of AB/HR was 7.88 (better than Stanton at 10.1) and his HRKAB was 4.73 (better than Stanton at 6.5). The sample size is too small to draw meaningful conclusions, but Olson even being on the list shows the advantage of using HRKAB as a measure instead of just the absolute number of home runs. HRKAB shows that Olson has the potential to be a very effective, possibly great, home run hitter.

HISTORIC COMPARISONS

Just as HRKAB can be used to compare power hitters in a given season, the measure can also be used to compare players across time. For example, Stanton's 6.46 is one of the best numbers for 2017, but how does it compare to other great power hitters? In order to answer this question, HRKAB is calculated each season for every player who hit more than 580 career home runs. The 11 players in this group are the epitome of power hitters. Their HRKAB results are therefore a good baseline for comparison. The data for the season in which each of these players reached his carer high in home runs are shown in Table 3.

Table 2. 2017 Season, top 10 in HRKAB for players with at least 20 home runs

	At-bats	HR	AB/HR	K	AB/K	HRKAB
Matt Olson	189	24	7.88	60	3.15	4.73
J.D. Martinez	432	45	9.60	128	3.38	6.23
Giancarlo Stanton	597	59	10.12	163	3.66	6.46
Mike Trout	402	33	12.18	90	4.47	7.72
Aaron Judge	542	52	10.42	208	2.61	7.82
Joey Gallo	449	41	10.95	196	2.29	8.66
Mike Moustakas	555	38	14.61	94	5.90	8.70
Joey Votto	559	36	15.53	83	6.73	8.79
Josh Donaldson	415	33	12.58	111	3.74	8.84
Cody Bellinger	480	39	12.31	146	3.29	9.02

Table 3. HRKAB for top 11 career HR hitters as of 2017 in best HR season

	Career HR	Year	At-bats	HR	AB/HR	K	AB/K	HRKAB
Barry Bonds	762	2001	476	73	6.52	93	5.12	1.40
Hank Aaron	755	1971	495	47	10.53	58	8.53	2.00
Babe Ruth	714	1927	540	60	9.00	89	6.07	2.93
Alex Rodriguez	696	2002	624	57	10.95	122	5.11	5.83*
Willie Mays	660	1965	558	52	10.73	71	7.86	2.87
Ken Griffey Jr.	630	1997	608	56	10.86	121	5.02	5.83
Ken Griffey Jr.	630	1998	633	56	11.30	121	5.23	5.83
Albert Pujols (a)	614	2006	535	49	10.92	50	10.70	0.22*
Jim Thome	612	2002	480	52	9.23	139	3.45	5.78*
Sammy Sosa	609	1998	643	66	9.74	171	3.76	5.98
Frank Robinson	586	1966	576	49	11.76	90	6.40	5.36*
Mark McGwire	583	1998	509	70	7.27	155	3.28	3.99*

*Career best; (a) Active

A natural place to start is to look at the seasons that immediately come to mind when thinking about great home run seasons. Babe Ruth's best year in terms of home runs is 1927, when he hit 60 balls out of the park. He had 540 at-bats that year so he averaged a home run exactly every nine at-bats. He struck out roughly every six at-bats and finished with 2.93 HRKAB. Interestingly, this is not Ruth's best year in terms of HRKAB. In 1931 he did even better with a figure of 1.14. Roger Maris (not shown in Table 3 because his career total for home runs is 275) had a mark of 0.87 HRKAB when he broke Ruth's record in 1961 with 61 home runs. That was the record until 1998, when Mark McGwire and Sammy Sosa orchestrated one of the most famous home run races in baseball history. Both players broke Maris' record, with McGwire hitting 70 home runs and Sosa hitting 66. McGwire also beat Sosa in terms of HRKAB that year, with 3.99 to Sosa's 5.98. Three years later, Barry Bonds broke McGwire's record when he hit 73 home runs. Bonds hit a homer at the impressive rate of one every 6.5 at-bats that year and finished with a mark of 1.40 HRKAB.

As great as all of these seasons are, in terms of the total number of home runs, they are not the best seasons in Table 3 in terms of HRKAB. The best season in the table by this measure is the 0.22 that Albert Pujols had in 2006. That was not a product of home run frequency. Pujols needed more than 10 at-bats to hit a home run that season, but his HRKAB number was very low because of the low frequency with which he struck out. Pujols struck out every 10.7 at-bats. That's roughly two to three times less frequent than many of the other AB/K numbers in Table 3, and indicates that Pujols—despite playing in a higher-strikeout era than any of the others in that group—did not need to tolerate a lot of strikeouts in order to hit a lot of home runs.

An HRKAB number so close to zero raises a question: Have there been any power hitters who struck out less frequently compared to the rate at which they hit home runs? Or in terms of this article, has anybody had a negative HRKAB figure? This question is examined by expanding the pool of players to those who have hit more than 520 career home runs and requiring a minimum of 100 at-bats to qualify. This doubles the size of the pool of players to 22. Take a minute to think about the answer before reading further.

The answer is yes, there have been two players in this expanded group who accomplished the feat. Bonds is one of them. He actually had a better season in 2004 in terms of HRKAB than he did in 2001. He hit 45 home runs in 2004, but his HRKAB figure is -0.81. The only other player to have a negative number is, not surprisingly, Ted Williams, who did it three times, in 1941, '50, and '55, when he had HRKAB figures of -4.56, -3.98, and -1.90 respectively. And, just like Pujols in 2006, he did it by rarely striking out. He only struck out 27, 21, and 24 times respectively those seasons, resulting in AB/K marks of 16.89, 15.90, and 13.33 respectively.

CONCLUSION

The purpose of this article is to explore power hitter effectiveness. To do so we introduced the metric HRKAB. While we acknowledge there are other aspects of total hitting production not included in HRKAB, it improves on the simple measure of total home runs by adjusting for the frequency of home runs per at-bat and by subtracting the strikeout rate, because a strikeout is usually a non-productive out. HRKAB allows us to compare hitters on an apples-to-apples basis. For example, in 2017, Giancarlo Stanton hit 59 home runs and had an HRKAB of 6.46. This number is worse than the 1.40 HRKAB of Barry Bonds in 2001, the year he hit 73 home runs. ∎

Acknowledgement

I would like to thank King Kaufman for his careful reading of the article and his help with developing the acronym HRKAB. The paper is much better because of his insightful comments.

Note

1. For example, Michael Bein has a web site that allows many batting and pitching statistics since 1900 to be easily plotted. See http://michaelbein.com/baseball.html; For an interesting discussion of the increase in offense that occurred between 1915 and 1920, see http://web.colby.edu/ baseball/files/2016/04/Final_LiveBall_Post.pdf; Cory Wagner discusses MLB home run totals between 1990 and 2014 in the following post: https://www.sportingcharts.com/articles/mlb/ total-home-runs-in-major-league-baseball-since-1990.aspx; For a good discussion of how pitching dominated in the 1960s, see http://www.thisgreatgame.com/1968-baseballhistory.html; David Schoenfield analyzes why pitching dominated in the 2014 season in this post: http://www.espn.com/mlb/story/_/id/ 12842711/ mlb-hurlers-rise-dominance.

Ron Hunt, Coco Crisp, and the Normalization of Hit-by-Pitch Statistics

Gary Belleville

It's a basic rule that's familiar to all baseball fans: A batter, when struck by a pitched ball, shall be awarded first base. While some people may dismiss the hit-by-pitch as a relatively minor aspect of the game, a hit batsman can have significant consequences. As an extreme example, the Tommy Byrne pitch that struck the foot of Nippy Jones in the 10th inning of Game Four of the 1957 World Series ignited a thrilling come-from-behind rally by the Milwaukee Braves, and it is generally regarded as the turning point of the series. Certain batters, such as the indomitable Ron Hunt, intentionally used the hit-by-pitch on a regular basis to boost their on-base percentage; in Hunt's case, his HBP prowess helped prop up a faltering career, extending his time in the big leagues by several years.

Aside from Hunt, many other batters throughout baseball history have routinely used the hit-by-pitch as an offensive weapon. This brings up an obvious question: Who was the best of all time at reaching base on an HBP? Previous research on this topic has relied on rudimentary statistics, such as the total number of hit-by-pitches in a season or career. While these traditional measures do provide some insight, their inherent drawbacks limit their usefulness. This article will briefly outline these deficiencies and introduce a new and improved metric for effectively comparing hit-by-pitch statistics of players, including those from different eras. This metric will then be used to identify the players who employed the hit-by-pitch to their greatest (or least) advantage. A discussion section of this paper will focus on the most noteworthy performances identified and describe some of the reasons why those players stood out so much from their peers.

DEVISING A NEW HBP METRIC
One obvious drawback with simply comparing players based on their HBP totals is that those figures do not

factor in how many opportunities each player had to get plunked. Even among the group of players with enough plate appearances to qualify for the batting title in a given season, there may be some players with roughly 50 percent more plate appearances than others. Effectively comparing career HBP totals is even more problematic using these traditional methods, since some players may enjoy 20-year careers (or more), while others may be forced to retire after only a dozen or so years in the major leagues.[1] Clearly, the formula devised for an improved HBP metric must include the total number of plate appearances.

Another significant issue that limits the effectiveness of using raw HBP totals to compare players from different eras is the fact that hit-by-pitch rates have varied significantly over the years, as shown in Figure 1. The graph, which was generated from statistics in the Lahman Baseball Database, demonstrates that hit-by-pitch rates have ebbed and flowed throughout baseball history, from an all-time high of 1.24 percent of all plate appearances in 1899 to a low of 0.32 percent in 1941.[2]

Since HBP rates have fluctuated so dramatically over the years, simply dividing the number of hit-by-pitches by the number of plate appearances to calculate a HBP average wouldn't be sufficient to effectively compare

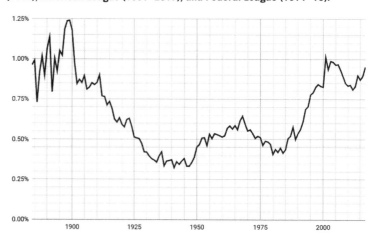

Figure 1. HBP Percentage per Plate Appearance. Yearly rates combined for the American Association (1884–91), National League (1887–2017), Players League (1890), American League (1901–2017), and Federal League (1914–15).

HBP statistics across the different eras. For instance, a batter getting hit in 5 percent of his plate appearances in 1941 would be far more significant than someone being plunked at the exact same rate in 2001, when hit batsmen were roughly three times more common. A better approach would be to devise a metric that also adjusts for the HBP rate of the corresponding season.

However, a closer look at the numbers shows that there are many seasons in which the individual leagues have had significantly different HBP rates. For example, the American League HBP rate in 1909 was roughly 40 percent higher than the corresponding National League rate. Conversely, the senior circuit's HBP rate was 21 percent greater than in the American League in 2013. Refer to Figure 2 for a graph of the HBP percentages of the individual leagues over time."

Due to the disparate HBP rates of the individual leagues, the proposed metric will adjust for the hit-by-pitch rate of the corresponding league and season instead of using a combined rate for all leagues. This will allow players to be compared relative to their league peers rather than those who may have played under markedly different conditions (e.g. opposing pitchers, fastball usage rates, and umpire strike-zone interpretations that may alter the percentage of pitches delivered high in the zone).

METHODOLOGY

Adjusted HBP, also known as HBP +, will be used to normalize hit-by-pitch numbers across leagues and seasons. Single-season HBP + numbers can be calculated for a player using the following formula (1):

$$Adjusted\ HBP = \frac{HBP}{Expected\ HBP} \times 100$$

$$where\ Expected\ HBP = \sum_{for\ all\ team\ stints} PA \times \frac{Total\ League\ HBP}{Total\ League\ PA}$$

This formula adjusts HBP numbers so that players who get hit with pitches at the same rate as the league average will have an HBP + of 100. Players who are struck twice as often as league average will have an HBP + of 200, and those who are hit at half of the league rate will have an HBP + of 50.

Career HBP + numbers can be calculated for a player using a similar formula (2):

$$Career\ Adjusted\ HBP = \frac{Career\ HBP}{\sum_{for\ all\ seasons} Expected\ HBP} \times 100$$

Please note that Expected HBP is calculated as per the single-season HBP + formula.

DATA ANALYSES

Data were downloaded from the Lahman Baseball Database and loaded into an Oracle database.[3] The author wrote several SQL queries to produce the data for the tables and figures in this article.

The Lahman Baseball Database contains complete hit-by-pitch data for the following leagues/seasons: American Association (1884–91), National League (1887–2017), Players League (1890), American League (1901–2017), and Federal League (1914–15). Batting data from other seasons and leagues were excluded from the SQL queries.

Figure 2. HBP Percentage per Plate Appearance. Data shown for the American Association (1884–91), National League (1887–2017), and American League (1901–2017). Data for the Players League (1890) and Federal League (1914–15) are not shown due to legibility issues.

DISCUSSION
Single-Season HBP Leaders (Traditional Metric)
Before we turn our attention to the single-season HBP + leaders, let's take a brief look at the top marks in our traditional metric, the total number of hit-by-pitches in a season, as shown in Table 1.

The list is dominated by Baltimore Orioles from the 1890s such as Hughie Jennings, Dan McGann, and Curt Welch. The Orioles of that era were a juggernaut, winning three consecutive National League pennants from 1894 to 1896 using an aggressive brand of small ball. The architect and manager of those teams, Ned Hanlon, was a strong proponent of using the hit-by-pitch as an offensive weapon, and his clubs led the National League in hit-by-pitches for seven consecutive seasons: the 1894–98 Orioles and the 1899–1900 Brooklyn Superbas.[4] The hit batsmen on Hanlon's squads peaked in 1898, when the Orioles were plunked an astounding 160 times in 154 games, more than the combined total of the St. Louis Browns and Pittsburgh Pirates, who finished second and third in hit-by-pitches respectively.

Single-Season HBP + Leaders
Calculating the single-season HBP + leaders across baseball history produces quite a different list than using the traditional metric. These rather eye-popping results can be found in Table 2 (opposite). Not only

does Hunt hold the top two spots of all time and five of the top 15 entries, but his 1971 season surpasses all others by an exceedingly wide margin. That year, Hunt was hit by a pitch almost 15 times more frequently than a league-average batter. To put that figure in perspective, to surpass the league-average home-run rate by a similar multiple, he would have had to have slugged a whopping 175 home runs in 1971, a season in which Willie Stargell led the National League with 48 round-trippers. Of course, Hunt was anything but a power hitter; the slap hitter spent most of his career batting leadoff or second in the order, and he was clever enough to understand his limitations and use every tool at his disposal to get on base, including intentionally getting in the way of a pitch.[5]

Hunt was quite open about his hit-by-pitch techniques. "First, I would blouse the uniform—this big, wool uniform, I would make sure it was nice and loose," he recalled in a 2015 interview. "Then I'd choke way up on the bat and stand right on top of the plate. That way, I could still reach the outside pitch. That was the Gil Hodges philosophy on hitting: The two inches on the outside corner were the pitcher's, the rest was his. I thought, 'If I can take away those two inches, and he's not perfect, I can put the ball in play and get some hits. And if he comes inside, I can get on base that way, too.'"[6]

Rule 5.05(b)(2) of the *Official Baseball Rules* clearly states that a batter hit by a pitched ball is not entitled to first base when "the batter makes no attempt to avoid being touched by the ball." To get around this stipulation, Hunt developed a spin move to help deceive the plate umpire. "The ball would be headed toward his elbow or his ribcage," said Dave Van Horne, the longtime Montreal Expos broadcaster. "He would turn his back away from the pitcher and deflect the ball with that spin move, so that he avoided those direct hits. To the average person, it would look like he was trying to get out of the way of the pitch, when, in fact, he just wanted to stand in there and take it."[7]

Another aspect that may have boosted Hunt's hit-by-pitch totals was the fact that the feisty player was almost universally disliked by both opponents and teammates.[8] He had a mean streak and a short temper, and he was not averse to resorting to fisticuffs on the field.[9] One habit that didn't exactly endear Hunt to other players in the league was his routine of picking up the ball after getting

Table 1. Single-season HBP leaders

Player	Year	Team(s)	HBPs
Hughie Jennings	1896	Baltimore Orioles	51
Ron Hunt	1971	Montreal Expos	50
Hughie Jennings	1897	Baltimore Orioles	46
Hughie Jennings	1898	Baltimore Orioles	46
Dan McGann	1898	Baltimore Orioles	39
Dan McGann	1899	Brooklyn Superbas, Washington Senators	37
Curt Welch	1891	Baltimore Orioles	36
Don Baylor	1986	Boston Red Sox	35
Curt Welch	1890	Athletics (Phila.), Baltimore Orioles	34
Craig Biggio	1997	Houston Astros	34
Tommy Tucker	1889	Baltimore Orioles	33
Hughie Jennings	1895	Baltimore Orioles	32
Brandon Guyer	2016	Tampa Bay Rays, Cleveland Indians	31
Jason Kendall	1997	Pittsburgh Pirates	31
Jason Kendall	1998	Pittsburgh Pirates	31
Steve Evans	1910	St. Louis Cardinals	31
Anthony Rizzo	2015	Chicago Cubs	30
Craig Wilson	2004	Pittsburgh Pirates	30
Chief Roseman	1890	St. Louis Browns, Louisville Colonels	29
Tommy Tucker	1891	Boston Beaneaters	29
Tommy Tucker	1887	Baltimore Orioles	29
Curt Welch	1888	Athletics (Phila.)	29

plunked and casually flipping it back to the pitcher in an act of defiance. One opponent, San Diego Padres catcher Bob Barton, took exception to Hunt's attempt to return the ball to pitcher Steve Arlin after he got plunked in consecutive at-bats in an August 1971 game, which led to Hunt yanking off Barton's mask and punching him in the face. The benches emptied, and when order was restored, Hunt was the only player ejected from the game.[10]

While Hunt was an average hitter who used the hit-by-pitch to help extend a middle-of-the-road career, the same cannot be said of Don Baylor. In a stellar 19-year career, Baylor slugged 338 home runs, won the Silver Slugger award three times, and was named the American League MVP in 1979. He was also quite happy to stand in the batter's box and let pitches hit him. Not only did he lead the American League in HBPs in eight different seasons, but in a three-year period from 1984 to '86, Baylor posted three of the top five single-season HBP+ marks in history, getting hit almost nine times more often than his American League peers. "My first goal when I go to the plate is to get a hit," he said in a 1987 interview. "My second goal is to get hit."[11]

The primary reason Baylor was hit so often was that he crowded the plate. "When the ball is inside, I don't

back away," he said. "Common sense says back away, but I guess common sense isn't that common. I just stiffen up and take the blow."[12] Baylor had a stubborn streak and he refused to be intimidated by the opposing pitcher. "There was always that confrontation," he said. "You're not going to beat me, and I'm not going to give in. I'm going to be right here. If you hit me, I'm coming right back again. I'm going to be right on the plate and you're not going to move me off the plate."[13]

Other than Hunt and Baylor, the only name that appears more than twice on the single-season HBP+ leaders in Table 2 is Chet Lemon, the Detroit Tigers and Chicago White Sox center fielder who was known for both his outstanding fielding and potent bat. Lemon's raw HBP numbers from 1981 to '83 may be rather modest, but they were partially masked by a moderate number of plate appearances and the fact that he played at a time of relatively low HBP rates. Although he led the American League in hit-by-pitches four times, Lemon spent most of his career in Baylor's HBP shadow, and he is not particularly well known as an HBP specialist by baseball fans today. Like Baylor, Lemon stood almost on top of the plate. "I actually didn't mind being pitched inside, I *wanted* to be pitched inside," he said. "I felt I could always turn on pitches. If you look at my hits, like all those doubles,

Table 2. Single-season HBP + leaders (min. 3.1 PAs per team game)

Player	Year	Team(s)	HBPs	HBP+
Ron Hunt	1971	Montreal Expos	50	1,463
Ron Hunt	1972	Montreal Expos	26	968
Don Baylor	1986	Boston Red Sox	35	885
Don Baylor	1985	New York Yankees	24	878
Don Baylor	1984	New York Yankees	23	854
Hughie Jennings	1896	Baltimore Orioles	51	829
Ron Hunt	1969	San Francisco Giants	25	733
Mike Macfarlane	1994*	Kansas City Royals	18	716
Hughie Jennings	1897	Baltimore Orioles	46	713
Chet Lemon	1983	Detroit Tigers	20	712
Frank Robinson	1956	Cincinnati Redlegs	20	704
Chet Lemon	1981*	Chicago White Sox	13	692
Chet Lemon	1982	Detroit Tigers	15	685
Ron Hunt	1968	San Francisco Giants	25	663
Ron Hunt	1974	Montreal Expos, St. Louis Cardinals	16	649
Steve Evans	1910	St. Louis Cardinals	31	627
Carlton Fisk	1981*	Chicago White Sox	12	621
Jason Kendall	1997	Pittsburgh Pirates	31	612
Jimmy Dykes	1933	Chicago White Sox	12	603
Jason Kendall	1998	Pittsburgh Pirates	31	601

* Strike-shortened season.

I think you'll find that I went down the left-field line in most of them."[14]

Career HBP Leaders (Traditional Metric)

Table 3 contains a list of the career hit-by-pitch leaders. Hall of Fame shortstop Hughie Jennings holds the record with 287, while Biggio, another Hall of Famer, is in second with 285 during his 20 seasons with the Houston Astros. As expected, the career leaders in this traditional metric are dominated by batters who played in an era of relatively high HBP rates and/or those who enjoyed lengthy careers.

Career HBP + Leaders

Table 4 (opposite), contains a tally of the top 20 hitters in career HBP + and, not surprisingly, Hunt appears in the top spot. Although his career HBP + of 713 is still comfortably ahead of Baylor's 550, the figure is considerably lower than Hunt's peak single-season numbers. In his first five years in the major leagues, Hunt "only" registered an HPB + of 372, but his use of the hit-by-pitch as an on-base tool really kicked into gear following his trade to the San Francisco Giants just prior to the 1968 season.[15] From that point on, Hunt led the National League in hit-by-pitches every year

Table 3. Career HBP leaders

Player	Years Active	HBPs
Hughie Jennings	1891–1903, 1907, 1909–10, 1912, 1918	287
Craig Biggio	1988–2007	285
Tommy Tucker	1887–99	272
Don Baylor	1970–88	267
Jason Kendall	1996–2010	254
Ron Hunt	1963–74	243
Dan McGann	1896, 1898–1908	230
Chase Utley*	2003–17	199
Frank Robinson	1956–76	198
Minnie Miñoso	1949, 1951–64, 1976, 1980	192
Jake Beckley	1888–1907	183
Jason Giambi	1995–2014	180
Andres Galarraga	1985–98, 2000–04	178
Alex Rodriguez	1994–2013, 2015–16	176
Curt Welch	1884–93	173
Carlos Delgado	1993–2009	172
Derek Jeter	1995–2014	170
Kid Elberfeld	1898–99, 1901–11, 1914	165
Fernando Viña	1993–2004	157
Fred Clarke	1894–1911, 1913–15	154
Brady Anderson	1988–2002	154

* Active as of 2018.

for the rest of his career, posting an HBP + of 941 in those seven bruising seasons.

Jennings holds the third-best career HBP + at 477. In the five-year period 1894–98, he was hit by a stunning 202 pitches, a figure that represents over 70 percent of his career total. Jennings also stood extremely close to home plate when he batted. "Hughie had a way of riding the plate, standing up as close as he could get and shoving his body out over it," said his Orioles teammate Jack Doyle.[16] While some may dismiss the hit-by-pitch statistics from this rough-and-tumble era, the achievements of Jennings, along with McGann, Tommy Tucker, and Kid Elberfeld, should not be minimized. For instance, if one excludes the batters on Hanlon's Orioles, the HBP rate for the rest of the league was 1.1 percent of all plate appearances in 1898, which is not that much different from the HBP rate in the American League in 2001 (1.05) or the National League in 2006 (1.03).

Aside from the trio of Hunt, Baylor, and Jennings, both Frankie Crosetti and Minnie Miñoso merit special mention as being head and shoulders above all others in career HBP + . Crosetti, a player and coach with the New York Yankees for 37 seasons, led the American League in hit-by-pitches eight times, including 1942, when he appeared in a mere 74 games. Crosetti was proud of his hit-by-pitch accomplishments, which were made possible by one of his coaches, Art Fletcher, who taught him the art of avoiding injury while getting hit.[17] Fletcher, ranked 11th overall in career HBP + , had an opportunity to perfect that technique years earlier as a member of the New York Giants, a team managed by the former third baseman of those pugnacious Orioles of the 1890s, John McGraw.

As baseball's first Latin American superstar, Minnie Miñoso possessed a lethal combination of speed and power. Miñoso, along with Willie Mays, helped reintroduce speed as an offensive weapon in the 1950s, and in addition to his other talents, he led the American League in hit-by-pitches a record 10 times. Like most other HBP + leaders, Miñoso crowded the plate, and he was not opposed to leaning into a pitch to "steal first."[18] He was also fearless in the batter's box; after having his skull fractured on a pitch from Bob Grim in 1955 that hit him above the left eye, he bounced back and hit better than ever upon his return.[19]

When Miñoso broke in with the Cleveland Indians in 1949, he became only the eighth openly black player in major-league history, a

Table 4. Career HBP + leaders (min. 5,000 PAs)

Player	Years Active	HBPs	HBP +
Ron Hunt	1963–74	243	712.8
Don Baylor	1970–88	267	549.7
Hughie Jennings	1891–1903, 1907, 1909–10, 1912, 1918	287	477.3
Frankie Crosetti	1932–48	114	468.0
Minnie Miñoso	1949, 1951–64, 1976, 1980	192	464.5
Dan McGann	1896, 1898–1908	230	385.1
Chet Lemon	1975–90	151	369.7
Sherm Lollar	1946–63	115	357.4
Tommy Tucker	1887–99	272	356.9
Kid Elberfeld	1898–99, 1901–11, 1914	165	352.5
Art Fletcher	1909–20, 1922	141	350.7
Gene Tenace	1969–83	91	337.4
Lonnie Smith	1978–94	92	336.7
Jason Kendall	1996–2010	254	327.1
Frank Robinson	1956–76	198	303.7
Frank Chance	1898–1914	137	298.0
Rickie Weeks	2003, 2005–17	134	296.1
Andres Galarraga	1985–98, 2000–04	178	291.7
Bucky Harris	1919–29, 1931	99	290.0
Craig Biggio	1988–2007	285	287.9

mere two years after Jackie Robinson broke the color barrier. In April 1951, he was traded to the White Sox, making the Cuban native the first black player on either of Chicago's MLB teams. Much like the seven black players before him, Miñoso endured discrimination and segregation, although he also had to deal with language and cultural issues that the others did not. Years later, Orlando Cepeda would refer to Miñoso as "the Jackie Robinson of Latino players."[20] "He was everybody's hero," Cepeda reminisced. "I wanted to be Miñoso. [Roberto] Clemente wanted to be Miñoso."[21]

Racism may have contributed to Miñoso's elevated hit-by-pitch rate, a subject he broached in a 2015 interview, mere days before he passed away suddenly. "What was I doing wrong in the game, that they'd purposefully want to hit me? They didn't do it because I'm nice-looking, and I didn't do it to get the record. I crowded the plate, because if you only have to look middle-outside, you can kill a pitcher, and if it's outside it's a ball," he said. "My father and my mother taught me there was a way to pay somebody back if they tried to break your arm or break your face: Pay them back on the field with a smile on your face."[22]

Biggio holds the modern-day high for the most career hit-by-pitches, so it is a bit of a surprise to see him only ranked 20th in career HBP + . However, he did make 12,504 plate appearances during his lengthy career, much of which was played at a time of relatively high HBP rates.[23] Fans looking for a relatively recent example of a HBP machine would be wise to refer to Jason Kendall, the rugged catcher who played most of his career with the Pirates. Not only did Kendall place well ahead of Biggio with a career HBP + of 327, but he is the only player since 1900 to have been hit by 30 or more pitches twice in a season (as of the end of 2017). Two other twenty-first century players, Rickie Weeks and Andres Galarraga, also rank higher than Biggio in career HBP + .

Career HBP + Laggards

If Hunt was the most distinguished hitter at reaching first base on a hit-by-pitch, then who was plunked the least often compared to his peers? The answer to that question can be found in Table 5 (see next page), which lists the batters with the lowest career HBP + in baseball history.

Coco Crisp, who was hit only five times in his 15 years in the big leagues, holds the distinction of having the lowest career HBP + for players with more than 5,000 plate appearances. His HBP + of 8.4 means that he was hit with a pitch roughly 12 times less often than his contemporaries. There are several reasons why Crisp was hit so infrequently, starting with the structural advantage of being a switch-hitter, which means that he was always batting against an opposite-handed pitcher. Due to typical pitch trajectories, hurlers hit opposite-handed batters significantly less often than they do same-handed hitters.[24]

Table 5. Lowest career HBP + (min. 5,000 PAs)

Player	Years Active	HBPs	HBP +
Coco Crisp	2002–16	5	8.4
Garret Anderson	1994–2010	8	9.7
José Cruz Jr.	1997–2008	5	9.9
Sandy Alomar	1964–78	3	10.1
Ruben Sierra	1986–98, 2000–06	7	11.0
Otis Nixon	1983–99	5	13.0
Neifi Pérez	1996–2007	7	13.9
Ozzie Guillén	1985–2000	7	15.0
José Reyes*	2003–17	11	15.4
Lance Johnson	1987–2000	7	16.9
Jim Hegan	1941–42, 1946–60	4	17.0
Jerry Mumphrey	1974–88	4	17.2
Joe Tinker	1902–16	10	17.3
Luis Castillo	1996–2010	12	17.8
Bones Ely	1884, 1886, 1890–91, 1893–1902	11	18.2
José Cruz	1970–88	7	18.4
Chipper Jones	1993, 1995–2012	18	19.3
Sam West	1927–42	5	19.8
Pete O'Brien	1982–93	7	20.0
Rollie Hemsley	1928–44, 1946–47	4	20.3

* Active as of 2018.

However, the fact that Crisp hit from both sides of the plate doesn't explain why he was struck by pitches so much less frequently than other switch-hitters in the American League. Crisp, an agile center fielder, also had a willingness to scoot out of the way of inside pitches, and a video review of a half-dozen examples from 2012 to 2016 of extreme inside pitches that he successfully dodged shows his quickness and dexterity at work.[25] However, perhaps the most significant reason for his extremely low HBP + is the fact that the book on Crisp was to feed him a steady diet of outside pitches. An analysis of PITCHf/x data from the last 10 years of his career shows that only 22 percent of pitches thrown to him were on the inner third of the plate or further inside.[26]

One of the more obscure players listed in Table 5 is Bones Ely, who at 6-foot-1 was the tallest man to play shortstop regularly in the big leagues during the nineteenth century.[27] The steady-fielding Ely was 155 pounds soaking wet, so his low HBP numbers could at least be partially chalked up to self-preservation. A controversial figure throughout his career, he was let go by the Pirates during the 1901 season on suspicion of recruiting players to join the upstart American League. Ely's release led the way for Honus Wagner to be converted from an outfielder to a shortstop, a move that the 27-year-old Wagner was initially hesitant to make due to Ely's popularity with Pittsburgh fans.[28]

CONCLUSIONS

By factoring in the number of plate appearances and the league-wide HBP rate, the HBP + metric provides an effective means of comparing hit-by-pitch numbers of players from different eras.

Although the HBP rates in the late nineteenth century were the highest ever recorded, the hit-by-pitch accomplishments of players of that era should not be downplayed. Ned Hanlon's Baltimore Orioles and Brooklyn Superbas were among the first teams to use the HBP as an offensive weapon, and his club skewed the hit-by-pitch rates of the entire National League for several seasons. Of all of Hanlon's batters, none were as proficient at leveraging the hit-by-pitch as Hughie Jennings, although Dan McGann was also among the very best of all time at taking one for the team. In addition, two other nineteenth-century ballplayers, Tommy Tucker and Kid Elberfeld, appear in the top 10 for career HBP + .

When viewed through an HBP + lens, Ron Hunt's modern-day record of 50 HBPs in 1971 stands out as one of the most impressive single-season records in baseball history. His feat represents an HBP + of 1,463, which means that he was plunked at a rate that was almost 15 times greater than his National League peers that season. His career HBP + of 713 easily surpasses all others, a clear indication that Hunt is worthy of being referred to as baseball's all-time HBP king. Perhaps the Montreal Expos press guide summed it up best with its cheeky assessment of Hunt: "He gets good flesh on the ball," it said.[29]

Aside from Hunt, nobody had a penchant for getting hit with a pitch like Don Baylor. Between 1984 and 1986, Baylor notched an HBP + of 854 or greater, giving him three of the top five single-season marks. By a comfortable margin, his career HBP + of 550 is the second best of all time. Chet Lemon, whose hit-by-pitch skills were overshadowed by Baylor in the 1980s, quietly posted exceptional HBP numbers. Lemon ranks seventh all time with a career HBP + of 370.

Hughie Jennings, Frankie Crosetti, and Minnie Miñoso put up equally impressive career HBP + numbers despite playing under considerably different conditions. While the trio is well behind Hunt and Baylor in career HBP + , they are still significantly ahead of all other major-leaguers.

In recent years, no batter had a better knack for reaching first base on a hit-by-pitch than Jason Kendall. Other players from the early part of the twenty-first century with a similar aptitude include Rickie Weeks, Andres Galarraga, and Craig Biggio. ■

Notes

1. This paper will use a similar approach as *The SABR Baseball List and Record Book* and only consider players with at least 5,000 plate appearances for the list of career leaders in the new HBP metric. Single-season leaders will require at least 3.1 plate appearances per team game. Society for American Baseball Research, *The SABR Baseball List and Record Book* (New York: Scribner, 2007).
2. This paper does not offer opinions on why HBP rates have fluctuated across the different eras of baseball history. While that topic may be of interest to some and it may be the subject of further research, this article will focus on the development of an improved HBP metric and the resulting insights from reviewing the all-time leaders in this metric.
3. Lahman Baseball Database, March 31, 2018, http://www.seanlahman.com/baseball-archive/statistics.
4. Jack Smiles, *"Ee-Yah": The Life and Times of Hughie Jennings, Baseball Hall of Famer* (Jefferson, NC: McFarland, 2005), 48.
5. Jonah Keri, "The Year Ron Hunt Got Hit By 50 Pitches," FiveThirtyEight, February 3, 2015, https://fivethirtyeight.com/features/the-year-ron-hunt-got-hit-by-50-pitches.
6. Keri.
7. Keri.
8. Bill James, *The New Bill James Historical Baseball Abstract* (New York: Free Press, 2001), 520.
9. Keri, "The Year Ron Hunt Got Hit By 50 Pitches."
10. Keri.
11. Jack Friedman, "For Don Baylor, Baseball Is a Hit or Be Hit Proposition," *People*, August 24, 1987, https://people.com/archive/for-don-baylor-baseball-is-a-hit-or-be-hit-proposition-vol-28-no-8.
12. Friedman.
13. Jose De Jesus Ortiz, "Don Baylor brings rugged style back to game," *Houston Chronicle*, March 28, 2004, https://www.chron.com/sports/astros/article/Baseball-Notebook-Don-Baylor-brings-rugged-style-1959380.php.
14. Mark Liptak, "Flashing Back…with Chet Lemon," White Sox Interactive, ND, http://www.whitesoxinteractive.com/rwas/index.php?category=11&id=2719.
15. Benjamin Pomerance, "Where Are They Now: Ron Hunt," Baseball Savvy, January 14, 2011, http://www.baseballsavvy.com/w_hunt.html.
16. Smiles, *"Ee-Yah,"* 79.
17. Tara Krieger, "Frankie Crosetti," SABR Bio Project, https://sabr.org/bioproj/person/460d26a7.
18. Mark Stewart, "Minnie Minoso," SABR Bio Project, https://sabr.org/bioproj/person/796bd066.
19. Larry Moffi and Jonathan Kronstadt, *Crossing the Line: Black Major Leaguers, 1947–1959* (Lincoln, NE: University of Nebraska Press, 2006), 43.
20. Jay Jaffe, "Baseball pioneer and seven-time MLB All-Star Minnie Minoso dies," *Sports Illustrated*, March 1, 2015, https://www.si.com/mlb/2015/03/01/minnie-minoso-chicago-white-sox-cubs-mlb-cuban-obituary.
21. *Los Angeles Times*, "Minnie Minoso dies; Chicago's first black big-league baseball player," March 1, 2015, http://www.latimes.com/local/obituaries/la-me-minnie-minoso-20150302-story.html.
22. Christina Kahrl, "'If Jackie Could Make It, I Could Too,'" ESPN.com, http://www.espn.com/mlb/story/_/page/blackhistoryMLBminoso/white-sox-great-minnie-minoso-integration-fanappreciation-cuba-hof-slight.
23. As of the beginning of the 2018 season, Craig Biggio ranked 11th in baseball history with 12,504 career plate appearances. Biggio's 34 HBP in 1997 translates into an HBP+ of 516; although that was the highest single-season HBP+ mark of his career, it was still well out of the top 20 of all time due to his extraordinary 744 plate appearances and a robust league-wide HBP rate of 0.88 percent.
24. Mike Fast, "Spinning Yarn: Why are Batters Hit by Pitches?" Baseball Prospectus, August 17, 2011, https://www.baseballprospectus.com/news/article/14807/spinning-yarn-why-are-batters-hit-by-pitches.
25. Neil Weinberg, "The Man Who Hasn't Been Hit in Almost Six Years," Fangraphs, January 13, 2017, https://www.fangraphs.com/blogs/the-man-who-hasnt-been-hit-in-almost-six-years.
26. The PITCHf/x data was extracted from the two 5x5 heat maps (from both the right and left sides of the plate) for the 2007 to 2016 seasons on Coco Crisp's Fangraphs player page at https://www.fangraphs.com/statss.aspx?playerid=1572.
27. Jacob Pomrenke, "Bones Ely," SABR Bio Project, https://sabr.org/bioproj/person/3a97d15b.
28. Pomrenke.
29. Jonathan Fraser Light, *The Cultural Encyclopedia of Baseball*, 2nd ed. (Jefferson, NC: McFarland, 2005), 412.

The Bats...They Keep Changing!

Steve Bratkovich

INTRODUCTION

Over the centuries, baseball bat shapes have undergone all kinds of contortions: Bat diameters have expanded and contracted and lengths have varied. Even bat wood species have transitioned from hickory and the traditional ash to maple, which dominates today in major-league baseball (MLB).

As baseball and its people have changed, the use of wood to make bats has not. In fact, at the highest level of baseball—and its blood-brother cricket—the object used to strike the ball is fashioned from a tree.[1]

The book *Baseball as America*, issued jointly by the National Baseball Hall of Fame and Museum and the National Geographic Society, argues that professional baseball has stuck with a wooden bat for numerous reasons, including safety, competitiveness, and the preservation of tradition.[2] This article focuses on MLB bats and the renewable material called wood.

SIZES, SHAPES, AND SPECIES OF WOOD

During the mid-1840s, when the Knickerbockers were playing the game under their rules, all players were responsible for their own bat. This "bring your own bat" to the game resulted in many different sizes, shapes, and species of wood.[3]

The earliest bats were quite primitive, akin more to a "club" than what we think of as a bat in the twenty-first century. Some bats came from tree limbs and some began their life as ax handles. Early bats were often flat—like cricket bats—and most were handmade from various trees such as sycamore, cherry, spruce, chestnut, poplar, and basswood. For a short time, the cricket-favored willow was the preferred choice.[4] Ash, maple, and pine were also favorite woods of batters in the earliest days of the game.[5]

By trial and error, ash and hickory emerged as the most popular woods for bat-making in the 1870s and '80s.[6] Even though hickory is a very dense, strong wood, ash eventually held the advantage since it has an unusually high strength-to-weight ratio. Physicist Robert Adair, in his book *The Physics of Baseball*, wrote, "Ash was celebrated in medieval times as the only proper wood from which to construct the lances of knights-errant; an ash lance was light enough to carry and wield and strong enough to impale the opposition."[7] Roger Maris used a 33-ounce ash bat to hit 61 home runs in one season; a hickory bat of the same dimensions would weigh about 42 ounces.[8]

In 1884, the year the modern fountain pen was invented, the first Louisville, Kentucky-manufactured bat was made. As legend has it, John "Bud" Hillerich, shaped a baseball bat on a lathe out of white ash for the American Association's Louisville slugger, Pete Browning. Browning, who had a .341 career batting average, had broken his favorite bat earlier in the day. Hillerich spoke with Browning after the game, promising to make the slugger a new bat in his father's shop. Browning went 3-for-3 the next day with Hillerich's bat. This simple event gave birth to a new Hillerich industry: baseball bat manufacturing.[9]

From the beginning, the Hillerich firm, later to become Hillerich & Bradsby, tried different tree species for bat-making. Eventually, the company settled on white ash (northern range of species) as the best.[10] For roughly a century, white ash (*Fraxinus americana*) dominated the bat market for all manufacturers and players. Within the first few minutes of Ken Burns's (originally) 18-hour documentary series *Baseball*, narrator John Chancellor intones, "The bat is made of turned ash, less than 42 inches long, not more than 2¾ inches in diameter."[11]

But players and entrepreneurs kept tinkering with bat dimensions and types of wood. In the late 1880s, many bat manufacturers were seeking new sources of raw material. The durable wood used for wagon tongues—which connects a wagon's wheel base to the draft animals—was considered fine material, and as Americans became less dependent on the horse and buggy, more of them were becoming available.[12] Even newspaper ads advertised for wagon-tongue wood. As an example, A.G. Spalding & Brothers purchased wagon tongues from the general population with the specific intent of "turning [shaping the tongues] into bats." In one ad, Spalding noted that he wanted to buy 100,000 old wagon tongues for use in his company's Wagon Tongue Brand of baseball bats. Spalding warned that he only wanted "straight grained, well-seasoned, second growth ash."[13]

At least one historian speculates that an early form of European baseball might not have included a bat at all. David Block, in the Our Game blog, writes, "The question of when a bat was first introduced to the pastime remains a mystery. It is certainly possible, if not probable, that, at its outset, the game of baseball [in Europe] did not employ a bat, and that a bare hand was used to strike the pitched ball." Block muses that the difference in baseball in Europe and the United States might be due to different social underpinnings. In England, baseball was played primarily by girls and young women, whereas in America, baseball became a sport for boys and men. The American version of the game—faster, rougher, and on a larger scale—might have accompanied the adoption of the bat perhaps perceived in England as too un-lady-like.[14]

Regardless of when a bat was first introduced in Europe, the vast Atlantic Ocean did not negate the appeal of baseball in the New World. The sport grew, and with the expanding interest in baseball came many modifications in bat dimensions. While players were making the switch to wagon-tongue wood, another revelation appeared to them: A ball could be hit much more solidly with a round bat. This observation led to the adoption of a round bat as the standard that exists to this day.

David Magee and Philip Shirley explain in their book *Sweet Spot* that the design of a bat, including a round barrel, was not "a given" in the early days of the game:

> Some players used square bats for bunting, while others played with square-handled bats. Others preferred thick handles, resulting in a bat that was nearly uniform in width from handle to barrel. Players selected their bat of choice often based on little more than a hunch; if they happened to connect solidly in a game with one, they often used that one bat until someone convinced them otherwise. The bat, in other words, was still evolving by trial and error.[15]

Henry "Heinie" Groh spent 16 seasons in the major leagues, mostly with the New York Giants and Cincinnati Reds. He debuted in 1912 with the Giants and wrapped up his career with a one-year stint in Pittsburgh. Groh posted a lifetime batting average of .292 and hit .474 in the 1922 World Series against the New York Yankees. He batted over .300 four times in a five-year span and was a part of five pennant winners, including two World Series championships. However, Groh is best remembered not for these or other accomplishments but for his famed "bottle bat," which had about a 17-inch barrel that tapered sharply to a thin, roughly 17-inch handle. Groh had small hands, and because thin handles were not commonly made in the early twentieth century, Groh devised a bat he could get his fingers around. The advantage of Groh's long barrel gave him a greater hitting zone. Although Groh's unique bat didn't catch on with many of his contemporaries, the "bottle bat" worked for him.[16]

As the twentieth century gave way to the twenty-first, more and more major-league players switched to hard (sugar) maple. When the 2017 big-league season began, about 75 percent of major-league batters swung maple (*Acer saccharum*). Ash bats had dramatically fallen to 10–15 percent of the big-league market.[17] Also, the number of firms supplying bats to MLB skyrocketed from the days of Pete Browning and Heinie Groh to 32 different licensed manufacturers for the 2017 season.[18]

RULES

As the game spread in America, more and more men were organized into clubs, or teams, for the purpose of playing baseball. In 1857, clubs gathered in lower Manhattan to discuss rules and competition between one another (a year later a permanent body was formed: the National Association of Base Ball Players).[19] One of the rules adopted stated that a bat "must be round, and must not exceed two and half inches in diameter in the thickest part. It must be made of wood, and may be of any length to suit the striker."[20] Prior to this bat rule, a player could lug a piano leg to the plate if he wished.

However, flat bats were legalized by the National League in 1885, and became ideal for bunting.[21] In 1893, the 1857 rule requiring a round bat was reinstated.[22] Soft woods (like pine) were banned as well.[23]

In 1868, a rule setting the maximum length at 40 inches was established. A year later the length was extended to 42 inches. In 1895, the National League allowed the bat diameter to expand to two and three-quarters inches.[24] As of the 2018 MLB season, the maximum length remains at 42 inches and the diameter is capped at 2.61 inches.[25]

A bat altered by scooping out an ounce or so of wood from the end of the barrel is known as a cupped bat. Cupped bats were originally manufactured in the late 1930s by the Hanna Manufacturing Company of

Athens, Georgia, but weren't legalized in MLB until 1975. Cupping results in a lighter bat and shifts the center of gravity farther down the barrel.[26] Jose Cardenal signed the first contract with Louisville Slugger for a cupped bat. Because the handle was not too thin and the barrel not too heavy, Cardenal said, "It's just a very well-balanced bat. You put it in your hands and you can feel it."[27] Many major leaguers in the twenty-first century use a cupped bat. The 2018 MLB rule book limits the "cup" to one and one-quarter inches in depth and between one and two inches in diameter.[28]

The bat handle rules can be traced all the way back to the late 1800s, according to baseball historian John Thorn. In 1885, a rule was put into place by the National League that limited twine on the handle end of the bat to 18 inches. The next year, the rule was modified to account for gritty stuff like rosin and dirt. Like the previous year's rule, 18 inches was the maximum length these substances could be applied to the bat handle.[29]

In 1976, the rule was updated. Team owners had discovered that pine tar on bat handles was the leading culprit for the increasing number of soiled baseballs being thrown out of play by umpires. Led by Calvin Griffith of the Minnesota Twins (formerly the Washington Senators), the owners, with an eye on saving money, pushed for a more specific rule that mentioned the sticky substance. According to Fillip Bondy's book *The Pine Tar Game*, the updated rule stated:

> The bat handle, for not more than eighteen inches from its end, may be covered or treated with any material or substance to improve the grip. Any such material, including pine tar, which extends past the eighteen inch limitation, in the umpire's judgment, shall cause the bat to be removed from the game. No such material shall improve the reaction or distance factor of the bat.[30]

The new language was tested on July 24, 1983, when George Brett of the Kansas City Royals connected with a two-run homer off Goose Gossage of the Yankees in the top of the ninth inning with two out and New York clinging to a one-run lead. Yankees manager Billy Martin popped out of the dugout and insisted to the umpires that Brett had used an illegal bat, since the pine tar on the handle extended well beyond 18 inches. After much discussion and arguing, including screaming and cursing by both teams, the umpires agreed with Martin, and Brett was called out, nullifying the home run that had put the Royals ahead. Several days later, after a lengthy review, American League President Lee MacPhail sided with Brett and the Royals and called for a make-up of the game's conclusion, replayed from the point of Brett's home run. Since the 1976 rule (1.10) said nothing about a player using a bat like Brett's being called out, the home run was ruled legal.[31]

After that famous "Pine Tar Game," a note was added to the rule book. It states that if an umpire discovers a bat that has any material or substance beyond 18 inches from its end *after* it has been used in play, the batter will not be ruled out or ejected from the game. Furthermore, the rule book states, that action on the field will not be nullified and protests will not be allowed (a new numbering system was implemented in 2015; for the 2018 season, the updated rule is 1.10).[32]

BATS IN MLB

The first baseball bats in America, even before the formation of the Knickerbockers, were heavy, thick, and barely tapered. To a baker, as well as to baseball players and fans, the bats looked like long rolling pins.[33]

Deadball Era (prior to 1920)

This era was called "deadball" primarily because of the baseball. According to Lawrence Ritter:

> The game was played differently then simply because the ball was different. It looked just like today's baseball, but when it was hit, no matter how hard, it did not carry long distances.... With such a dead ball, batters didn't swing with all their might.... They practiced bunting and place hitting...they punch[ed] line drives... and slapp[ed] hard ground balls.[34]

Also, the extremely heavy bats favored in the first decade of the twentieth century were made primarily of hickory, a very dense wood.[35] However, some players used ash as their lumber of choice since ash had the reputation as the best wood for a baseball bat.

Wee Willie Keeler, standing only 5'4" and weighing a mere 140 pounds, used a bat characteristic of the time regarding weight. Keeler's bat often weighed 46 ounces (although because of his small stature, the length was a Little League size of 30 inches). In 1897, he batted .424 and set a National League record with a 45-game hitting streak. (According to the SABR bio-project site, Keeler's streak stretched from the last game in 1896 through 44 games to begin the 1897 season.) Keeler, who batted .341 between 1892 and 1910, espoused the hitting philosophy of the day: "Hit 'em where they ain't."[36]

Another MLB star who exemplified the Deadball Era of "hit 'em where they ain't" was Ty Cobb, the 11-time American League batting champion and all-time leader in batting average (.366). As an 11-year-old, one of Cobb's first bats was crafted for him with scrap wood by his next-door neighbor, a coffin maker. Supposedly, the wood used was black mountain ash.[37] Since local names for different trees can vary, and since the only tree in the twenty-first century called a "mountain ash" is a smallish ornamental tree that isn't really an ash at all, the guess is that Cobb's "coffin-wood" bat was actually white ash (or perhaps green ash), native to his home state of Georgia. Regardless, Cobb brought his "lucky" bat in a cloth bag to the big leagues in 1905.[38]

In the majors, Cobb wielded a 34½-inch bat that weighed a hefty 40 ounces (although he used a lighter bat near the end of his career). He spread his hands a few inches apart on the handle, which made the heavy bat easier to control as well as providing stability to slap at the ball. Cobb explained in 1910, as quoted in the Charles Leerhsen book *Ty Cobb: A Terrible Beauty*, "The great hitters of our time grab their batting sticks a foot or more from the handle and, instead of swinging, aim to meet the ball flush.... I stick to the sure system of just meeting the ball with a half-way grip."[39]

In the early twentieth century, Cobb wasn't the only superstar to swing a heavy bat or use a "split-grip" at the plate. Honus Wagner, who won eight National League batting average titles with the Pittsburgh Pirates between 1900 and 1911, also held his hands apart on the handle and wielded a bat that weighed up to 38 ounces. Although Wagner's bat was two ounces lighter than Cobb's, his "stick" was a tad longer, measuring 35 inches in length.[40]

Another Hall of Famer, Edd Roush, who started his 18-year big-league career in 1913, explained that his 48-ounce hickory bat with a thick handle was important to his success.[41] As quoted in *Good Wood*, Roush said, "I only take a half swing at the ball, and the weight of the bat rather than my swing is what drives it."[42]

Live-ball Era (approximately 1920 to 1940)

The Deadball Era ended for a host of reasons, including the elimination of the spitball (1920), the use of more (and cleaner) baseballs per game (1921), and the center of the baseball featuring a rubber-coated cork core instead of a pure rubber core (introduced in

Wee Willie Keeler reportedly stood 5' 4" and weighed 140 pounds. His 46-ounce bat was a typically hefty weight for the time, but because of Keeler's small stature, the length was only 30 inches.

1910).[43] Not only was the heavy hickory bat gradually replaced by the lighter ash as the preferred tree species for MLB bats, but two other major shifts occurred.

First, a trend of tapered bat handles began. Rogers Hornsby is often overlooked as the player who popularized the practice of using a thin-handled bat. Hornsby realized that a thin handle enabled him to get the bat head through the hitting zone more quickly. He hit 36 home runs in his first five full seasons (1916–20) but changed his ways in the roaring '20s. Hornsby ripped 21 homers in 1921 while also leading the National League in batting average (.397), hits (235), doubles (44), triples (18), runs (131), and RBIs (126). He followed up that spectacular season by clubbing a league leading 42 home runs in 1922 while batting .401 and driving in 152 runs. For six consecutive seasons starting in 1920, Hornsby led his league in batting average, on-base percentage, and slugging average.[44] With Hornsby's success at the plate, coupled with the rise of a certain other superstar, the trend toward tapered handles had begun in earnest.

Although Babe Ruth swung a heavy bat (40 to 47 ounces), especially in his early playing days, he realized that a thin handle (patterned after Hornsby) and big barrel gave him more of an opportunity to swing from his heels.[45] (Ruth sometimes used bats heavier than 50 ounces, but mostly in spring training.)[46] Since Ruth was paid to hit home runs rather than advance runners one base at a time, he wanted a large barrel on his bat so he could clobber the "lively" ball. He once said, "There's nothing that feels as sweet as a good, solid smash."[47] A thick bat handle—favored by many Deadball Era stars—did little for what Ruth wanted to accomplish at the plate.

The 714th and last home run Ruth ever hit was in 1935 with the Boston Braves, when he was experimenting with, in his mind, a lightweight bat, 36 ounces.

Ruth's blast was the first time a baseball cleared the right field roof at Pittsburgh's Forbes Field.[48]

Author Charles Leerhson pointed out major differences between slugger Ruth and deadball place-hitter Cobb:

> [Ruth] held [the] bat very differently than Cobb gripped his much thicker club—all the way down at the knob end—and swung it differently, too, with a decisive uppercut motion, and with such force that if his spikes stuck in the clay around home plate, he could, and sometimes did, wrench his back. When he made contact with…the "jackrabbit ball," the results were electrifying.[49]

Some deadball stars frowned on the home run since the game they played depended on place hitting, advancing the runner, bunting, and speed. It's important to recognize that baseball started out as a meadows game. Once it was realized that people would dole out money to watch the game, fences were erected to eliminate non-payers. To preserve baseball's character, it was not uncommon to build the fences far away to keep them out of play. Consequently, batters—with the encouragement of coaches, managers, and owners—attempted to hit line drives, not out-of-the-park home runs.[50]

To shed a perspective on distant outfield fences, consider the original Braves Field in Boston. The left-field foul line was an incredible 402.5 feet from home plate, and the right-field line measured 375 feet (though some books and websites list the ballpark's opening-day distance between 369 and 402 feet). Center field measured a whopping 461 feet, with right-center a gigantic 542 feet from home plate. A 10-foot wall rimmed the park. When Cobb saw the new Braves Field in 1915, he exclaimed, "Nobody will ever hit a baseball out of *this* park." Cobb's prediction was a bit sarcastic but it did take a batter two years before a home run sailed over the wall.[51]

Cobb was one of the deadball players who initially believed Ruth's swing-for-the-fences mentality was the wrong way to play baseball.[52] Even many managers, writers, and fans argued that Ruth's bombastic show lessened the game and wasn't effective baseball strategy. They preferred the more chess-like game played since the late 1800s.[53] However, Cobb finally relented and said Ruth's style was a legitimate, alternative, and crowd-pleasing way to play the game and should be encouraged.[54] Consequently, and with the blessings of two of the all-time greats of the game (Ruth and Cobb), thinner handled bats changed the game for the next century.

Bat-Speed Era (approximately 1940 to 2000)

Another milestone in the history of MLB bats occurred when Ted Williams came to the majors. Williams, a rookie in 1939, batted .327, smacked 31 home runs and led the American league in RBIs with 145.[55] Williams said many times that hitting a baseball properly is the most difficult thing to do in all of sports, and succeeding three times out of 10 is a great performance.[56] If so, Williams did very well at the task. He posted a lifetime .344 batting average in a career that spanned from 1939 to 1960.[57]

Williams swung a bat crafted from ash, the favored wood of that era. His bat weighed 33–34 ounces for much of his career, a light bat compared to Ruth, Cobb, and most players in the early days of baseball.[58] The bat length for Williams was 35 inches, comparable to the length of many deadball stars.[59] However, the "secret" for Williams was the speed he generated with a light bat.

Williams' theory was that a lighter bat could still produce plenty of power because a hitter generates more bat speed. One story that Williams told in his own book, *My Turn At Bat*, is that as a minor-leaguer in 1938, he was feeling tired near the end of the season. By chance, Williams picked up a teammates' light bat and liked the feel of it. Williams wrote, "It had a bigger barrel than mine, but lighter by two ounces at least." Williams got the approval of his teammate to use the bat that night with the bases loaded. Against a left-handed pitcher, Williams wrote, "I got behind two strikes. I choked up on the bat, thinking that I would just try to meet the ball…. The pitch was low and away, just on the corner of the plate. *Unnh.* I give this bat a little flip and gee, the ball flew over the center-field fence." A 410-foot grand slam and Williams' theory of a light bat was solidified.[60] As the old saying goes: The rest is history.

Williams was meticulous (some might say paranoid) about the weight of his bats. He urged the Red Sox to install a scale in the clubhouse so he could precisely weigh his bats, saving a trip to the post office.[61] One time, as legend has it, J.A. Hillerich Jr., laid out six bats on a motel bed in front of Williams. Hillerich then asked Williams to close his eyes and pick out the heavy bat, which was only a half-ounce heavier than the other five, a difference likely imperceptible to most humans, but not to the Splendid Splinter. Williams wrote in *My Turn At Bat*, "I picked it out [the heavy bat] twice in a row."[62]

Williams was meticulous about more than just the weight of his bats. He once got a new shipment of bats from the Hillerich & Bradsby factory. Displeased with the handles, he returned the set of Louisville Sluggers with a short note that said, "Grip doesn't feel just right." Upon receipt at Hillerich & Bradsby, employees used calipers to measure the bat handles. Williams was right: The handles were five thousandths of an inch thinner than he had ordered![63]

Ted Williams was a perfectionist as a hitter beyond just the "feel," heft, and end-to-end distance of his bats. As Magee and Shirley wrote in their book, *Sweet Spot*:

> He wanted the very best bat, from the best wood, with the perfect weight and length. He wanted to know what made a bat as good as it could be and spent time with the craftsmen who made [his] Louisville Sluggers to understand how to maximize their potential. In fact, he once called his first visit to Hillerich & Bradsby's Louisville Slugger bat factory "…one of the greatest things I ever did in my life."[64]

Williams always seemed to be looking for the slightest edge over pitchers. He was known by bat factory employees at Hillerich & Bradsby as the player who climbed over piles of lumber, looking for the perfect piece, which included 10 growth rings or fewer per inch. When he found it, he showed the lumber to one of the craftsmen, and demanded that *his* bat be made from this particular chunk of wood. Williams wanted the best tools of the trade, and he got them. "Everybody said I got the best bats in the league," he said.[65]

Williams wasn't the only MLB player to demand a particular piece or type of wood. The man who signed Williams on a scouting trip to California in the 1930s was also very particular about his lumber.

Eddie Collins, then the general manager of the Boston Red Sox, had enjoyed a 25-year career beginning in 1906 and spanning the Deadball Era and the roaring '20s.[66] He hit third and played second base for both Philadelphia and Chicago in the American League, collecting over 3,300 hits and leading the Athletics to three World Series championships. But Collins was remembered by Louisville Slugger employees for probing through stacks of wood for just the right cut.[67]

Collins wanted all of his bats made from the heart of the tree. Since heartwood is darker than the lighter-colored sapwood, his bats often were reddish or dark brown on one side and white on the other. Input—or special requests—from major leaguers to bat-makers is encouraged as long as the contribution

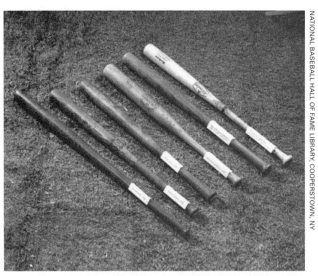

From left to right, bats of Dan Brouthers (1880s), Charles Comiskey (1886), a 1910 model, Heinie Groh's Bottle Bat (1915), Max Carey (1920–25), and Willie Mays's 500th home run bat from 1962.

conforms to the rules of the game. Williams and Collins are two prolific hitters who stand out for their finicky, but legal, demands.[68]

Heavy bats made a short-lived comeback in the 1960s with a few marquee players. Roberto Clemente sometimes swung a 39-ouncer, and Orlando Cepeda and Dick Allen hefted bats that weighed 40 ounces or more.[69] Clemente often took a couple of bats to the on-deck circle, making his final selection on "feel," intuition, and the tendencies of the pitcher. In spite of these star players, lighter weight bats were in MLB to stay. For example, Hank Aaron primarily used a 31–32 ounce bat, and Rod Carew won seven batting average titles swinging a 32-ouncer.[70] Joe Morgan carried a lightweight, 30-ounce bat to the plate.[71] Even David Ortiz swung a 32-ounce bat early in his career, and later switched to 31½ ounces.[72] More recent stars like Bryce Harper (31–33 ounces), Mike Trout (average of 31¾ ounces), Kris Bryant (31 ounces) and Joe Mauer (31–33 ounces) swing light lumber.[73]

In 1920, most bats used by major leaguers were typically no lighter than 36 ounces. At the beginning of the twenty-first century, bat racks in MLB held few bats heavier than 36 ounces. Of course, the range of weight, length, wood type, shape, handle diameter, and other bat factors vary from player to player.[74]

Maple-Bat Era (approximately 2000 to present)

When Derek Jeter broke into the big leagues in 1995, he used a 32-ounce white ash Louisville Slugger with a length of 34 inches.[75] The Jeter bat is one of many examples of the dominance of ash as the preferred wood for bat-making through the twentieth century.

However, wood enthusiasts and bat gurus continued to experiment with new innovations, including looking for a new wood that would give the batter an advantage. One such innovation was hard maple.

Joe Carter of the Toronto Blue Jays was the first MLB player to use a maple bat in a game, in 1997. He was also the first to hit a homer with one.[76] Carter said, "When you first use them, it's a totally different feel from a normal [ash] bat. I mean, totally different. After you use them, you don't want to go back."[77]

Maple has long been a fixture in the sporting world because of its hardness and durability. Many of the hardwood floors used for basketball courts are made from maple. The different shades of maple (called "grades") give many courts a distinct appearance. Of the 30 National Basketball Association courts, 29 are made from maple (the Boston Celtics court is oak).[78]

In the middle of the 1999 season, Barry Bonds of the San Francisco Giants began using a maple bat full-time. In 2001, he used a 34-inch, 32-ounce hard sugar maple model with a half-cupped barrel. Bonds' bat was crafted for him by Canadian Sam Holman, who had the experience of over two decades in the carpentry business. In the 2001 season, Bonds crushed single-season records for home runs (73) and slugging average (.863) using his custom-made Sam Bat. After Bonds' power display, maple bats surged in popularity in the major leagues. Many players believed that maple added home runs to their totals (although an exit velocity study demonstrated otherwise).[79] As of the 2017 season, approximately three-fourths of big leaguers strode to the plate carrying a maple bat.[80] Ash was a distant second-most popular, followed by the up-and-coming yellow birch (*Betula alleghaniensis*).[81]

Maple is denser, and thus heavier, than ash. But since most players want lighter lumber, maple bats tend to have thinner handles. As any player, at any level, knows, a thin-handled bat is more likely to break on an inside-pitch. Also, the grain pattern of maple is more difficult to see than ash, leading to inferior bats and difficult-to-detect hairline fractures creeping into the game. Consequently, broken, shattered, and snapped bats were becoming more common in the professional game in the first decade of the twenty-first century.[82]

In 2008, a wave of incidents involving flying shards of shattered bats swept baseball. On April 15, 2008, Pirates hitting coach Don Long had his left cheek

Heinie Groh is remembered for his famed "bottle bat," which had about a 17-inch barrel that tapered sharply to a thin, roughly 17-inch handle. Groh had small hands, and because thin handles were not commonly made in the early twentieth century, he devised a bat he could get his fingers around. The long barrel gave him a greater hitting zone.

slashed; on April 25, a fan's jaw was broken in two places when the barrel of Todd Helton's bat hit her in the face; and in June umpire Brian O'Nora's forehead was cut when Kansas City catcher Miguel Olivo's bat shattered.[83]

MLB funded a study that explored, among other topics, the likely reason for the high incidence of shattered bats. One of the study's key findings centered on the anatomical differences between ash (easy to see grain slope) and maple (difficult to see grain slope). MLB adopted recommendations based on this finding, particularly regarding maple. One of the recommendations adopted by MLB was to rotate where the trademark on maple and similar species appeared by 90 degrees, so that hitters would make contact with the hardest wood. MLB also required manufacturers of non-ash bats to place a clear, quarter-sized spot on the traditional trademark side of the bat handle to help inspectors see the grain. These policy changes reduced maple bat "flying shard incidents" from about one per game in 2008 to to less than one every three games in 2016.[84]

Pests have also wreaked havoc on North American trees in the maple-bat era. The emerald ash borer (EAB) and Asian longhorned beetle (ALB) are two invasive insects that have devastated woodlands that supply bat wood to MLB. Because EAB is often spread via the transport of firewood, Hillerich & Bradsby teamed with the Nature Conservancy on a campaign to limit the movement of wood called "Buy It Where You Burn It."[85] As opposed to EAB's single species preference for ash, ALB feeds on numerous trees, including elm, birch, willow, poplar, and black locust. Unfortunately for baseball, one of its favorite trees to dine on is maple. The US Department of Agriculture soberly reported that the Asian longhorned beetle could inflict worse damage than Dutch elm disease, chestnut blight, and gypsy moths.[86] Fortunately, yellow birch has not had the ALB complete a life cycle on it.[87]

FINAL THOUGHTS

Baseball, and in particular the baseball bat, has changed over time. But in the twenty-first century, major-league bats continue to be made from a single piece of wood. As we near the beginning of that century's third decade, some fans wonder if aluminum or other materials will replace wood as the choice for major-league bats.[88] Will maple continue its dominance in the game? What is the future of ash? Are insects like the emerald ash borer, the Asian longhorned beetle, or other invasive pests a serious threat to the trees that produce MLB bats? Is there an alternative species for bat wood, perhaps yellow birch, that will require serious discussion in 20, 50, or 100 years?

However, what is known, and not debated or challenged, is that the sizes, shapes, and species of wood, bat rules, and player bat preferences change over time. ∎

Notes

1. Beth Hise, *Swinging Away: How Cricket and Baseball Connect* (London: Scala Books, 2010), 10, 48.
2. John Odell, ed., *Baseball as America* (Washington: National Geographic Society and Cooperstown, NY: National Baseball Hall of Fame and Museum, 2002), 260–61.
3. Bernie Mussill, "The Baseball Bat: From the First Crack to the Clank," *Oldtyme Baseball News*, no. 2 (1998), 21–25.
4. Stuart Miller, *Good Wood: The Story of the Baseball Bat* (Chicago: ACTA Publications, 2011), 83.
5. Josh Leventhal, *A History of Baseball in 100 Objects: A Tour Through the Bats, Balls, Uniforms, Awards, Documents, and Other Artifacts That Tell the Story of the National Pastime* (New York: Black Dog & Leventhal Publishers, 2015), 201.
6. Miller, *Good Wood*, 84.
7. Robert Adair, *The Physics of Baseball*, 3rd ed. (New York: Perennial, 2002), 114, 138.
8. Adair, 114.
9. Dan Gutman, *Banana Bats & Ding-Dong Balls: A Century of Unique Baseball Inventions* (New York: Macmillan, 1995), xviii; Miller, *Good Wood*, 107.
10. Steve Rushin, *The 34-Ton Bat* (New York: Little, Brown and Company, 2013), 60.
11. "Baseball: A Film By Ken Burns," Episode 1, "First Inning: Our Game," directed by Ken Burns, written by Geoffrey C. Ward, Burns, PBS, 1994.
12. Gutman, *Banana Bats*, 7; Miller, *Good Wood*, 84.
13. Bob Hill, *Crack of The Bat: The Louisville Slugger Story* (Champaign, IL: Sports Publishing, 2002), 7; Gutman, *Banana Bats*, 7. Second growth is a forest that grows up after a disturbance and leads to trees being replaced. In the case of ash, the tree replacement is typically from seed of nearby trees.
14. John Thorn, "A Peek into the Pocket-book," *Our Game*, April 19, 2016, https://ourgame.mlblogs.com/apeek-into-the-pocket-book-a9bd03dfe31d (accessed May 1, 2017).
15. David Magee and Philip Shirley, *Sweet Spot: 125 Years of Baseball and The Louisville Slugger* (Chicago: Triumph Books, 2009), 8.
16. Leventhal, *A History of Baseball in 100 Objects*, 2015; Adair, *The Physics of Baseball*, 130.
17. Scott Drake, vice president of business operations for baseball bat manufacturer PFS Teco, author interview, April 5, 2017.
18. Unnamed source, author interview, February 28, 2017.
19. Leventhal, *A History of Baseball in 100 Objects*, 37, 73. The NABBP was replaced by the National Association of Professional Base Ball Players (NA) in 1871. In 1876, the National League of Professional Base Ball Clubs was formed, and still exists today.
20. Leventhal, 37, 203.
21. Miller, *Good Wood*, 84.
22. Magee and Shirley, *Sweet Spot*, 22.
23. Gutman, *Banana Bats*, 10; Miller, *Good Wood*, 84.
24. Leventhal, *A History of Baseball in 100 Objects*, 203.
25. Tom Lepperd, ed. *Official Baseball Rules: 2018 Edition* (New York: Office of the Commissioner of Baseball, 2018), 5 (MLB rule 3.02 a).
26. Gutman, *Banana Bats*, 26.
27. Miller, *Good Wood*, 89.
28. Lepperd, ed. *Baseball Rules: 2018*, 5 (MLB rule 3.02 b).
29. Filip Bondy, *The Pine Tar Game: The Kansas City Royals, the New York Yankees, and Baseball's Most Absurd and Entertaining Controversy* (New York: Scribner, 2015), 5.
30. Bondy, 4.
31. Bondy, 4-6, 144–45, 148, 162–63.
32. Leppard, *Baseball Rules: 2018*, 5.
33. Hill, *Crack of the Bat*, 4–6.
34. Lawrence Ritter, *The Story of Baseball*, 3rd ed. (New York: Morrow Junior Books, 1999), 26–27.
35. Adair, *The Physics of Baseball*, 114.
36. Hill, *Crack of the Bat*, 6; Miller, *Good Wood*, 22–23.
37. Charles Leerhsen, *Ty Cobb: A Terrible Beauty* (New York: Simon & Schuster, 2015), 36.
38. Leerhsen, 96.
39. Hill, *Crack of the Bat*, 10; Miller, *Good Wood*, 84; Leerhsen, *Ty Cobb*, 201, 324, 361. In *Sweet Spot*, Magee and Shirley, note that the first bat order Cobb placed for his Louisville Slugger was 32 ounces, and that Cobb got most of his hits with a Louisville Slugger.
40. Miller, *Good Wood*, 84.
41. Miller, 21–22.
42. Miller, 21–22.
43. Ritter, *The Story of Baseball*, 26, 28; "Spitball," Baseball Reference Bullpen, https:// www.baseball-reference.com/bullpen/Spitball; "Baseball (ball)," Wikipedia, https://en.wikipedia.org/wiki/Baseball_(ball) (both sites accessed August 22, 2018).
44. Ritter, 86; Leventhal, *A History of Baseball in 100 Objects*, 197.
45. Hill, *Crack of the Bat*, 11; Miller, *Good Wood*, 86.
46. Miller, 21.
47. Miller, 7.
48. Adair, *The Physics of Baseball*, 115.
49. Leerhsen, *Ty Cobb*, 307.
50. Adair, *The Physics of Baseball*, 105–106.
51. Ron Selter and Phil Lowry, author interviews, August 25, 2018; Curt Smith, *Storied Stadiums: Baseballs History Through its Ballparks* (New York: Carroll & Graf Publishers, 2001), 123. Thanks also to an anonymous reviewer of an earlier article draft.
52. Leerhsen, *Ty Cobb*, 308.
53. Leventhal, *A History of Baseball in 100 Objects*, 194; Leerhsen, Ty Cobb, 309.
54. Leerhsen, 308.
55. "Ted Williams," Baseball Reference, https://www.baseball-reference.com/players/w/willite01.shtml (accessed August 19, 2018).
56. Magee and Shirley, *Sweet Spot*, 68; Ritter, *The Story of Baseball*, 117.
57. "Ted Williams," Baseball Reference.
58. Ted Williams, *My Turn at Bat: The Story of My Life* (New York: Simon and Schuster, 1969), 54, 173; Hill, *Crack of the Bat*, 10.
59. Miller, *Good Wood*, 13; Hill, *Crack of the Bat*, 10.

60. Williams, *My Turn*, 54.
61. Williams, 54–55, 109.
62. Williams, 55; Magee and Shirley, *Sweet Spot*, 71.
63. Gutman, *Banana Bats*, 33; Magee and Shirley, 71.
64. Magee and Shirley, 64, 68.
65. Magee and Shirley, 68; Miller, *Good Wood*, 13.
66. Paul Mittermeyer, "Eddie Collins," SABR Biography Project, http://sabr.org/bioproj/person/c480756d (accessed June 13, 2017).
67. Magee and Shirley, *Sweet Spot*, 29.
68. Magee and Shirley, 29.
69. Miller, *Good Wood*, 87.
70. Adair, *The Physics of Baseball*, 115 (Aaron's bat); Hill, *Crack of the Bat*, 10 (Carew's bat).
71. Miller, *Good Wood*, 23.
72. Miller, 55.
73. "Bryce Harper's Bat;" "Mike Trout's Bat;" "Kris Bryant's Bat;" Bat Digest, https://www.batdigest.com/mlbbats (accessed September 1, 2018); "Joe Mauer," VintageBats.com, http://www.vintagebats.com/feature_page-JoeMauer.htm (accessed August 4, 2017).
74. Adair, *The Physics of Baseball*, 113.
75. Magee and Shirley, *Sweet Spot*, 128.
76. Miller, *Good Wood*, 53–54.
77. Miller, 91.
78. Tim Newcomb, "Facts about floors: Detailing the process behind NBA hardwood courts," *Sports Illustrated*, December 2, 2015, https://www.si.com/nba/2015/12/02/nba-hardwood-floors-basketball-court-celtics-netsmagic-nuggets-hornets (accessed June 26, 2017).
79. Miller, *Good Wood*, 91–92; Stephen Canella, "Against the Grain," *Sports Illustrated*, March 25, 2002, https://www.si.com/vault/issue/703412/108/2 (accessed November 27, 2017).
80. Scott Drake, author interview; Everett Rogers, *Diffusion of Innovations*, 3rd ed., (New York: Free Press, 1983).
81. Scott Drake, author interview.
82. Miller, *Good Wood*, 91–93.
83. Lou Dzierzak, "Batter Up: Shattering Sticks Create Peril in MLB Ballparks," *Scientific American*, July 14, 2008, https://www.scientificamerican.com/article/baseball-bat-controversy (accessed August 26, 2018); Dave van Dyck, "Danger: Flying Objects," *Chicago Tribune*, May 25, 2008, http://articles.chicagotribune.com/2008-05-25/sports/0805240422 _1_maple-bats-major-league-baseball-darts/2 (accessed September 1, 2018).
84. Scott Drake, unnamed source, author interviews.
85. "Transported firewood can spread devastating invasive species," the Nature Conservancy https://www.nature.org/ourinitiatives/urgentissues/land-conservation/forests/firewood-buy-it-where-you-burn-it.xml; "About," DontMoveFirewood.org, https://www.dontmovefirewood.org/ about (both accessed August 26, 2018).
86. US Forest Service personnel, author interview, March 6, 2017.
87. "Asian Longhorned Beetle: Annotated Host List," US Department of Agriculture, January 2015, https://www.aphis.usda.gov/plant_health/plant_pest_info/asian_lhb/downloads/ hostlist.pdf (accessed August 26, 2018).
88. In 1989, Peter Gammons wrote in *Sports Illustrated*: "Like it or not, the crack of the bat is inevitably being replaced by a ping. By the turn of the century even the majors will probably have put down the lumber and picked up the metal." Gammons, "End of an Era," *Sports Illustrated*, July 24, 1989.

Racial Parity in the Hall of Fame

Dr. David J. Gordon

HISTORICAL BACKDROP

Although the first all-professional baseball organization, the National Association, was established in 1871, only six years after the Civil War, Major League Baseball began with the establishment of the National League in 1876. MLB's first seven decades took place against of backdrop of Reconstruction, Jim Crow laws, and lynchings, and MLB was a creature of its time. Black players were unwelcome from the beginning. In 1883, Chicago White Stockings team captain Cap Anson refused to let his team take the field for an exhibition game against a Toledo team that employed an African American catcher named Moses Fleetwood Walker.[1] Although Anson relented when faced with the loss of his share of gate receipts, incidents of this sort were repeated through the 1880s until there was a de facto ban of players of color from MLB.

This ban was enforced through 1946 by a "gentlemen's agreement" among team owners, with the support of league presidents and, after 1920, Commissioner Kenesaw Mountain Landis.[2] The lack of a formal policy enabled Landis to proclaim disingenuously, "There is no rule, formal or informal, or any understanding—unwritten, subterranean, or sub-anything—against the hiring of Negro players by the teams of organized ball."[3] Although widely circulated allegations that Landis scuttled an attempt by Bill Veeck to purchase and integrate the Phillies in 1943 are probably untrue (or at least greatly exaggerated), Landis clearly did not use his power to promote integration during his nearly 25 years as Commissioner.[4]

Integration of MLB gained traction only after Landis died in November 1944 and was succeeded by former Kentucky Senator Albert "Happy" Chandler, who proclaimed that if black men "can fight and die in Okinawa, Guadalcanal, and in the south Pacific, they can play baseball in America."[5] When Brooklyn Dodgers general manager Branch Rickey signed Jackie Robinson, assigned him to Montreal in 1946, and promoted him to Brooklyn, where he debuted on April 15, 1947, integration of MLB finally became a reality.[6]

Now that MLB has been integrated for 72 years (about half its history), it is appropriate to ask how black players have fared—not so much in their achievements on the field, which are obviously impressive, but in receiving equal recognition for their accomplishments in the Hall of Fame. There are two aspects to this question:

1. Among players who made their major league debuts on or after April 15, 1947, are black, Latino, and white players with comparable on-field accomplishments equally likely to win election to the Hall of Fame?

2. Does the number of Negro League players chosen for the Hall of Fame in 1971–2006 represent a fair ratio to the number of white Hall of Famers who debuted before April 15, 1947?

METHODS

Classification as Pre- or Post-Integration

The date when MLB was integrated is marked by a bright line on April 15, 1947. The simplest way to delineate between players who belong to the pre- or post-integration eras is by whether the player debuted before Robinson (when segregation was in full force) or afterward, under the new paradigm of racial integration. However, many of the players who debuted before Robinson played much of their careers in the post-integration era. I have calculated the midpoint of every player's career, defined as the year when that player's cumulative Wins Above Replacement (WAR) first exceeded half of his eventual career total.[7] For the purpose of these analyses, I have assigned every player who reached his career midpoint in 1947 or earlier to the pre-integration category, and every player who reached his career midpoint after 1947 to the post-integration category.

JAWS

To answer the two questions posed above, one needs an objective, race-neutral metric of a player's credentials for the Hall of Fame. No single metric is perfect for this purpose, but I believe the Jaffe WAR Score (JAWS) is probably the best single published metric available.[8] JAWS, which is based on WAR, is derived by adding a player's total career WAR to the total WAR for his seven best seasons and dividing the sum by two.

JAWS shares many of the limitations of the underlying WAR statistic. It does not consider postseason performance and it systematically undervalues catchers and relief pitchers. I have set the JAWS standard for the HOF to 36 for relief pitchers, 40 for catchers, and 48 for everyone else. Players with JAWS equaling or exceeding these thresholds are deemed JAWS-Plus, while those below these thresholds are deemed JAWS-Minus.

By these standards, there are 206 HOF-eligible JAWS-Plus players, compared to 226 men who were actually elected to the HOF as MLB players (not including managers, executives, umpires, and Negro League players). Although I use JAWS in this article as a dichotomous standard for HOF credentials, I will readily concede that there are some JAWS-Minus players who deserve enshrinement and some JAWS-Plus players who do not. But the JAWS-Plus vs. JAWS-Minus dichotomy is useful to characterize groups of players on the average by a single objective metric, even though it provides only a partial picture of any single player's HOF qualifications. An additional 29 pre-1947 Negro League players have been elected to the HOF, but detailed statistical records of their careers are lacking and objective comprehensive metrics like JAWS are unavailable. My analysis includes steroid users, but not banned players Pete Rose or the eight banned players from the Black Sox scandal.[9]

Demographic Categories

Baseball's segregation policy from the 1880s through 1946 was directed mainly at players of post-Columbian African descent and was based primarily on skin color. Fair-skinned players with Latino ancestry (e.g., Ted Williams, whose mother was Mexican) and American Indians (of whom Baseball Almanac lists 49 examples) were not banned.[10] For the purpose of this article, I have followed the US Census demographic classification by race and ethnicity, which divides the population into Hispanic or Latino (persons whose ancestry derives from the Spanish-speaking countries of the Americas and Caribbean, regardless of race), black or African American (non-Latinos with African ancestry, including Canadians and natives of English-, French-, and Dutch-speaking Caribbean islands with African ancestry), and white or European American (non-Latinos of European ancestry).[11]

Only two American Indians—Chief Bender (Ojibwe) and Zack Wheat (Cherokee)—are in the Hall of Fame; both were JAWS-Minus. The other categories (Alaska Natives, Asians, Pacific Islanders) are not germane to this discussion, since they were never banned from MLB and have produced no candidates for the Hall of Fame. Since the Census allows persons to self-identify, and most Latino immigrants are fluent in English and identify as American in a generation or two, I have counted only players who were themselves born outside the United States or whose parents were born outside the United States as Latino.

RESULTS

Members of the Hall of Fame: Tables 1 and 2 list the players elected to the Hall of Fame by the Baseball Writers Association of America (BBWAA) and the various versions of the Veterans Committee (VET).[12] The latter body was formed in 1939 as the Old-Timers Committee. From 1953 to 2009 it was known as the Veterans Committee. Since 2010 there have been three separate committees that each focus on a different era. This article uses Veterans Committee as shorthand for the entire process.[13] Tables 1 and 2 are subdivided into JAWS-Plus and JAWS-Minus Players. The higher proportion of JAWS-Plus players among BBWAA (83 percent) than VET (38 percent) electees is not entirely surprising, since the BBWAA had the first crack at most post-1900 players, with the Veterans Committee only voting on the "leftovers." However, the Veterans Committees also had more "relaxed" HOF standards than the BBWAA for pre-World War II players, especially for friends and teammates of ex-players who served on the committee.[14] This obvious cronyism had a far bigger impact in the pre-integration era, when 67 percent of Hall of Famers were put there by the Veterans Committee, than in the post-integration era, when only 14 percent were. The large number (59) of JAWS-Minus pre-integration Hall of Famers, 52 of whom were put there by the Veterans Committee, has made the Hall of Fame considerably whiter than it would otherwise be.

Table 3 shows the 29 players elected to the Hall of Fame based on their careers in Negro Leagues. The list includes 26 African American players and three Latino players. Some of them had limited major-league exposure late in their careers; most had no opportunity at all to play in the major leagues. The nine players elected between 1971 and 1977 were chosen by the Committee on Negro Baseball Leagues. Longtime Negro League manager Rube Foster (1981) and the eight players elected in 1987–2001 were chosen by the Veterans

Table 1. Baseball Writers Association of America (BBWAA) Electees to the Hall of Fame

	JAWS-Plus* (n=106)									JAWS-Minus* (n=22)		
Year**	Name (Posn)	Race***	Year**	Name (Posn)	Race***	Year**	Name (Posn)	Race***		Year**	Name (Posn)	Race***
1899	Young, Cy (SP)	W	1951	Robinson, Jackie (2B)	AF	1978	Fisk, Carlton (C)	W		1899	Keeler, Willie (RF)	W
1906	Lajoie, Nap (2B)	W	1953	Spahn, Warren (SP)	W	1979	Ryan, Nolan (SP)	W		1919	Maranville, Rabbit (SS)	W
1906	Wagner, Honus (SS)	W	1954	Wynn, Early (SP)	W	1979	Gossage, Rich (RP)	W		1924	Pennock, Herb (SP)	W
1908	Mathewson, Christy (SP)	W	1954	Berra, Yogi (C)	W	1980	Schmidt, Mike (3B)	W		1928	Traynor, Pie (3B)	W
1915	Cobb, Ty (CF)	W	1954	Snider, Duke (CF)	W	1980	Brett, George (3B)	W		1931	Terry, Bill (1B)	W
1915	Collins, Eddie (2B)	W	1954	Roberts, Robin (SP)	W	1981	Winfield, Dave (RF)	AF		1935	Dean, Dizzy (SP)	W
1915	Johnson, Walter (SP)	W	1958	Mantle, Mickey (CF)	W	1982	Dawson, Andre (RF)	AF		1937	Medwick, Joe (LF)	W
1917	Speaker, Tris (CF)	W	1959	Banks, Ernie (SS)	AF	1982	Carter, Gary (C)	W		1949	Kiner, Ralph (LF)	W
1917	Alexander, Grover (SP)	W	1959	Mathews, Eddie (3B)	W	1982	Eckersley, Dennis (RP)	W		1952	Campanella, Roy (C)	AF
1920	Sisler, George (1B)	W	1961	Wilhelm, Hoyt (RP)	W	1983	Yount, Robin (SS)	W		1952	Lemon, Bob (SP)	W
1923	Hornsby, Rogers (2B)	W	1962	Mays, Willie (CF)	AF	1984	Murray, Eddie (1B)	AF		1960	Ford, Whitey (SP)	W
1924	Heilmann, Harry (RF)	W	1962	Kaline, Al (RF)	W	1987	Smith, Ozzie (SS)	AF		1963	Koufax, Sandy (SP)	W
1926	Ruth, Babe (RF)	W	1962	Drysdale, Don (SP)	W	1987	Raines, Tim (LF)	AF		1964	Aparicio, Luis (SS)	LA
1926	Frisch, Frankie (2B)	W	1963	Aaron, Hank (RF)	AF	1988	Henderson, Rickey (LF)	AF		1968	Brock, Lou (LF)	AF
1927	Vance, Dazzy (SP)	W	1964	Robinson, Frank (RF)	AF	1988	Molitor, Paul (DH)	W		1971	Stargell, Willie (LF)	AF
1930	Simmons, Al (LF)	W	1965	Marichal, Juan (SP)	LA	1988	Boggs, Wade (3B)	W		1972	Perez, Tony (1B)	LA
1931	Gehrig, Lou (1B)	W	1966	Clemente, Roberto (RF)	LA	1989	Gwynn, Tony (RF)	AF		1973	Hunter, Catfish (SP)	W
1931	Cochrane, Mickey (C)	W	1966	Killebrew, Harmon (1B)	W	1989	Ripken, Cal (SS)	W		1977	Fingers, Rollie (RP)	W
1932	Lyons, Ted (SP)	W	1967	McCovey, Willie (1B)	AF	1989	Sandberg, Ryne (2B)	W		1979	Rice, Jim (LF)	AF
1932	Grove, Lefty (SP)	W	1967	Williams, Billy (LF)	AF	1994	Larkin, Barry (SS)	AF		1979	Sutter, Bruce (RP)	W
1932	Waner, Paul (RF)	W	1967	Robinson, Brooks (3B)	W	1995	Alomar, Roberto (2B)	LA		1989	Puckett, Kirby (CF)	AF
1933	Hartnett, Gabby (C)	W	1968	Gibson, Bob (SP)	AF	1996	Griffey, Ken (CF)	AF		1998	Hoffman, Trevor (RP)	W
1934	Gehringer, Charlie (2B)	W	1969	Yastrzemski, Carl (LF)	W	1996	Thomas, Frank (DH)	AF				
1934	Foxx, Jimmie (1B)	W	1972	Jenkins, Fergie (SP)	AF	1996	Maddux, Greg (SP)	W				
1934	Cronin, Joe (SS)	W	1972	Perry, Gaylord (SP)	W	1996	Biggio, Craig (2B)	W				
1934	Hubbell, Carl (SP)	W	1974	Morgan, Joe (2B)	AF	1997	Glavine, Tom (SP)	W				
1936	Ruffing, Red (SP)	W	1974	Jackson, Reggie (RF)	AF	1997	Smoltz, John (SP)	W				
1936	Ott, Mel (RF)	W	1974	Seaver, Tom (SP)	W	1997	Bagwell, Jeff (1B)	W				
1936	Dickey, Bill (C)	W	1974	Bench, Johnny (C)	W	1997	Piazza, Mike (C)	W				
1938	Greenberg, Hank (1B)	W	1975	Carew, Rod (2B)	LA	1999	Rodriguez, Ivan (C)	LA				
1940	Appling, Luke (SS)	W	1975	Carlton, Steve (SP)	W	1999	Johnson, Randy (SP)	W				
1941	DiMaggio, Joe (CF)	W	1975	Palmer, Jim (SP)	W	2000	Martinez, Pedro (SP)	LA				
1941	Feller, Bob (SP)	W	1976	Niekro, Phil (SP)	W	2001	Thome, Jim (1B)	W				
1944	Boudreau, Lou (SS)	W	1976	Sutton, Don (SP)	W	2002	Guerrero, Vladimir (RF)	LA				
1948	Williams, Ted (LF)	W	1977	Blyleven, Bert (SP)	W	2002	Jones, Chipper (3B)	W				
1950	Musial, Stan (LF)	W										

* "JAWS-Plus" refers to relief pitchers with JAWS ≥ 36, catchers with JAWS ≥ 40, and all other players with JAWS ≥ 48. "JAWS-Minus" refers to players who are not JAWS-Plus.

** The midpoint of the player's career (See Methods—"Classification as Pre- or Post-Integration" for detailed definition).

*** W = White, AF = African American, LA = Latino (See Methods—"Demographic Categories" for detailed definitions).

Table 2. Veterans and Old-Timers Committee (VET) Electees to the Hall of Fame (Players Only)

JAWS Plus* (n=37)						JAWS Minus* (n=61)					
Year**	Name (Posn)	Race***	Year**	Name (Posn)	Race***	Year**	Name (Posn)	Race***	Year**	Name (Posn)	Race***
1883	Ward, John Montgomery (SS)	W	1904	Wallace, Bobby (SS)	W	1879	White, Deacon (3B)	W	1924	Rice, Sam (RF)	W
1884	Galvin, Pud (SP)	W	1907	Plank, Eddie (SP)	W	1884	O'Rourke, Jim (LF)	W	1926	Sewell, Joe (SS)	W
1884	Radbourn, Old Hoss (SP)	W	1908	Brown, Mordecai (SP)	W	1885	Kelly, King (RF)	W	1927	Bottomley, Jim (1B)	W
1885	Keefe, Tim (SP)	W	1908	Crawford, Sam (RF)	W	1887	Ewing, Buck (C)	W	1927	Haines, Jesse (SP)	W
1885	Welch, Mickey (SP)	W	1910	Walsh, Ed (SP)	W	1891	McCarthy, Tommy (RF)	W	1927	Hoyt, Waite (SP)	W
1886	Anson, Cap (1B)	W	1913	Baker, Home Run (3B)	W	1891	McPhee, Bid (2B)	W	1929	Combs, Earle (CF)	W
1888	Brouthers, Dan (1B)	W	1920	Coveleski, Stan (SP)	W	1892	Thompson, Sam (RF)	W	1929	Cuyler, Kiki (RF)	W
1888	Connor, Roger (1B)	W	1922	Faber, Red (SP)	W	1894	Duffy, Hugh (CF)	W	1929	Jackson, Travis (SS)	W
1889	Clarkson, John (SP)	W	1928	Goslin, Goose (LF)	W	1896	Beckley, Jake (1B)	W	1929	Lindstrom, Freddie (3B)	W
1893	Rusie, Amos (SP)	W	1937	Vaughan, Arky (SS)	W	1897	Jennings, Hughie (SS)	W	1929	Manush, Heinie (LF)	W
1894	Hamilton, Billy (CF)	W	1941	Mize, Johnny (1B)	W	1897	Kelley, Joe (LF)	W	1929	Wilson, Hack (CF)	W
1895	Nichols, Kid (SP)	W	1942	Gordon, Joe (2B)	W	1901	Collins, Jimmy (3B)	W	1930	Hafey, Chick (LF)	W
1897	Delahanty, Ed (LF)	W	1946	Newhouser, Hal (SP)	W	1903	Flick, Elmer (RF)	W	1931	Lazzeri, Tony (2B)	W
1899	Burkett, Jesse (LF)	W	1949	Reese, Pee Wee (SS)	W	1904	Chesbro, Jack (SP)	W	1931	Waner, Lloyd (CF)	W
1899	Davis, George (SS)	W	1954	Ashburn, Richie (CF)	W	1905	Chance, Frank (1B)	W	1932	Klein, Chuck (RF)	W
1902	McGinnity, Joe (SP)	W	1964	Bunning, Jim (SP)	W	1906	Joss, Addie (SP)	W	1934	Averill, Earl (CF)	W
1903	Clarke, Fred (LF)	W	1966	Santo, Ron (3B)	W	1907	Bresnahan, Roger (C)	W	1935	Ferrell, Rick (C)	W
1903	Willis, Vic (SP)	W	1986	Trammell, Alan (SS)	W	1908	Tinker, Joe (SS)	W	1935	Gomez, Lefty (SP)	W
1904	Waddell, Rube (SP)	W				1909	Evers, Johnny (2B)	W	1937	Herman, Billy (2B)	W
						1914	Marquard, Rube (SP)	W	1938	Lombardi, Ernie (C)	W
						1917	Schalk, Ray (C)	W	1946	Doerr, Bobby (2B)	W
						1918	Hooper, Harry (RF)	W	1948	Slaughter, Enos (RF)	W
						1919	Bender, Chief (SP)	AI	1949	Rizzuto, Phil (SS)	W
						1919	Carey, Max (CF)	W	1950	Kell, George (3B)	W
						1919	Wheat, Zack (LF)	AI	1952	Doby, Larry (CF)	AF
						1920	Roush, Edd (CF)	W	1953	Schoendienst, Red (2B)	W
						1921	Bancroft, Dave (SS)	W	1957	Fox, Nellie (2B)	W
						1921	Youngs, Ross (RF)	W	1963	Cepeda, Orlando (1B)	LA
						1923	Rixey, Eppa (SP)	W	1963	Mazeroski, Bill (2B)	W
						1924	Grimes, Burleigh (SP)	W	1985	Morris, Jack (SP)	W
						1924	Kelly, High Pockets (1B)	W			

*   "JAWS-Plus" refers to relief pitchers with JAWS ≥ 36, catchers with JAWS ≥ 40, and all other players with JAWS ≥ 48. "JAWS-Minus" refers to players who are not JAWS-Plus.

**   The midpoint of the player's career (See Methods—"Classification as Pre- or Post-Integration" for detailed definition).

*** W = White, AF = African American, LA = Latino (See Methods—"Demographic Categories" for detailed definitions).

Table 3. Negro League Players Elected to the Hall of Fame (1971–2006)

African American Players						Latino Players	
Elected	Name	Elected	Name	Elected	Name	Elected	Name
1971	Satchel Paige	1995	Leon Day	2006	Andy Cooper	1977	Martin Dihigo
1972	Josh Gibson	1996	Bill Foster	2006	Frank Grant	2006	Jose Mendez
1972	Buck Leonard	1997	Willie Wells	2006	Pete Hill	2006	Cristobal Torriente
1973	Monte Irvin	1998	Bullet Rogan	2006	Biz Mackey		
1974	Cool Papa Bell	1999	Smokey Joe Williams	2006	Louis Santop		
1975	Judy Johnson	2000	Turkey Stearnes	2006	Mule Suttles		
1976	Oscar Charleston	2001	Hilton Smith	2006	Ben Taylor		
1977	Pop Lloyd	2006	Ray Brown	2006	Jud Wilson		
1987	Ray Dandridge	2006	Willard Brown				

Committee. The remaining 12 players and five executives were chosen by the Special Committee on Negro Leagues in 2006. The interested reader may find more information about these players (including incomplete statistical records) in Lawrence Hogan's *Shades of Glory*.[15]

To complete the picture, Table 4 lists the 63 eligible JAWS-Plus players (as of January 2018) who have not

been elected to the Hall of Fame, broken down by era and race.

It is not surprising that there are more such players in the post-integration era, since the post-integration lists include 12 players who were on the 2017 BBWAA ballot and many others who might still be elected by the Veterans Committee, while the HOF window has probably closed for most pre-integration players.

Table 4. JAWS-Plus Players Who Are Not in the Hall of Fame

Mid-Career	Name (Posn)	Mid-Career	Name (Posn)	Mid-Career	Name (Posn)	Mid-Career	Name (Posn)
1874	Mathews, Bobby (SP)	1960	Boyer, Ken (3B)	1968	Allen, Dick (1B)	1972	Tiant, Luis (SP)
1877	Bond, Tommy (SP)	1972	Bando, Sal (3B)	1969	Davis, Willie (CF)	1995	Palmeiro, Rafael (1B)
1882	McCormick, Jim (SP)	1972	Wood, Wilbur (SP)	1969	Wynn, Jim (CF)	1996	Martinez, Edgar (DH)*
1883	Whitney, Jim (SP)	1974	Munson, Thurman (C)	1973	Bonds, Bobby (RF)	1999	Sosa, Sammy (RF)*
1887	Caruthers, Bob (SP)	1976	Grich, Bobby (2B)	1973	Smith, Reggie (RF)	2001	Ramirez, Manny (LF)*
1887	Glasscock, Jack (SS)	1976	John, Tommy (SP)	1983	Randolph, Willie (2B)	2006	Santana, Johan (SP)*
1887	Mullane, Tony (SP)	1976	Nettles, Graig (3B)	1986	Whitaker, Lou (2B)		
1888	Buffinton, Charlie (SP)	1976	Simmons, Ted (C)	1996	Bonds, Barry (LF)*		
1889	King, Silver (SP)	1976	Tenace, Gene (C)	1997	Lofton, Kenny (CF)		
1895	Breitenstein, Ted (SP)	1978	Evans, Darrell (3B)	2000	Sheffield, Gary (RF)*		
1899	Dahlen, Bill (SS)	1978	Reuschel, Rick (SP)	2002	Jones, Andruw (CF)*		
1910	Magee, Sherry (LF)	1978	Tanana, Frank (SP)				
1922	Shocker, Urban (SP)	1980	Bell, Buddy (3B)				
1926	Uhle, George (SP)	1982	Evans, Dwight (RF)				
1932	Ferrell, Wes (SP)	1982	Hernandez, Keith (1B)				
1937	Walters, Bucky (SP)	1984	Stieb, Dave (SP)				
		1988	Hershiser, Orel (SP)				
		1989	Saberhagen, Bret (SP)				
		1994	Appier, Kevin (SP)				
		1994	Clemens, Roger (SP)*				
		1994	Cone, David (SP)				
		1994	Finley, Chuck (SP)				
		1995	McGwire, Mark (1B)				
		1997	Brown, Kevin (SP)				
		1997	Walker, Larry (RF)*				
		1998	Olerud, John (1B)				
		1999	Mussina, Mike (SP)*				
		2001	Edmonds, Jim (CF)				
		2001	Schilling, Curt (SP)*				
		2003	Rolen, Scott (3B)*				

* On BBWAA ballot in 2017 election; and therefore not yet considered by the Veterans Committee.

RACIAL PARITY IN THE HALL OF FAME

Let us now return to our original two questions concerning racial parity in the Hall of Fame. Table 5 compares the number of JAWS-Plus players in each racial/ethnic group in the post-integration era with the number that would be expected if the distribution of JAWS matched the underlying racial/ethnic makeup of MLB. Clearly, it does not. There have been almost twice as many JAWS-Plus black players (32) in the post-integration era as the 17.2 that would have been expected based on the fact that black players comprised about 14 percent of MLB players during this period.[16] A statistical test comparing the percentage of black players in the JAWS-Plus group (25.8 percent) with the percentage of black players in MLB during this period yields a Z-score of 3.8 (P < 0.001), indicating that black Hall of Famers are significantly more likely than whites to be found in the JAWS-Plus group.[17] By contrast, the number of JAWS-Plus Latino players (13) is almost exactly as expected, while the number of JAWS-Plus white players (79) is 86 percent of the 92.2 expected.

There are no eligible JAWS-Plus Asian players yet—and won't be until five years after Ichiro Suzuki retires. Also, the explosion of the Latino contingent in MLB, from 11.8 percent in 1986 to 27.4 percent in 2016, is only beginning to be reflected in the population of HOF-eligible players. As players like Mariano Rivera, Alex Rodriguez, David Ortiz, Carlos Beltran, Albert Pujols, and Adrian Beltre become HOF-eligible, the increase in JAWS-Plus Latino players is likely to outpace the increase in black or white players.

The disproportionate success of socioeconomically disadvantaged minorities with limited opportunities for advancement elsewhere is not unprecedented in baseball or in other sports. One need only look back to the preeminence of Irish immigrants in nineteenth-century baseball as a prime example. Indeed, of the 41 players in the Hall of Fame who began their careers before 1900, 15 (37 percent) were the sons of Irish immigrants.[18] In any case, the remarkable success of black players in post-integration baseball has certainly put the lie to the old canard that they lacked the capacity to compete with white players on the major-league level. Despite Commissioner Landis's absurd insistence that the absence of black players in MLB for more than 60 years had nothing to do with a deliberate policy of racial discrimination, most MLB executives, like P.K. Wrigley of the Cubs, admitted that their real fear was that attendance by white fans would be affected adversely by integration, and they rationalized that they had to wait for the right time to integrate.[19]

Having established the disproportionate representation of black players among the best players in MLB during the past 70-plus years, what about their representation in the Hall of Fame? Table 6 shows that black players are at least equally well represented during this period.

Table 5. Observed vs. Expected Prevalence of JAWS-Plus by Race

Race	% of MLB Players	JAWS-Plus Players*	
		Expected**	Actual
White	74.4%	92.2	79
African American	13.9%	17.2	32
Latino	11.6%	14.4	13
Asian	0.1%	0.1	0
Total	100%	124	124

*   "JAWS-Plus" refers to relief pitchers with JAWS ≥ 36, catchers with JAWS ≥ 40, and all other players with JAWS ≥ 48.

**   Based on distibution of 124 JAWS-Plus players in proportion to their representation in the MLB Population.

Table 6. Post-Integration Demographics of the Hall of Fame

Race	% of MLB Players	Hall of Famers	
		Expected*	Actual
White	74.4%	75.1	64
African American	13.9%	14.0	27
Latino	11.6%	11.7	10
Asian	0.1%	0.1	0
Total	100%	101	101

*   Based on distibution of 101 JHOF players in proportion to their representation in the MLB Population.

Table 6 is parallel to Table 5 and compares the numbers of post-integration white, black, and Latino players in the Hall of Fame to the numbers of each group that would have been expected based on their representation in the MLB population as a whole. Almost twice as many black players (27) from this period have been elected to the Hall of Fame than the 14 who would have been expected based on proportional representation ($Z = 3.7$, $P < 0.001$). Conversely, the number of white players elected to the Hall of Fame in this period (64) is 85 percent of the 75.1 who would have been expected based on proportional representation. The numbers of Latino players (10) and Asians (0) in the Hall of Fame are in line with their representation in the population of all MLB players, although (as in Table 5) the number of Latino players in the Hall of Fame will likely exceed expectations as more of the top Latino players of the past 30 years retire and become eligible for consideration by the BBWAA.

Table 7 addresses the equity of the post-integration Hall of Fame voting process by asking whether the best players of the three major racial/ethnic groups (i.e., the JAWS-Plus players) are equally likely to win election to the Hall of Fame or whether there is a lingering racial bias. The voting process is, of course, sequential. First, players who have been retired for five or more years appear on the BBWAA ballot, whereupon they have up to 10 years (it used to be 15) to be elected or rejected. Rejected players then enter the purview of the Veterans Committee, where currently they are considered in batches of 10 by era, with eras rotating from year to year. The BBWAA has treated black players well, electing 66 percent of JAWS-Plus black players compared to 56 percent of JAWS-Plus white players and 54 percent of JAWS-Plus Latino players. The small black-white difference is not statistically significant ($Z = 0.98$, 2-sided $P = 0.33$).[20] The BBWAA has also elected five JAWS-Minus black players, as well as eight white players and two Latino players, from the post-integration era. Clearly, African Americans, who comprise one-third of JAWS-Minus post-integration players elected by the BBWAA to the Hall of Fame, are well represented there as well.

However, the report card for the Veterans Committee, which has elected no JAWS-Plus (and only two JAWS-Minus) minority players to the Hall of Fame, is mixed at best. Although the numbers are small due to the tightening of the Veterans Committee's standards in the past two decades, the committee has elected five of the 30 JAWS-Plus post-integration white players under their purview, as well as seven JAWS-Minus white players. This racial difference in voting patterns is statistically significant ($Z = -2.45$, 2-sided $P = 0.014$).

Now, one could hypothesize that the reason for that difference may be that the Veterans Committee never gets to consider most of the elite minority players because they have already been elected by the BBWAA, but there are some deserving Hall of Fame candidates among the 10 minority players who have thus far been denied election by the Veterans Committee, including Lou Whitaker, Luis Tiant, Kenny Lofton, and perhaps Dick Allen. If the Veterans Committee had elected only one of these players, the racial difference in voting would not be statistically significant; if they had elected two, we would not be having this discussion at all.

In their defense, we should note that the Veterans Committee did put eight Negro League players in the Hall of Fame between 1987 and 2001, a period during which they also elected six white pre-integration players, of whom only the first four were JAWS-Plus. This seems superficially like a more than equitable distribution, but must be taken in the context that that the Negro Leagues were almost virgin territory at that time, while pre-integration MLB had been well ploughed over before 1987. Indeed, MLB and the HOF had to empanel a special committee in 2006 to finish their work by electing 12 more Negro League players and five executives. This is not necessarily an indictment of the Veterans Committee, since it requires special expertise and a lot of historical research to do the job properly, but it does suggest that the Veterans

Table 7. Post-Integration Electoral Behavior of BBWAA and   Veterans Committee for JAWS-Plus Players

Racial/Ethnic Group	JAWS-Plus*	BBWAA			Veterans Committee	
		Elected	On ballot**	Rejected	Elected	Rejected
White	79	44 (56%)	5	30	5 (17%)	25
African American	32	21 (66%)	3	8	0 (0%)	8
Latino	13	7 (54%)	4	2	0 (0%)	2
Total	124	72 (58%)	12	40	5 (13%)	35

*   "JAWS-Plus" refers to relief pitchers with JAWS $\geq$ 36, catchers with JAWS $\geq$ 40, and all other players with JAWS $\geq$ 48.

**   Denotes players who were on BBWAA ballot in 2017, including Johan Santana, who failed to get 5% of the votes.

Committee was less than thorough in the execution of its charge. The Veterans Committee has elected only five players of any era—all of them white—since 2001.

In Table 8, we take a speculative look at the demographics of the pre-integration Hall of Fame. At first, this issue seems like a non-starter, since MLB (with the exception of a few American Indians and fair-skinned Latinos) was all white. However, we can also bring the 29 Negro League Hall of Famers into the discussion. Did the well-intentioned effort by MLB and the Hall of Fame to honor the greatest Negro League players achieve a fair racial balance in the pre-integration portion of the Hall of Fame? We can apply the analytic techniques used above to address this question.

The percentage of black players in the pre-integration Hall of Fame is only 16.9, mainly because of the profligacy of the Veterans Committee in electing 54 JAWS-Minus players (52 white and two American Indian), including 30 from the period between the two world wars. I have addressed this issue by adjusting the pre-integration ratio of JAWS-Plus to JAWS-Minus Hall of Famers to match the 5:1 ratio of the post-integration era. So, without specifying which players to remove, we are left with 13 instead of 59 JAWS-Minus pre-integration Hall of Famers, in addition to 66 JAWS-Plus pre-integration Hall of Famers. So, when the 29 Negro Leaguers are added in, you now have 24 percent of the pre-integration Hall of Famers being black players—a percentage that is not very different from the 27 percent in the post-integration era.

The percentage of Latinos (three percent) in the "adjusted" pre-integration era is of course far less than the post-integration 10 percent, reflecting the fact that Latinos represented only about one percent of the US population at that time.[22] In short, the pre-integration "shortfall" in the percentage of black players in the Hall of Fame is more reflective of the surplus of JAWS-Minus pre-integration white players elected by the Veterans Committee than a paucity of Negro League honorees. That being said, some worthy Negro Leaguers are still out there, and the HOF can probably accommodate a few more.[21]

SUMMARY

It is abundantly clear that black players have succeeded in MLB far beyond what would be expected given their numbers. This will hardly surprise anyone who has been paying attention during the past seven decades. But it is less obvious and quite reassuring that the BBWAA voters (but not necessarily the Veterans Committee) have been even-handed in giving deserving black players of the post-integration era their full due in the Hall of Fame and even honoring five black (vs. eight white and two Latino) JAWS-Minus players. The Hall of Fame and MLB also stepped in to mitigate the injustice of prior racial segregation by recognizing many highly deserving Negro League players in the Hall of Fame, although no one can fully redress the injustice of so many promising careers that either never happened or happened in relative obscurity. Still, recognition in the Hall of Fame is an important step for descendants of these players and their fans, if not for the players themselves.

This analysis does not address the 23 managers, 35 pioneers/executives, and 10 umpires (68 members in all) who have been elected to the Hall of Fame, whose accomplishments cannot be encapsulated in a statistical metric. The list of honorees includes several MLB executives (led by Commissioner Landis) who were complicit in implementing and maintaining the "gentlemen's agreement" to segregate MLB or who were slow to hire black players after integration. It might be appropriate for the Hall of Fame to consider removing or at least adding an asterisk to a few of

Table 8. Pre-Integration Demographics of the Hall of Fame

Source	Raw		Adjusted*	
	In HOF	Proportion	In HOF	Proportion
MLB				
JAWS-Plus**	66	42.9%	66	61.0%
JAWS-Minus**	59	38.3%	13.2	12.2%
Negro Leagues				
African American	26	16.9%	26	24.0%
Latino	3	1.9%	3	2.8%
Total	154	100%	108.2	100%

*   Adjusting ration of JAWS-Plus/JAWS-Minus MLB players to post-integration ration of 5:1..

**   "JAWS-Plus" refers to relief pitchers with JAWS ≥ 36, catchers with JAWS ≥ 40, and all other players with JAWS ≥ 48.
      JAWS-Minus refers to players who are not JAWS-Plus.

those plaques. On the other hand, the Hall of Fame can be proud to have honored a few boat-rocking executives and managers (Chandler, Rickey, Veeck, Durocher)—the real "gentlemen"—who had the courage to stand up for the integration of MLB in the 1940s. ∎

Notes

1. David Fleitz, "Cap Anson," SABR Biography Project, https://sabr.org/bioproj/person/9b42f875.
2. Wikipedia. Kenesaw Mountain Landis. https://en.wikipedia.org/wiki/Kenesaw_Mountain_Landis#cite_note-FOOTNOTEPietrusza406-141.
3. Lawrence D. Hogan, *Shades of Glory* (Cooperstown, NY: National Baseball Hall of Fame, 2006), 331–32.
4. David M. Jordan, Larry R. Gerlach, and John P. Rossi. "A Baseball Myth Exploded, https://sabr.org/cmsFiles/Files/Bill_Veeck_and_the_1943_sale_of_the_Phillies.pdf, accessed September 2018.
5. Hogan, *Shades of Glory*, 334.
6. Andy McCue, "Branch Rickey," SABR Biography Project, https://sabr.org/bioproj/person/6d0ab8f3; Rick Swaine, "Jackie Robinson," SABR Biography Project, https://sabr.org/bioproj/person/bb9e2490.
7. "WAR Explained," Baseball-Reference, https://www.baseball-reference.com/about/war_explained.shtml.
8. Jay Jaffe, *The Cooperstown Casebook* (New York: St. Martin's Press, 2017), 22–27.
9. Andy Sturgill, "Pete Rose," SABR Biography Project, https://sabr.org/bioproj/person/89979ba5; Eliot Asinov, *Eight Men Out: The Black Sox and the 1919 World Series* (New York: Henry Holt & Company, 1963).
10. "American Indian Baseball Players," Baseball Almanac, http://www.baseball-almanac.com/legendary/american_indian_baseball_players.shtml, accessed August 2018.
11. "Demographic Trends of the 20th Century," US Census Bureau, Figure 3.3, 77, November 2002, https://www.census.gov/prod/2002pubs/censr-4.pdf; "Hispanic or Latino origin," US Census Bureau, https://factfinder.census.gov/help/en/hispanic_or_latino_origin.htm, accessed August 2018.
12. "Hall of Famers by Election Method," BaseballHall.org, https://baseballhall.org/discover-more/stories/hall-of-famer-facts/hall-of-famers-by-election-method, accessed August 2018.
13. Wikipedia, Veterans Committee, https://en.wikipedia.org/wiki/Veterans_Committee, accessed September 2018.
14. Jaffe, *The Cooperstown Casebook*, 48–61.
15. Hogan, *Shades of Glory*.
16. Mark Armour and Daniel R. Levitt, "Baseball Demographics, 1947–2016," SABR, https://sabr.org/bioproj/topic/baseball-demographics-1947-2012.
17. "One-Sample Z-Test for Proportions," Free Statistics Lectures, http://www.statisticslectures.com/topics/onesamplezproportions.
18. The 15 were: Jim O'Rourke, Pud Galvin, King Kelly, Dan Brouthers, Mickey Welch, Tim Keefe, Tommy McCarthy, Ed Delahanty, Hugh Duffy, George Davis, Joe Kelley, Willie Keeler, Jimmy Collins, Roger Bresnahan, and Joe McGinnity. The SABR Biography Project has biographies of all but Brouthers, searchable at https://sabr.org/bioproj_search; For Brouthers: Roy Kerr, *Big Dan Brouthers: Baseball's First Great Slugger* (Jefferson, NC: McFarland, 2013), 4.
19. Hogan, *Shades of Glory*, 332.
20. "Z-Test for Proportions, Two-Samples," Free Statistics Lectures, http://www.statisticslectures.com/topics/ztestproportions.
21. "Demographic Trends of the 20th Century," US Census Bureau; Graham Womack, "Baseball Hall of Fame Could Do More for Negro Leaguers," *The Sporting News*, February 27, 2017, http://www.sportingnews.com/us/mlb/news/negro-leaguers-in-the-baseball-hall-of-fame-cooperstown-buck-oneil-gus-greenlee/1p766f7lpmxio1x06l6lv0qkry.

Why Has No True DH Been Elected to the Hall of Fame—Yet?

John Cronin

The Designated Hitter has been the way of life in the American League since 1973. With this extensive history, it prompts the question "Why has no true DH been elected to the Hall of Fame—yet?" Naturally, the next is "Will there be a DH in the Hall, and when and who will that be?"

First, it is necessary to determine how many players have played enough games at DH to be considered Hall of Fame material. From 1973 to the conclusion of the 2017 season, only nine players appeared in 1,000 or more games at DH. All of them are retired from the game, and two are in the Hall of Fame: Frank Thomas and Paul Molitor. As shown below, Thomas was the designated hitter in only 56.42 percent of the games he played in, while Monitor's percentage was even lower at 43.76.

Clearly, neither Thomas nor Molitor was a "true" DH. Their election to the Hall of Fame was based upon career numbers that went way beyond their DH stats. Their plaques don't even mention their DH activities.

Here are some other interesting facts about the players with at least 1,000 games at DH:

- David Ortiz is the only who has appeared in at least 2,000 games, and he's the only one with 2,000 hits, 250 home runs, or 1,500 runs batted in.

- Only Edgar Martinez and Molitor have a batting average over .300.

- Edgar Martinez is the only one who has an OBP of .400.

- Four of them (Ortiz, Martinez, Thomas, and Travis Hafner) have an SLG over .500.

- Don Baylor is the only one with an OPS under .800.

- Only Ortiz and Martinez have an OPS over .900.

Frank Thomas/Paul Molitor Comparison

Player		Hits	HR	RBI	PA	AVG
Frank Thomas	While DH	1,288 (52%)	269 (52%)	881 (52%)	5,698	.275
	Career Total	2,468	521	1,704	10,075	.301
Paul Molitor	While DH	1,457 (44%)	102 (44%)	654	5,338	.308
	Career Total	3,319	234	1,307	12,167	.306

Data Source: Baseball-Reference.com

Table 1. Players with 1,000 or more games as a DH: Selected Stats

Player	G	Hits	HR	RBI	AVG	OBP	SLG	OPS
David Ortiz	2,027	2,191	485	1,569	.289	.383	.559	.942
Harold Baines	1,643	1,690	236	981	.291	.370	.467	.837
Hal McRae	1,426	1,555	145	823	.294	.357	.463	.820
Edgar Martinez	1,403	1,607	243	1,003	.314	.428	.532	.959
Frank Thomas	1,310	1,288	269	881	.275	.394	.505	.899
Don Baylor	1,287	1,210	219	803	.259	.344	.449	.792
Paul Molitor	1,174	1,457	102	654	.308	.374	.454	.828
Chili Davis	1,160	1,175	200	736	.282	.382	.483	.864
Travis Hafner	1,043	1,036	200	689	.275	.378	.504	.882

Data Source: Baseball-Reference.com

Table 2. Games as DH as a percentage of games played (min. 1,000 games)

Player	Games as DH	Total Games	% as DH
Travis Hafner	1,043	1,183	88.17
David Ortiz	2,027	2,408	84.18
Hal McRae	1,426	2,084	68.43
Edgar Martinez	1,403	2,055	68.27
Harold Baines	1,643	2,830	58.06
Frank Thomas	1,310	2,322	56.42
Don Baylor	1,287	2,292	56.15
Chili Davis	1,160	2,435	47.64
Paul Molitor	1,174	2,683	43.76

Data Source: Baseball-Reference.com

As previously discussed, there have only been nine players who appeared in 1,000 or more games at DH from its introduction in 1973 through 2017. How does this compare to defensive positions during that same time frame? Table 3 shows that there were almost four times as many left fielders and right fielders, five times as many third basemen and catchers, six times as many center fielders, first basemen and second basemen and seven times as many shortstops.

Table 3. Players appearing in 1,000 or more games by position or role (1973–2017)

Position	Number of Players
Shortstop	65
Second Base	54
First Base	53
Center Field	52
Catcher	48
Third Base	47
Right Field	38
Left Field	34
Designated Hitter	9

Data Source: Baseball-Reference.com

Based upon this analysis, designated hitter has not been a "full-time" baseball role like the positions. The DH has been considered a one-dimensional player throughout its 45 year-history, and carries a stigma as such. It starts with the fundamental ideology of baseball. Wade Boggs said it best recently:

I think everyone who plays this game wants to be recognized as a complete ballplayer, not as a one-dimensional player. It's everything rolled into one. Basically, you have two jobs. One of them is four or five plate appearances each game; the other is playing defense for eight or nine innings.[1]

Baseball is a game steeped in tradition and slow to change. Boggs's statement echoes this mind-set.

The DH was not considered a career option in the period from 1973 to 1990.

Players in the DH role during that time frame can be divided into five categories.

1. Players such as Molitor, Harold Baines, and Andre Thornton, who transitioned to DH after beginning their careers as everyday players in the field. The reason for the switch was usually an injury that would have resulted in the end of the player's career if not for the new DH rule. This category would also include players such as Tony Oliva, who after years of wear and tear on his knees would have been a defensive liability if he had been forced to play in the field to keep his bat in the lineup. Oliva was able to extend his career for four years (1973–76) by becoming a full-time DH.

2. Older players like Reggie Jackson and Ted Simmons, who began their transition by playing some time in the field and some at DH to give them what is today considered a half-day off to rest their legs.

3. Former National Leaguers such as Hall of Famers Hank Aaron, Orlando Cepeda, and Billy Williams, who switched to the American League to extend their careers as designated hitters.

4. Players like Greg Luzinski, who would be classified as "professional hitters" because they were a liability to their team defensively.

5. A few players, such as Thomas and Eddie Murray (who both also fit in the second category above), who started out as designated hitters to get their bats in the lineup before their defensive position became available.

Prior to the introduction of the DH, the players in the first three categories had two options, either retire or become a pinch-hitter limited to one at-bat a game. Now, as a DH, they could get four or five at-bats per game. A new mind-set for the player was created since he no longer played a defensive position. The best way to describe this mind-set is the advice given to Ron Blomberg, major league baseball's first DH, by Elston

Howard, his coach on the New York Yankees, who gave him these sage words: "Go hit and then sit down."[2]

The data in Table 4 support what was just discussed. Clubs for the most part have not had full-time DHs

Table 4. Enough plate appearances as DH to qualify for the batting titles

Year	Qualifying DHs	Teams	% with full-time DH	DHs 35 or older	% of DHs 35 or older
1973	4	12	33.33	2	50.00
1974	3	12	25.00	3	100.00
1975	4	12	33.33	3	75.00
1976	1	12	8.33	1	100.00
1977	5	14	35.71	1	20.00
1978	4	14	28.57	2	50.00
1979	3	14	21.43	2	66.67
1980	0	14	0.00	0	N/A
1981	5	14	35.71	1	20.00
1982	6	14	42.86	2	33.33
1983	4	14	28.57	2	50
1984	5	14	35.71	3	60.00
1985	5	14	35.71	3	60.00
1986	2	14	14.29	2	100.00
1987	3	14	21.43	1	33.33
1988	2	14	14.29	1	50.00
1989	3	14	21.43	2	66.67
1990	3	14	21.43	2	66.67
1991	6	14	42.86	3	50.00
1992	4	14	28.57	2	50.00
1993	4	14	28.57	2	50.00
1994	6	14	42.86	4	66.67
1995	3	14	21.43	2	66.67
1996	5	14	35.71	4	80.00
1997	3	14	21.43	2	66.67
1998	5	14	35.71	2	40.00
1999	4	14	28.57	2	50.00
2000	3	14	21.43	1	33.33
2001	2	14	14.29	1	50.00
2002	2	14	14.29	1	50.00
2003	3	14	21.43	2	66.67
2004	4	14	28.57	1	25.00
2005	2	14	14.29	0	0.00
2006	4	14	28.57	2	50.00
2007	6	14	42.86	3	50.00
2008	1	14	7.14	1	100.00
2009	2	14	14.29	1	50.00
2010	3	14	21.43	1	33.33
2011	4	14	28.57	3	75.00
2012	1	14	7.14	0	0.00
2013	4	15	26.67	1	25.00
2014	1	15	6.67	1	100.00
2015	6	15	40.00	2	33.33
2016	4	15	26.67	3	75.00
2017	4	15	26.67	2	50.00
TOTALS	**158**	**627**	**25.20**	**82**	**51.90**

1) To qualify for the batting title, the rules require 3.1 at-bats for every game the team plays. For a 162-game season, 502 plate appearances are required.
2) The 1981 and 1994 seasons were shortened by strikes. For those seasons, the number of plate appearances was calculated for each team based upon the number of games played.
Data Source: Baseball-Reference.com

Edgar Martinez is popularly thought of as a designated hitter, but only nine seasons of his career included over 502 plate appearances at DH.

since its inception. To clarify, a full-time DH is a player who has enough plate appearances in that role during the season to qualify for the league's batting title. Since 1973, only 25 percent of American League teams (158 of 627) have employed a full-time DH. The rest have rotated players in that job. Further review discloses a low of 0 percent in 1980 to a high of 43 percent achieved in four seasons (1982, '91, '94, and 2007). It is hard to fathom that no team utilized a full-time DH during the 1980 season! In five seasons (1976, '80, 2008, '12, and '14), fewer than 10 percent of the teams had a full-time DH, with three of those five seasons occurring within the past 10 years. Throughout its history, the DH has largely been a rotational position used to give players a semi-day off.

Table 4 also supports the thinking that the DH is for older players whose defensive skills have deteriorated. As it shows, 52 percent of the full-time DHs since 1973 were 35 years old or older. This ranges from a low of 0 percent in three seasons (1980, 2005, and '12) to a high of 100 percent in five seasons (1974, '76, '86, 2008, and '14). Furthermore, in 18 of the 45 seasons (40 percent), the full-time DHs over 35 made up 60 percent or more of the total. Those statistics begin to explain why there have been no DHs elected to the Hall of Fame.

In order for the Baseball Writers of America to elect a player to the Hall of Fame, the player must have been active for 10 major-league seasons. If you consider that 1,000 games over 10 seasons is 100 games, or about 62 percent of a season's games, that does not leave many full-time DH candidates eligible for consideration. A better yardstick would be to see how many DHs over the 45-year span had at least 10 seasons where they had sufficient plate appearances (502) to qualify for a batting title.

Table 5. Most seasons as DH with 502 plate appearances

Player	Number of Seasons
David Ortiz	11
Edgar Martinez	9
Chili Davis	7
Paul Molitor	6
Frank Thomas	6
Don Baylor	5
Harold Baines	4
Travis Hafner	4
Billy Butler	4
Kendrys Morales	4
Rico Carty	4
Hal McRae	4
Brian Downing	3
Dave Parker	3
George Brett	3
Jim Thome	3
Willie Horton	3
Andre Thornton	3
Dave Kingman	3
12 Players Tied	2
35 Players Tied	1

Data Source: Baseball-Reference.com

A review of the table explains why no true full-time DH has been elected. There has been only one true full-time DH with a career of at least 10 seasons. David Ortiz is that one player, but he is not even eligible for election to the Hall of Fame until 2022. Edgar Martinez is probably the other best-known DH, but two key points to keep in mind are the fact that he only played 68.27 percent of his games as a DH, and he only had nine seasons in which he had enough plate appearances as a DH to qualify for the batting title.

Baseball, in addition to being a game governed by statistics, has a subjective and intangible nature to it. So while we look at the statistics for answers, there are other factors that provide clues to why no true DHs are Hall of Famers yet. When asked this question, John Thorn, the official historian of Major League Baseball, replied by quoting Branch Rickey:

Baseball people are generally allergic to new ideas; it took years to persuade them to put

61

numbers on uniforms, and it is the hardest thing in the world to get Major League Baseball to change anything—even spikes on a new pair of shoes—but they will eventually....They are bound to.[3]

Jeff Idelson, president of the Hall of Fame, answered the same question this way:

The BBWAA has the daunting responsibility of determining which players earn election to the Hall of Fame. The electorate has elected three players who spent a great deal of time as designated hitters, Paul Molitor, Frank Thomas, and Jim Thome, who played more than 800 games as a DH. Edgar Martinez, who has had great support, spent more than 1,400 games in that role. So designated hitters do get consideration for Cooperstown and are represented, and rightfully so.[4]

This raises the question "Does a DH belong in the Hall of Fame"?
Thorn responded to that:

Yes, because this is the way that the game has been played for 45 years. Resistance is akin to that once facing relief pitchers, which prompted me to write *The Relief Pitcher* eons ago.[5]

Idelson answered:

I believe that all eligible players should be considered for Cooperstown regardless of position and I am very comfortable with whomever the writers chose to elect. They have done a fabulous job.[6]

Looking into the baseball crystal ball, it would appear that Martinez will be the first "almost" true DH to be enshrined in Cooperstown. The definition of a true DH for this article is a player who has at least 10 seasons with enough plate appearances as a DH to qualify for the batting title. Martinez, as previous discussed, had nine. Even though Martinez has been classified as an almost-true DH, there are extenuating circumstances that must be considered. First, Martinez's career started with cups of coffee in 1987 and '88, and then he played mostly third base from 1989 to '94. Then, from 1995 to his retirement after the 2004 season, he was the DH in 1,323 of the 1,403 games that he played. This represented 94.30 percent of those games. Also,

he may have gotten the 10 seasons with enough plate appearances to qualify for the batting title if he had not ruptured his left hamstring, requiring surgery, in 2002. Martinez was limited to 97 games (91 as a DH) and had 407 plate appearances that season.

During the period from his first year of eligibility in 2010 to 2015, Martinez had a low of 25.2 percent of the votes in 2014 to a high of 36.5 percent in 2012. Beginning with the 2016 election, his candidacy picked up steam, with 43.4 percent, followed by 58.6 percent in 2017 and then 70.4 percent in 2018—20 votes short. The only caveat is that 2019 will be Martinez's last year of eligibility for election by the BBWAA writers.

If Martinez cannot gain the necessary 75 percent of the votes in 2019, it appears that Ortiz will be elected as the first true DH when he becomes eligible in 2022. His career stats at DH, including a .942 OPS and 485 home runs, are generally better than those of Martinez.

After that, who could or would be next? Table 6 lists the most games as a DH among active players through the end of 2017. The player's age has been included in order to do an interpolation to try to determine if the player will have enough games at the end of his career to qualify as a true DH.

Table 6. Most games as a DH among active players (through 2017)

Player	Age at end of 2017 Season	Games as DH
Victor Martinez	38	801
Kendrys Morales	34	643
Edwin Encarnacion	34	607
Albert Pujols	37	509
Nelson Cruz	37	501
Adam Lind	34	418
Evan Gattis	31	291
Joe Mauer	34	287
Mark Trumbo	31	267
Carlos Santana	31	222

No player is even close to the 1,000-game mark. Victor Martinez has announced that he will retire as an active player after the 2018 season, so he will not appear in 1,000 games as a DH in his career. Only five active players even have 500 games or more at DH. It is interesting to note that the average age of those five players is 36, so one wonders how many more games they'll play. There is quite a drop off at sixth place, with 418 games, and then another in seventh through tenth place. They are all in the 200-game range. The average player's age in this group is 32. The stats in this table further solidify that the DH is a rotational position.

As analytics continue to be utilized, baseball executives believe that it is best to limit the starting pitcher to facing the opponent's lineup about two times. Along with this thinking, they feel it is best to use a series of hard throwing relievers in the final innings of the game. Therefore, there is a constant need for bullpen help. A consequence of carrying more pitchers on the roster is that teams are playing games with a bench of three or four players. It becomes necessary that these bench players can play multiple positions. As a result, a full-time DH has become even rarer than in the past.[7]

Martinez and Ortiz are not only likely to be the first players to enter the Hall of Fame as designated hitters, they also may be the only such players inducted into Cooperstown for the foreseeable future. ∎

Notes

1. Hal Bodley, "Horse Sense—Triumphant Image of Wade Boggs on Horseback Remains a Lasting Memory of a Hall of Fame Career," *Memories and Dreams* 40, no. 2 (2018): 33.
2. George Vescey, *Baseball: A History of America's Favorite Game* (New York: Random House, 2006), 181.
3. John Thorn, email correspondence with the author, May 10, 2018.
4. Jeff Idelson, email correspondence with the author, May 2, 2018.
5. Thorn, email.
6. Idelson, email.
7. Buster Olney, "Hitters Who Can't Beat The Heat Getting Left Behind," ESPN.com, May 20, 2018. http://www.espn.com/blog/buster-olney/post/_/id/18519/olney-hitters-who-cant-beat-the-heat-getting-left-behind.

Why Do Games Take So Long?

David W. Smith

This article is based on the presentation I gave at SABR48 in Pittsburgh in 2018 to address the issue of game length which has become a hot issue in recent years. In 2014, then-commissioner Bud Selig announced the formation of a committee to investigate the issue. Since taking office, current commissioner Rob Manfred has taken steps to reduce game time including rules changes that limit mound visits, a countdown clock between innings, and has spoken openly about the possibility of introducing a "shot clock" for every pitch.

The commissioner's concerns are not new. Ban Johnson, the original and long-time president of the American League, was agitated by what he considered slow games as long ago as 1909. As the headline in a December 2, 1909, issue of *The Sporting News* reads: "Why Games Drag: Too Much Practice Time Taken Between Innings."

In the article, Johnson had noted that several games had exceeded two hours and he decided that teams took too much time throwing the ball around the infield at the start of each inning after the pitcher's warmup throws. He was supported by veteran umpire Tom Brown who said: "The practice work does not belong in the game."

In 1925, Johnson was still banging that drum. The *St Louis Post-Dispatch* had a story headed: "President Johnson of American League Moves to Speed up Games."

The article noted:

> Contests in the A.L. this season have frequently run more than two hours and Johnson wants to know the reason why. A report must be sent to President Johnson on all games running over two hours, with the reasons for the delays. If it is because of arguments, the guilty athletes will be punished.

For the record, 269 of the 616 AL games that year were over 120 minutes—44%—and the league average was 120.8 minutes.[1] One can only imagine what Johnson's reaction would be to our current average game time, which is now over three hours! Why do games take so long? Various culprits have been blamed depending on who's answering, making it high time for a sabermetric look at the issue. I decided to take a long view to examine many years to look for patterns and trends that can be measured quantitatively.

The data for this study come from Retrosheet (www.retrosheet.org) and I was able to study 183,224 games over the course of 108 seasons, 1908 through 2017 minus 1918–19.[2] In order to make fair comparisons, it is necessary to remove games whose times were skewed, including extra-inning games, and games that ended early due to rain, curfew, or other reasons. The remaining "regulation-length" games are then divided into those where the home team does or does not bat in the bottom of the ninth.

The Sporting News, *1909*

St. Louis Post-Dispatch, *1925*

Table 1. Regulation-length Games

Length	Games	Percentage
8.5	80,968	44.3
9.0	83,516	45.7
All	164,484	90.0

How has the length of the average game changed? It has definitely grown over time. Figure 1 shows the data from 1908-2017, excluding 1918 and 1919, but including the extra innings games this time to see the extreme values.

Figure 1. Average minutes for all games, 1908–2017

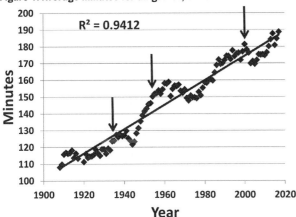

The figure shows the expected annual variations and periods of rise as well as decline. However, when a linear regression is performed to determine the best fit line, the result shows an extremely strong direct relationship with the R^2 value (coefficient of determination) indicating that 94% of the variance in the game length is accounted for by the passage of the years. Highlights along this 110 year trip are marked with arrows and summarized here.

Table 2. Landmarks in game length

Year	Avg. in Minutes	Landmark
1934	123.6	First year with average of over 2 hours
1954	150.3	First year with average of over 2½ hours
2000	181.4	First year with average of over 3 hours
2017	188.7	Longest average game time

At SABR47 in New York, Steve Steinberg [a SABR researcher who has an article elsewhere in this volume –Ed.] asked me what the relation was between number of pitches and game length. Retrosheet's pitch data have two distinct components. For the years 1947–64 we have 2,739 games from Allan Roth of the Dodgers, and from 1988 to present we have 68,566 games from Project Scoresheet, Baseball Workshop and MLBAM. Figure 2 shows the answer to Steve's

question for all regulation-length games from this entire period, covering more than 64,000 games and over 18 million pitches.

There are several points to make about Figure 2.

Figure 2. Regulation game length and number of pitches.

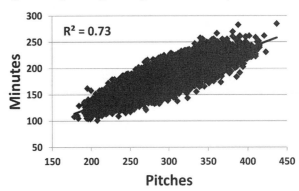

The R2 value of 0.73 means that the number of pitches in a game explains nearly three quarters of the variance in the time of game. That is a strong relation, although we would always like it to be more. I did analyze the 8.5- and 9-inning games separately and also the Roth games separately from the modern ones. The Roth data fit in extremely well with the modern information so there is no need to present separate graphs. Also the calculated slopes of the lines for 8.5 and 9 inning games are only slightly different and I therefore combined them in this one figure.

This figure includes very large ranges in both pitch totals and game times. These extremes and the averages are summarized in Table 3.

Table 3. Ranges and Averages of Pitch Totals and Game Length in Regulation-Length Games

	8.5 Innings	9 Innings
Minimum Pitches	145	178
Maximum Pitches	439	437
Minimum Minutes	93	101
Maximum Minutes	271	285
Average Pitches	274	289
Average Minutes	166	176

Playing the bottom of the ninth adds an average of 10 minutes and 15 pitches to the game.

Having seen this clear importance of the number of pitches on the time of game, I then set about looking for explanations of what would make the number of pitches increase. I checked several categories of offensive quantitative categories such as runs, hits, and walks, as shown in Figure 3. All values are for both teams combined.

Runs are, of course, the net result of all offensive action. As we see here, scoring has varied over the last

Figure 3. Figure 3. Major offensive categories, 1908–2017

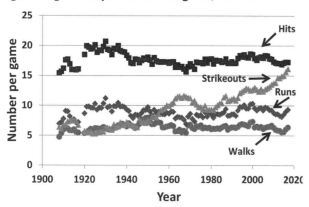

110 years, but there is no obvious upward trend to match the time of game. We have still not returned to the level of scoring seen in the first 15 years of the lively ball era although the average game length then was more than an hour less than it is now. So more scoring doesn't give us our answer.

The average number of hits per game and the changes there are pretty close to the pattern for runs, but once again there is no systematic upward trend.

Walks take more pitches than other kinds of events (more details on that in a moment), but they also show little systematic change. On the other hand, strikeouts have changed dramatically. As the lively ball era began, the number of strikeouts per game fell, being less than six per game for both teams combined until 1930. The average stayed in the mid-7 range until 1952 when it began a steady increase to a peak of 11.6 in 1967. After the mound was lowered and the strike zone reduced in 1969, the average began to drop, reaching 9.2 in 1981. However, since then there has been a steady rise (with some short-term oscillations) and the value really took off in 2006. The strikeout rate in 2017 was 16.2 per game, the first time it has passed 16.

We must address home runs as well and those annual rates are in Figure 4.

Home runs have certainly increased since 1908, but there have been boom and bust years. As expected, there was a surge with the introduction of the lively ball in 1920, but that ended dramatically in 1940, with a drop of 42% to 0.7 per game in 1943, perhaps reflecting changes in the construction of the ball due to wartime shortages. That slack time was followed by a dramatic upsurge from 1945 to 1961 when it reached 1.9 per game. The next dramatic point was in 1987 (circled in Figure 4) which has been written about a great deal. There is no satisfactory explanation for this

Figure 4. Home runs per regulation-length game, 1908–2017, both teams combined.

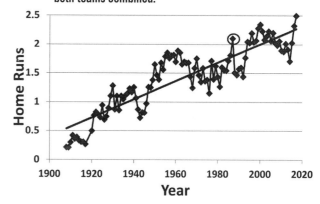

16% spurt in a single year although there was much speculation at the time about a "juiced" ball. *Sports Illustrated* published a study in which the physical properties of the 1987 ball were studied and nothing was detected to account for this large increase. The decline of 28% the next year is equally mysterious. At any rate, the next sustained increase was from 1992 to 2000, followed by a slow decline to 2014 when it was 1.7. In the four seasons since (2014 to 2017), we have seen an extraordinary 46% increase to last year's all-time high of just under 2.5 per game. The R^2 shows a strong relationship over time.

I go through all this detail to make the point that there is a strong relationship between home run increase and strikeout increase. This is shown clearly in Figure 5.

Figure 5. Home runs and strikeouts, 1908–2017

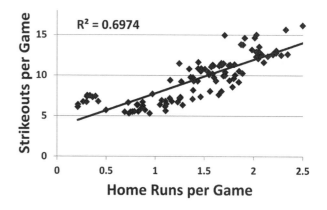

The R^2 value of 0.70 shows a strong relation. The only other pair of variables with this close relation are hits and runs. I am led to a conclusion that others have reached as well, namely that the correspondence between home run rate and strikeout rate is one of cause and effect. One consequence of sabermetric analysis has been that strikeouts no longer have the stigma they once did. Statcast data show launch angles and swing velocities and batters have clearly used this information to adjust their swings so that they hit the ball further. Of course, as these harder swings happen, it is much more likely that the ball will be missed, so we have a pretty clear all-or-nothing phenomenon.

I then calculated the average number of pitches for four types of event since 1988, the period for which we have pitch data for every game.

- balls in play

- strikeouts

- walks

- and hit by pitch

These are shown in Figure 6.

Figure 6. Number of pitches for each type of event

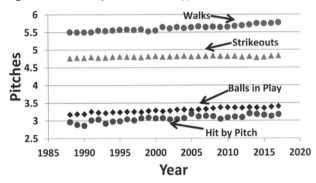

Balls in play, walks, and hit by pitch show a slight, but discernible increase with the average walk now taking 5.8 pitches to complete. These increases, especially in walks, may indicate greater patience on the part of hitters or greater concern ("nibbling") by pitchers. Strikeouts have not had a comparable increase in the average number of pitches, showing a remarkably stable pattern.

One last way to look at this is to examine how often each type of event occurs. Figure 7 has these results, again from 1988 to 2017. This time outs on balls in play are separated from hits.

There a clear inverse relation between outs on balls in play and strikeouts. Hits, walks, and hit by pitch have stayed quite steady. On average, strikeouts take 1.5 pitches more than other kinds of out, so this trade of strikeouts for outs on balls in play will also add time to the game. In fact, all of the factors point in the same direction of contributing to increasing game length.

Figure 7. Percentage of different events, 1988 to 2017

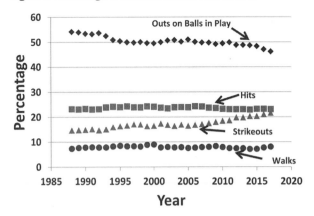

Another important measurement is the number of plate appearances per game and their pattern of change, shown in Figure 8. This is to be expected since the scoring of more runs necessarily requires more plate appearances. This pattern is rather similar to what we saw for scoring, which is reasonable since games with more runs will of necessity have more batters. The rapid increase in plate appearances as the lively ball was introduced and the decline with the pitching dominance and larger strike zone in the mid-1960s stand out, as did the changes in runs scored. The recent decline and subsequent rise also parallel scoring.

Figure 8. Plate Appearances per Game

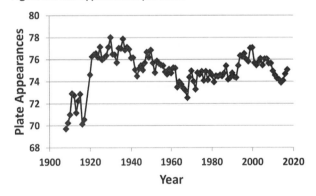

Finally we must consider actions affecting game length which are not directly related to the actual playing of the game. Many of these have been blamed for lengthening game times. My choices for these are as follows:

- Time between pitches (attributable to both batter and pitcher)

- Time between innings

- Replay reviews

- Visits to the mound

- Relief pitchers, especially mid-inning changes

Time between pitches has received attention from several sources in recent years. Baseball Prospectus has documented differences in pitch interval between bases empty situations and those with runners on base. Jim Albert has used PitchFX data very impressively to demonstrate among other thing that intervals are longer in the later stages of the game. Fangraphs published overall data on the time between pitches for all games since 2008.[3] These results are especially interesting to me. They measured an increase in the average time between pitches of 21.6 to 24.7 seconds between 2008 and 2017 with over 40% of the difference happening in 2017. The interval has both increased and decreased over this period. If we apply the full value of 2.6 seconds to the average number of pitches in a regulation game, the conclusion is that this increased interval has added 8 minutes to the average regulation game in these last 10 years. Since the average regulation game has increased by 14.5 minutes in that time, the 8 minutes are a significant part of the increase. Grant Bisbee published an intriguing article at SBNation.com in which he did an extraordinarily detailed analysis of two comparable games, one from 1984, the other from 2014, which were available on YouTube.[4] The more recent game was over 30 minutes longer and Bisbee's biggest conclusion is that he felt it was due to "lollygagging" by both pitchers and batters.

Time between innings is not routinely measured or reported so it is hard to know how long it takes to change sides, especially in earlier seasons. There have been various rules on the timing of these breaks and it is clear that the current limit of two minutes is being enforced more stringently.

Replays have been with us for about a decade now and so far this year they occur about one time for every two games, similar to the rate in 2017. They were somewhat more frequent earlier in the decade. For 2018, these reviews are formally listed through June 30 as taking one minute and 23 seconds, with an average on 59 seconds "on the headset." This does not count the potential delay of 30 seconds granted to teams to decide if they want to challenge. On the other hand, the replay system has greatly reduced the number of managerial arguments on the field, which will lead to

a shorter game. So, although it will be hard to get exact numbers for the time taken by reviews, this is obviously another factor that may make games longer.

Visits to the mound by the catcher, infielder, or someone from the bench (pitching coach or manager) also consume time, but I know of no data that systematically measure the time used by visits. MLB has taken some steps in this regard in 2018 by limiting mound visits to six per game per team. The visits were limited to 30 seconds beginning in 2016, the first restriction of this kind. There was consideration of imposing a 20 second limit between pitches as well this year, but that rule was not adopted.

Relief pitcher usage is potentially the biggest effect on time of game. There are two kinds of relief appearances: those at the start of an inning and those that happen during an inning. It seems reasonable that the mid-inning changes should take more time than a change at the start of an inning which should be virtually identical in terms of time consumed to having the same pitcher stay in the game. Figure 9 has the data for these two aspects of relief pitcher usage.

The line for total relievers per game goes back to 1908 because our data allow that determination. The line for mid-inning relievers starts in 1939 because that measurement requires full play by play for every game and Retrosheet's complete seasons currently begin with 1939.

The line for total relievers has several distinct portions. First, there is a dip during each of the World Wars, although the first drop was bigger. However, there is a fairly steady overall increase from 1908 through 1968 and then a decline for most of the next decade after the changes in mound height and strike zone. The advent of the DH had no immediate effect. From 1975 to the present, we have another long period of increase, much faster than the earlier one.

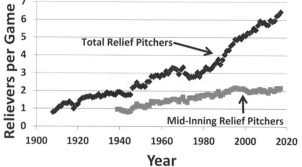

Figure 9. Average number of relief pitchers per game, both teams combined.

The average passed 6 relievers per game for the first time in 2015 and reached 6.4 in 2017. By the way, through games of June 30, 2018, the average in 2018 is over 6.5, right in line with the recent pace of an additional tenth of a reliever per game for each year.

However, the surprising results to me are the mid-inning changes. These have increased by more than a factor of two since 1939, but essentially not at all since 1994. This indicates to me that the use of additional relief pitchers has had minimal effect on the time of games. These extra pitchers appear to be the "role" players who are dedicated to the seventh, eighth, and ninth innings. Changes in bullpen use are not the culprit for why the game keeps getting longer.

Although there are more batters per game than there were a century ago, the biggest part of the increase is that each plate appearance besides strikeouts takes more pitches than 30 years ago. Perhaps this is a result of the "homer or strikeout" mentality or perhaps it just reflects greater plate discipline by batters in modern times. This conclusion is supported by the data in Figure 10 which covers 1947 to 2018, minus 1965–87.

Figure 10. Pitches per game

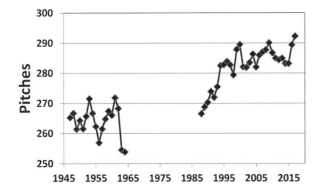

The inclusion of the Allan Roth data reveals interesting patterns.[5] The general average for his era is some 25 pitches fewer per game than current levels, but the first few years of the 1988 to 2017 interval are similar to his values. Of course, we do not know the shape of the line for 1965 to 1987, but I note that the last two years that Roth covered, 1963 and 1964, are clearly the lowest of any seasons for which we have data. These were, of course, the first two years of the altered strike zone. My major conclusion is that the single biggest factor contributing to the longer games is the number of pitches. The rise in strikeouts and related drop in outs on balls in play accounts for much of the difference over time. I have identified other factors (and other researchers have as well), but the number of pitches stands out as predominant. ∎

Notes

1. Of the 546 regulation-length game in 1925, 216 were over 120 minutes (40 %) and the average time was 118 minutes.
2. The exclusion of 1918 and 1919 reflects the unavailability of time of game for those two seasons for more than a handful of games. I checked several newspaper sources to no avail. The gap coincides with the demise of the *Sporting Life* weekly newspaper and the monopoly that resulted for *The Sporting News* beginning in 1918. *The Sporting Life* reported time of game faithfully, but *The Sporting News* did not fill this need until 1920. Most of my analysis will have those two seasons omitted.
3. Fangraphs, search: https://www.fangraphs.com/leaders.aspx?pos= all&stats=bat&lg=all&qual=0&type=22&season=2017&month= 0&season1=1871&ind=0&team=0,ss&rost=0&age=0&filter= &players=0&sort=1,d.
4. Grant Brisbee, "Why Baseball Games Are So Damned Long," SB Nation, 2017, https://www.sbnation.com/a/mlb-2017-season-preview/game-length
5. I must give proper respect to the first sabermetrician, Allan Roth, whose work with the Dodgers, initially with Branch Rickey, was truly groundbreaking and set the stage for the analytic revolution we currently enjoy.

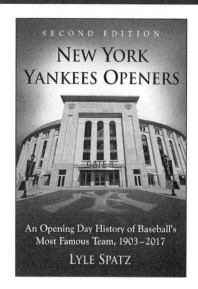
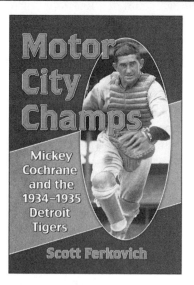
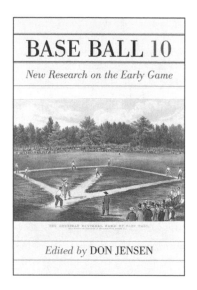
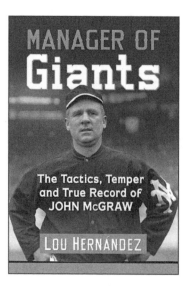
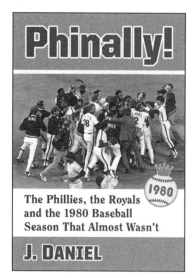

Shorty, Brother Lou, and the Dodgers Sym-phony

Rob Edelman

If Bob Sheppard, longtime public address announcer for the New York Yankees, was class personified, Tex Rickards, who held a similar slot with Dem Bums, reflected the spirit of the "woiking" class Brooklynite.[1] And while Robert Merrill, the classy Metropolitan Opera baritone, often sang "The Star Spangled Banner" at Yankee Stadium, at Ebbets Field the fans themselves were the artistes. They included Hilda Chester and her cowbell, Eddie Bettan and his police whistle, and the Dodgers Symphony (or, Sym-phony and Sym-phoney): a five-, six-, or seven-man unit of comically wacky amateur instrumentalists.

Away from Ebbets Field, the Sym-phony members, who changed across the years, toiled as truck drivers, clerks, and city workers of various stripes, and they hailed from such blue-collar communities as Williamsburg and Greenpoint. Their instruments included everything from snare drums, bass drums, and metal containers posing as drums to cymbals, bugles, trumpets, trombones, and washboards employed as noisemakers. "Sometimes the band sounds like a herd of elephants with whooping cough," wrote *The New York Times'* Murray Schumach in 1947, when the Sym-phony was at its zenith.[2] Dodger devotee Aaron Elkins, Brooklyn's Thomas Jefferson High School Class of 1952, added seven decades later: "For me, they were a given, so natural I never really thought about them… [I] just laughed and enjoyed them… I remember them all with much affection and nostalgia now…"[3]

The Sym-phony was founded in 1937 by Carmine "Shorty" Laurice, also known as "Jack" Laurice: a diminutive long-time Dodgers fan who toiled as a welder in the New York subway system. Laurice's verbiage was of the toidy-toid-and-toid variety. "Shorty is softspoken and even-tempered," observed Schumach, "and his speech is true Brooklynese. He favors the present tense and has a tendency to ignore grammatical links between verbs and nouns." Laurice explained his version of how the Sym-phony came into being:

Back in '37 I'm sittin' in my seat at Ebbets Field—the same seat I got for twenty-eight years, Section 8, Row 12, on the aisle—and I'm whistling, through my megaphone like always, when I run into this guy, a drummer. And that's the beginning of the band. It don't take much to start things in that Section 8 at the ball park, you know. Pretty soon I get myself a band. No, we don't get paid, just free ducats to the ball games.[4]

Originally, the Sym-phony called itself the Dodgers' Bums band. Legend has it that, in 1939, broadcaster Red Barber re-named it the Sym-phony to emphasize that their members were non-professionals.

Laurice was the star attraction in Section 8. "He is extremely visible, in the area behind the Brooklyn dugout, because he usually wears a silk hat, frock coat and orange pantaloons, and is perpetually in prancing motion," Schumach observed. His baton was a cane, until an uncle fashioned a real one from the branch of a tree in upstate New York. "Shorty thinks it elegant," Schumach added, "but he would have preferred a baton from a Brooklyn tree." Early on, Laurice's primary companion was forever-jitterbugging Jo Jo Delio, a little person who weighed only forty pounds. "Shorty would toss Jojo (sic) over his head, under his legs, make him cakewalk the guard rail. All this was done with consummate ease as his musicians wrestled with rhythm." However, by 1947, Jo Jo's weight had ballooned to 120 pounds: just five pounds less than Shorty. So their acrobatic act was history.[5] Laurice and company also regularly left the environs of Section 8 to parade through the stands during games and could be found atop the dugouts responding to on-field happenings.

The Sym-phony is best-recalled for serenading baseball's men in blue with a rendition of "Three Blind Mice." Predictably, the umps were not amused. "The Brooklyn Sym-Phony used to be the worst for us—they would always play 'The Three Blind Mice' when we'd walk out on the field," explained umpire Beans Reardon in 1949. "And that would eat up a feller like (umpire) Babe Pinelli. I said to the Babe, just ignore 'em, and he did and they stopped after a while. Fans like you to growl back at 'em."[6]

Opposing players also were subjected to the Sym-phony's taunts; "After all," Shorty claimed, "it's my job to rattle the other team."[7] If a Giant or Cub or Cardinal grounded out, the band comically imitated his gait as he returned to the dugout. If one sipped water from a drinking fountain, the Sym-phony lampooned him with "How Dry I Am." If one too-slowly returned to his dugout seat, he was loudly accompanied by the drums and cymbals. If one struck out, or if a pitcher entered or was taken out of a game, he was saluted with "The Worms Crawl In, The Worms Crawl Out," also known as "The Hearse Song," a ditty that exists in various incantations. A typical verse:

The worms crawl in, the worms crawl out,
The worms play pinochle on your snout.
A big black bug with two red eyes,
crawls up through your stomach and out through
      your eyes.
Your liver turns to a slimy green,
And looks and tastes like whipped cream.[8]

Shorty and his Sym-phony were nationally known. In 1947, *The New York Times* dubbed him "the Toscanini of Ebbets Field."[9] By all accounts, he was beloved and respected off the field. "Shorty would bring Jackie Robinson and Ralph Branca over to St. Lucy's Church," recalled his brother, Joe Laurice, "and he also managed a ball club at the Navy Yard. He'd do anything for anybody. He'd play basketball after the game was over on Friday nights, buy the kids sodas…"[10]

Shorty also was endlessly, unashamedly vocal in his support of the Dodgers. Six days before the start of the 1947 campaign, Commissioner Happy Chandler handed out a one-year suspension to Leo Durocher, the Dodgers skipper, and Shorty brandished a sign in which he informed one and all: "Open the door, Chandler, and let our Leo in."

Occasionally, Shorty and the Sym-phony trekked outside the boundaries of Ebbets Field. In 1941 and 1947, they were front-and-center in parades starting at Prospect Park, heading along Flatbush Avenue, and ending downtown, at Borough Hall, in celebration of the Bums copping National League pennants. In September 1946, they appeared at Sanford's, a Sheepshead Bay restaurant, to fête Pee Wee Reese and Eddie Stanky, and performed at an impromptu 36th birthday party for Dixie Walker.[11] Its members were invited to stroll the aisles of the 1948 Republican National Convention in Philadelphia. Thomas Dewey, New York governor and presidential nominee, promised to have them perform at the White House. (But Dewey lost to Democrat Harry Truman.)[12]

On August 21, 1948, Laurice was honored with a special "Shorty Laurice Day" at Ebbets Field. Tragically, however, the Sym-phony superstar died suddenly that November after undergoing ulcer surgery. Laurice was just 43 years old, and some of the money given him on his "Day" helped pay for his funeral. "Just as Shorty would have wished it, every member of the Dodger outfit who possibly could come was at the mass [at St. Ann's Roman Catholic Church], together with hundreds of Dodger fans, including several members of his impromptu band," reported the *Brooklyn Eagle*. Branch Rickey, Walter O'Malley, Jackie Robinson, and Roy Campanella were among those in attendance.[13]

Most poignantly, Shorty's cortege circled his beloved ballyard. It is not without irony that he had been felled by ulcers between the 1946 and 1947 seasons. "That ulcers, it's all in the head," Laurice told Murray Schumach. "Give me plenty of baseball and I don't never get ulcers."[14]

Laurice was not quickly forgotten. The following summer, he was honored at Ebbets Field on Opening Day. A plaque dedicated to his memory was erected on his favorite Section 8 seat and a memorial fund was instituted in his honor to help support underprivileged children. Five years later, the *Brooklyn Eagle* described Laurice as the "Brooklyn fan who 'cared' more deeply than anyone else" and a "wonderful little fellow," adding that a "gentle touch to the story of Shorty Laurice is that his memory is perpetuated by the association he formed and that his friends hold dances and parties to raise money to take orphans to Brooklyn games."[15]

Upon Laurice's death, snare drummer Lou Soriano became the Sym-phony's leader and director. Occasionally, "Brother Lou" (as he was called) accepted credit for founding the band; he just may have been the unnamed drummer that Laurice mixed with at Ebbets Field in 1937. As Soriano explained in a 1981 interview: "We were coming home from a picnic with our families… and it was so nice a day when we passed the park we went in. Instruments and all. People said: 'Give us a tune!' So we gave 'em a tune."[16]

In 1949, six musicians comprised the Sym-phony: Soriano (who worked as a civilian driver for the US military on Governors Island); trumpeter Phil Mason (a truck driver); clarinetist Bob Sharkey (a subway maintenance man); bass drummer Patsy Palma (a beer distributor); trombonist Pete Norman (a paper cutter);

and, of course, Jo Jo Delio (a grocer) who manned the cymbals. Their day jobs allowed them to play at Ebbets for approximately 35 games each season, on Sundays and holidays and during night games. Plus, they earned a write-up in the venerable *New Yorker* magazine. Here, Soriano (rather than Laurice) was cited as the band's founder. The Sym-phony "was started by Soriano," claimed the magazine. "He brought a trombone player [with him] one day [and] when the Dodgers had a man on base, he blew a few notes. Soriano kept adding instruments till they got what they have now. The band has a thematic music for nearly every Dodger player. It also plays 'Hearts and Flowers' when a visiting team is hollering about something to the ump."[17]

A minor flap occurred in July 1951, when Local 802 of the American Federation of Musicians demanded that the Sym-phony members be paid for their work and imposed a ban on their performances. It was lifted with one proviso: No union member could play with the band. Then on August 13, the Dodgers staged a "Music Depreciation Night." Of the 24,560 fans in attendance, 2,426 showed up with banjos, bongo drums, trombones, flutes, saxophones... All were admitted for free, and joined the Sym-phony in their music-making. Additionally, the band was honored that same month in a pre-game Ebbets Field ceremony. Fans were encouraged to donate $1 each for the purchase of new musical instruments and costumes.

On the rare occasion that the Sym-phony did cross the Brooklyn Bridge into Manhattan, it was usually to represent Brooklyn in some manner. They might show up at Penn Station to welcome Dem Bums after a successful road trip. In September 1951, they entertained the crowd at Times Square's Globe Theater during a screening of *Rhubarb*, a newly-released Brooklyn-set baseball film.

In 1956, the band included seven musicians: Soriano and Palma plus trumpeter Ziggy Rullo (a lithographer); clarinetist Frank Ambro (a Parks Department worker); cymbalist Louis Dallojacono (a bank clerk); trombonist Pete Dellaiacono (a tree pruner); and tenor saxophonist William "Cally" Califano (a high school student). The Sym-phony's act also had changed. When asked if they still serenaded umpires, Soriano responded: "Na. When they had three umpires we used to play 'Three Blind Mice.' But now they got four. And, what!—we can't come up with the fourth mouse! We leave 'em alone. If we don't, they holler at us."[18]

Even after the Dodgers left Brooklyn, the Sym-phony remained intact; they marched in parades and appeared at everything from store openings to old-timers' games.

In 1958, they accompanied a busload of Brooklyn diehards to Philadelphia, where the now-Los Angeles Dodgers were to battle the Phillies. On their way out of town, the Sym-phony performed "St. Louis Blues" and "Who's Sorry Now." Upon their arrival in the City of Brotherly Love, it was announced that the game had been rained out.[19]

As the years passed, Sym-phony members aged and died—and in 1989, Lou Soriano's passing merited a brief obituary in *The New York Times*. Unlike many of his brethren who by then had abandoned the city for the suburbs, at age 84 Soriano still resided in Greenpoint. "Mr. Soriano's most cherished possession," noted the *Times*, "was a plaque presented to him by the Brooklyn Dodgers organization... He was offered as much as $7,000 for the keepsake, but turned it down. Asked if he held on to it for sentimental reasons, he explained, 'Nah, I'm holding out for $10,000.'"[20]

In October 1995—the fortieth anniversary of the team's lone World Series triumph—the Sym-phony appeared at the Brooklyn Historical Society in an event accompanying a special Ebbets Field exhibit. The following year, they were found at a 92nd Street Y shindig honoring living Brooklyn Dodgers from Cal Abrams to Pee Wee Reese. In June 2001, they showed up at the KeySpan (now MCU) Park debut of the Brooklyn Cyclones, the Class A New York Mets farm team: the first professional baseball game in the borough since the departure of the Dodgers 44 years earlier. At one point, according to *The New York Times*, the Sym-phony members "huddled by a concession stand. The musicians were supposed to get prime seats, said Dan Wilson, a 79-year-old trumpeter, 'but somebody goofed; at our age, this we don't need.'"[21]

The Sym-phony performed several numbers—including "Three Blind Mice"—at the 2005 unveiling of a Jackie Robinson-Pee Wee Reese statue outside KeySpan Park. At a KeySpan gathering two years later, Rachel Robinson, Jackie's widow, saw and acknowledged Dan Wilson, whom *The New York Times* described as "the longest-tenured active member of the Dodgers Sym-phony—as in phony symphony..." On that occasion, the Sym-phony included Arnie Mig, also 85, playing cymbals; Lou Mento, 82, on bass drum; saxophonist Rex Sita, 77; and trombonist Nick Fiore, also 77.

Wilson admitted that he was not an official Symphony original. He was just 17 years old in 1939, and was enlisted as a fill-in musician. "...(the) Dodgers management did not want us at the ballpark," he recalled. "They felt we were a nuisance, but the players and the fans loved us, so we had to sneak into the ballpark. One guy paid the admission fee and lowered a rope over the side of the stadium, and we tied our instruments to the rope and had them hoisted up. Then we ran into the stands and started playing."

Wilson noted that, in 2007, he and Jo Jo Delio were the sole remaining living links to the original Sym-phony. Delio, then 87, resided in a Massapequa, Long Island nursing home.[22] He was 94—or, over twice the age of Shorty Laurice—when he passed away in January 2011. One year later, a *Newsday* tribute cited him as the "last member of the Brooklyn Dodgers Sym-Phony Band. Your legend will never be forgotten! From your loving family and friends from the Northside Williamsburg, Brooklyn, and Parkview Nursing Home."[23] Then in 2015, *Newsday* reported that the Sym-phony "has lost (one more) last surviving member" upon the passing of 87-year-old Armand Soriano, Lou Soriano's son. A cymbal-player, Armand had been recruited by Lou right after World War II, when he was 18. Armand's life was typical of most Sym-phony musicians. Brooklyn-born, he dropped out of school after completing eighth grade to support his family. He eventually worked in the stockroom at the Steuben Glass company, where he remained for three decades.[24]

"Over the years, as the original guys disappeared, we took their places," explained Nick Fiore in 2007. He reported that he had joined the Sym-phony in 1977, adding: "Danny and the rest of us are all trained musicians who performed with big bands, but we're still proud to keep this great tradition alive." And Rachel Robinson observed, "The Sym-Phony was one of the things people loved about Ebbets Field. They provided a kind a special character and loving warmth that few other ballparks had, so I'd recognize them anywhere."[25] ∎

Notes

1. Most famously, after a cluster of fans had placed their coats over the grandstand railing at Ebbets Field, Rickards requested that "the fans in the first row along the railing please remove their clothes." (One of a number of variations: "Will the ladies sitting along the first-base line please take off their clothes….") So as not to confuse anyone in the stands, Rickards—not to be mistaken for the legendary boxing promoter and founder of the New York Rangers, who passed away in 1929—appeared on the field garbed in a white wool sweater with the words "Dodgers Announcer" stitched on its front. It may have been 100 degrees in the shade, but Rickards always wore the wool. He inexplicably conjured up incorrect names in his announcements, referring to pitchers Ernie Johnson and Eddie Erautt as, respectively, "Cy" and "Herman," and infielder Gene Freese as "Augie"—which became Freese's nickname.
2. Murray Schumach, "Dodgers' Maestro," *The New York Times*, September 28, 1947; SM28.
3. Email from Aaron Elkins, March 10, 2017.
4. Schumach; SM28.
5. Schumach; SM28.
6. Adam K. Raymond, "How To Get Ejected From a Baseball Game," *Slate*, September 18, 2012.
7. Schumach; SM28.
8. "The Hearse Song," Wikipedia, https://en.wikipedia.org/wiki/The_Hearse_Song.
9. Schumach; SM28.
10. Bob McGee, *The Greatest Ballpark Ever: Ebbets Field and the Story of the Brooklyn Dodgers* (New Brunswick, New Jersey and London: Rivergate Books. 2005); 211.
11. "Dodgers' Party Followed by Fete For Dixie Walker," *Brooklyn Eagle*, September 25, 1946; 4.
12. McGee; 211.
13. "Dodger Leaders Attend Rites For Carmine (Shorty) Laurice," *Brooklyn Eagle*, November 29, 1948; 11.
14. Schumach; SM28.
15. Tommy Holmes, "Dazes and Knights," *Brooklyn Eagle*, July 8, 1953; 17.
16. Ken Denlinger, "Only Memories At Ebbets Field," *Washington Post*, October 28, 1981.
17. Frank Grisaitis and Rex Lardner, "Incidental Music," *The New Yorker*, September 3, 1949; 17.
18. William R. Conklin, "Dodgers' Music Score? Off-Pitch Sym-phoney Band Is Base," *The New York Times*, August 12, 1956; 161.
19. Gay Talese, "Like Old Times in Brooklyn: Safari All Awry," *The New York Times*, May 26, 1958; 34.
20. "Louis Soriano, 84, Dies; Led Dodger Band," *The New York Times*, April 12, 1989; B5.
21. Andy Newman, "It's Summer: The Boys Are Back in Town," *The New York Times*, June 26, 2001; D3.
22. Vincent M. Mallozzi, "Sour Notes Are Sweet for Sym-Phony of Brooklyn," *The New York Times*, August 14, 2007; B2.
23. "In Memoriam," *Newsday*, January 23, 2012.
24. Joan Gralla, "Armand Soriano dies; last of the Brooklyn Dodgers' razzing Sym-Phony was 87," *Newsday*, June 13, 2015.
25. Mallozzi; B2.

1948

When Baseball's Minor League Winter Meetings Came to Minneapolis

Sarah Johnson

It was an event *The Sporting News* said featured "Paul Bunyan hospitality."[1] Bringing nearly 1,200 visitors to the North Star state, the 48th annual gathering of the National Association of Professional Baseball Leagues was held in Minneapolis from December 8–10, 1948. Prior to the convention, Charles Johnson, sports editor at the *Minneapolis Tribune*, wrote in his "Lowdown on Sports" column, "There is no better group in the sports business than the baseball men. They are big spenders. Come what may in the way of actual results, this is the most important sports meeting this city has ever had or probably ever will have again."[2]

To introduce attendees to Minnesota's largest city, *The Sporting News* reported on the area's cultural aspects. "Minneapolis boasts, without fear of successful contradiction from any quarter, that it has more sports-minded citizens than any other big city in the country...Minneapolis fans combine their sports with a sound appreciation for culture, spelled with a small 'c' up here. When Dimitri Mitropoulos, the orchestra's world famed conductor, takes up his baton for his first concert, it will be a musical event here comparable to the first home game of the Millers."[3]

The Sporting News often referred to Minneapolis as either the Mill City or Millertown in homage to its history as a flour-making mecca, and the local minor league team was known as the Millers. For the female visitors, activities included a tea and style show sponsored by Dayton's (a well-known specialty department store, perhaps best known today as the progenitor of Target) and a tour of the milling district where "they may see where their favorite flour is made."[4] Convention headquarters were at the Nicollet Hotel in downtown Minneapolis. Temperatures during that week ranged from five degrees to 20 degrees with snow flurries: typical Minnesota winter weather.[5]

The convention showcased the history of minor league baseball in Minneapolis, with *Minneapolis Tribune* sports writer George Barton reporting that baseball executives were meeting in American Association territory for the tenth time since its organization.

Baseball commissioner Happy Chandler attended the meetings and told the press he had pitched a no-hitter in Minnesota in 1919, but evidence of the game's occurrence has eluded researchers.

"Millertown points with pride to the fact that in addition to finishing first seven times in the American Association since 1902, it is the only city in the league whose team has never finished last."[6]

The Millers were a New York Giants farm team in 1948, but had previously been associated with the Boston Red Sox. Nicollet Park in south Minneapolis had seen many future stars in the Millers dugout, most notably Ted Williams. "It was at Minneapolis in 1938 that Williams, a sliver-like 19-year-old, stamped himself as a coming star. The Kid led the American Association that year with a .366 average, socked 43 home runs and batted in 142."[7] Rosy Ryan, the Millers general manager, and Tommy Heath, the new Millers field manager (recently appointed in October from another Giants farm club), were in attendance at the winter meetings. Reported the *Star*, it would be "Heath's first visit to Minneapolis since his appointment during the World Series, although he is familiar with Nicollet Park from his years in the American Association with Columbus and Milwaukee."[8]

The day before the convention officially began on Wednesday, there was an opening luncheon held at the Nicollet Hotel. Halsey Hall, sports writer at the *Minneapolis Tribune* and future Twins broadcaster (and the man the Minnesota SABR chapter is named after), served as the master of ceremonies. The lunch featured guests including Carl Hubbell, Leo Durocher, Casey Stengel, and Bill Veeck. Hubbell told of the difficulties he had in pitching to Rogers Hornsby and related a story that included another banquet attendee, Frank Frisch. Per *The Sporting News*, "He asked Frisch, playing third, to tell how to pitch to the Rajah. After he had hurled three balls, fast and on the inside, as per instructions, he queried Frankie on what to do then. Frisch's answer, according to Hubbell, was: 'You're the pitcher, I'm just a third baseman.'"[9]

Frisch himself told a story involving Freddie Fitzsimmons and umpire Beans Reardon. When Fitzsimmons said something he shouldn't have to the umpire, and the umpire asked him to repeat what he said, Fitzsimmons replied, "You've been guessing all afternoon, now guess what I said."[10] The midday event was attended by 761 people and the *Minneapolis Star* reported, "it was unquestionably the finest sports affair this city has ever had. It was unfortunate that every real baseball lover in this area couldn't have sat in on this show for it will probably never be duplicated around here again."[11]

At 11:00 AM on Wednesday, the first official meeting got underway in the Nicollet Hotel's main ballroom, with Hubert Humphrey giving the welcome address. (Humphrey, who had been Mayor of Minneapolis, had just been elected to the United States Senate that November.) George Trautman, president of the National Association, declared that the number one problem in minor league parks was inadequate lighting. Even though more than $3 million was spent to upgrade facilities in 1948, many were still inadequately equipped for night play. "Poor lighting is hazardous to the player, not only from the standpoint of injury but also because it handicaps his efforts to perform at his peak. It is also distinctly unfair to the fan. Unquestionably, bad lighting is bad business," said Trautman.[12]

He also revealed that he had approached several colleges with the proposal of including courses covering the administration of professional ball in their physical education programs. "The administration of baseball is no longer seasonal," he said. "The employment of an ambitious, energetic and competent business manager for only seven or eight months, or less, affords him little security and certainly is not conducive to attracting capable and ambitious men into baseball's administrative field."[13]

Another topic of discussion was the argument that televising major league games was hurting minor league attendance—International League president Frank Shaughnessy said that televising night games was "simply advising the fans seeking and having time for recreation to get it at home without cost." So on the third day of the convention, the minor league representatives voted unanimously to ban radio and TV broadcasts beyond 50 miles from the station. This was largely a symbolic vote and was quickly voted down the next week at the major league winter meetings.[14]

Historically the winter meetings have seen some exciting trades or signings but few of any note took place in Minneapolis in 1948 despite Bob Beebe of the *Minneapolis Star* reporting that "there were as many trade rumors as citrus in a fruit cake."[15] Between meetings, attendees could view an exhibit that featured some of the most famous bats in baseball history, brought to Minneapolis by the Hillerich and Bradsby Bat Company from Louisville. They included bats used by Ty Cobb and the one Babe Ruth used to hit his 51st and 52nd home runs on his way to his record spree of 60. Bernie Swanson of the *Minneapolis Star* reported that the collection was "insured for $50,000, which is incidental because it never could be replaced."[16]

A crosstown dustup happened during the convention on Wednesday night between Babe Barna, a Minneapolis outfielder, and Dick Lanahan, a former St. Paul pitcher. According to witnesses, Barna was boasting, "There isn't a chucker I can't hit a home run off of." "Never hit one off me," Lanahan reportedly replied, which started a very mature back and forth of "Well, I'll bet I did." "You didn't." "Did." "Didn't." This ended with Barna punching Lanahan in the mouth and requiring a trip to a local hospital.[17]

Twin Cities Dunkers—a local sports boosters group still active today which includes SABR members on its roster—had its first meeting in conjunction with the convention as Gerald Moore, executive director of the Greater Minneapolis Chamber of Commerce, welcomed Lou Boudreau, Billy Southworth, Happy Chandler, and George Trautman to a breakfast meeting at the Minneapolis Athletic Club.[18]

In an article by Charles Johnson titled "Happy Chandler Just that at Convention," the baseball commissioner talked about his connection to Minnesota when he was a student. "In those days a collegian could make some money playing baseball during vacation time without being ineligible for amateur competition. I will never forget Minnesota—particularly Hallock. I pitched a no hit game for that team back in 1919 and I have been bragging about it ever since."[19] [Note: members of the Halsey Hall SABR chapter have tried to verify this account but so far have not found any additional evidence that this no-hit game occurred.]

Halsey Hall, in his column "It's a Fact," reported on the official scorers meeting: "It was voted hereafter that the starting pitcher must go five full innings to get the win regardless if it was a seven or nine inning game." Exceptions were made for a shortened game due to rain, curfew, or train catching: if the game went only five innings, four innings pitched would make a starter eligible to get the win. "If a starting pitcher doesn't go five innings, but is removed because of injury or illness, he may still be credited with a win. He also might have had he been kicked out by the umpire…the committee decided, however, to erase the umpirical clause because if a hurler gets booted out with a victory in sight, he doesn't morally deserve it."[20]

During the week, St. Louis Cardinals president Bob Hannegan and manager Eddie Dyer, along with Leo Durocher, visited some injured Duluth Dukes players at Bethesda Hospital in St. Paul. On July 24, 1948, a bus carrying the Dukes (then a minor league team of the Cardinals), had crashed in the Twin Cities, killing six and injuring 14 players.[21] Also, Ted Williams, referred to as the "Red Sox fence buster and former Miller," took in a Minneapolis Lakers game on Wednesday night. The Lakers (now known as the Los Angeles Lakers), were then a Basketball Association of America team (a forerunner of the NBA) who played at the Minneapolis Auditorium in downtown Minneapolis.[22]

After the final convention session on Friday, attendees left Minneapolis and made their way to Chicago for the major league winter meetings, held that year December 13–15. On Sunday, Charles Johnson wrote "Minneapolis's first minor league convention is history, but even a home towner can say that it was one of the biggest and most successful events ever staged."[23] Thirteen years before Minneapolis would become home to the major-league Twins (1961), it was briefly the epicenter of the minor-league world. ■

Notes

1. "1,100 Visitors and 1,100 Varieties of Entertainment," *The Sporting News*, December 15, 1948, 6.
2. Charles Johnson, "Lowdown on Sports," *Minneapolis Sunday Tribune*, December 5, 1948, 2.
3. "Minneapolis Chilly? Not In Its Welcome," *The Sporting News*, December 8, 1948, 7.
4. "Ladies may see where their favorite flour is made," *The Sporting News*, December 8, 1948, 3.
5. Weather, *Minneapolis Tribune*, December 6, 1948, 28.
6. George Barton, "Minneapolis Linked to Game Since '82," *The Sporting News*, December 8, 1948, 3.
7. Bob Beebe, "Twin Cities' Grads Read Like Who's Who of Game," *The Sporting News*, December 8, 1948, 8.
8. Jim Peterson, "Heath Here, Sees Ryan," *Minneapolis Star*, December 1, 1948, 46.
9. "Major Leaguers 'Cut Up' at Minor Loop 9 Luncheon," *The Sporting News*, December 15, 1948, 6. The Hubbell story is probably apocryphal.
10. "Major Leaguers 'Cut Up'".
11. Charles Johnson, "Lowdown on Sports," *Minneapolis Star*, December 9, 1948, 54.
12. E.G. Brands, "Better Lighting Minors' #1 Need—Trautman," *The Sporting News*, December 8, 1948, 2.
13. Brands, "Better Lighting."
14. Steve Weingarden and Bill Nowlin eds., *Baseball's Business The Winter Meetings : Volume 1: 1901–1957* (Society for American Baseball Research, 2016).
15. Bob Beebe, "Rumors Mostly, Not Deals, Mark Meeting," *Minneapolis Star*, December 9, 1948, 54.
15. Bernie Swanson, "History Carved in Hickory," *Minneapolis Star*, December 7, 1948, 1.
17. Marty Merrick, "Pitcher Out After Barna Punch," *Minneapolis Star*, December 9, 1948, 1.
18. Charles Johnson, "Happy Chandler Just That at Convention," *Minneapolis Star*, December 9, 1948, 1.
19. Johnson, "Happy Chandler."
20. Halsey Hall, "It's a Fact," *Minneapolis Tribune*, December 10, 1948, 22.
21. Halsey Hall, "Chairman Kelley Has Proud Hour," *Minneapolis Tribune*, December 9, 1948, 28.
22. Bill Carlson, "Caps Lucky? Just Great Club—Kundla," *Minneapolis Star*, December 9, 1948, 46.
23. Charles Johnson, "Lowdown on Sports," *Minneapolis Sunday Tribune*, December 12, 1948, 2.

Voices for the Voiceless

Ross Horning, Cy Block, and the Unwelcome Truth

Warren Corbett

The general public, or baseball fan, when he thinks of baseball thinks of the major leagues. He thinks of Joe DiMaggio and Ted Williams. He thinks of huge salaries, of terrific baseball parks and beautiful lights and marvelous conditions, hotels, trains. That is baseball. Only 5 percent of baseball players in the United States play that way.[1]

– Ross Horning

Behind the sentimental rhetoric of the national pastime, Organized Baseball grew into a $100 million industry in the boom times after World War II. With 59 minor leagues operating at the peak, and around 10,000 players, the professional game touched 46 of the 48 states. No one yet knew that the game stood on the brink of wrenching change that would continue into the twenty-first century.

By 1951 the attendance trend was pointing downward and the devastation of the minors had begun when Congress cracked open a window on the business of baseball for the first time. The House Judiciary Committee's Subcommittee on Study of Monopoly Power collected financial data, contracts, working agreements, and other internal documents that had never before been made public. The hearings were part of a broad investigation of economic concentration in industries including steel, newsprint, aluminum, and defense.

The subcommittee was considering three bills that would give congressional approval to baseball's exemption from antitrust laws and extend the exemption to other professional sports leagues. Chairman Emanuel Celler, a Democrat from Brooklyn, said his purpose was to "strengthen and fortify" baseball's legal position, which was under attack in court.[2] But as he listened to testimony, Celler sounded increasingly skeptical of the antitrust exemption and its companions: the reserve clause that denied players freedom to choose their employer and the territorial-rights rules that denied clubs freedom to move to a different city.

The first witness at the opening hearing on July 30 was Ty Cobb, a name guaranteed to attract press coverage. Cobb had little to offer, but he did endorse the reserve clause while saying veteran players should be permitted to take salary disputes to arbitration.

With the commissioner's office vacant—Happy Chandler had recently been dumped by unhappy owners—Organized Baseball's leadoff witness was National League President Ford Frick, who would be elected commissioner less than two months later.

"Frankly, gentlemen, I don't see why all the furor about the reserve clause," Frick declared. "Basically, it is a long-term contract which is nothing unusual where distinctive personal services are contracted for. I read by the papers that [comedian] Milton Berle has just signed such a contract for 30 years."[3] The subcommittee report noted that Berle had been free to negotiate with any television network before he signed with NBC—a choice not available to ballplayers.

Two unknown young men stepped forward to challenge Frick's benign view of owner-player relations. They were voices for the voiceless, the 95 percent in the minor leagues.

THE GRAD STUDENT

Ross Horning, called "Bumps" in his playing days, had his first collision with the reserve clause when he was a 21-year-old shortstop with Sioux Falls, South Dakota, in 1942, warming up for a road game in Duluth, Minnesota.[4] "I was playing catch with one of the players, and a fellow (from the Duluth team) came along the fence and said, 'What size uniform do you want?' I said, 'What do you mean? I've already got one.' And he said, 'Well, you've just been sold to us.'"[5]

The Sioux Falls club had just left home for a two-week road trip, meaning the team would be paying Horning's living expenses. But Duluth was beginning a two-week homestand, and he would have to rent a room. That extra expense would put a considerable dent in his $75-a-month paycheck. He told the Duluth owner he wanted to stay with Sioux Falls. "We argued until about 2 o'clock in the morning, and I knew before we finished that he would tell me the obvious fact, that I could not play for any other team in the United States anyway, and so I may just as well play for him."[6]

When Horning read about the upcoming hearings, he wrote a five-page letter to Chairman Celler urging him to investigate the reserve clause's role in oppressing minor leaguers. "If your committee only calls outstanding players, managers, and owners, it will not reach the core of the reserve clause controversy," he said.[7]

He had quit Organized Baseball after five seasons in Class C and D and service in the Army Air Forces. His .228 batting average in his first full professional season had convinced him that he would never join the 5 percent. He kept playing ball to earn money for college.

As a graduate student at The George Washington University in the nation's capital in the summer of 1951, Horning was preparing to take the State Department's Foreign Service entrance exam. The subcommittee's associate counsel, future Supreme Court Justice John Paul Stevens, interviewed him, and he was invited to testify on August 7. He had plenty to say.

Horning gave the congressmen a vivid and depressing picture of life in the low minors. The Sioux Falls Canaries traveled on a decrepit Ford bus known as "Stucker's Steamer" after the team owner, Rex Stucker. "We used to pile all our suitcases, baseball bats, and other things in this bus and leave Sioux City [Iowa, after a road game] about midnight and travel to Cheyenne, Wyo. It was about 600 miles away. And we were to get there about 4:30 the following afternoon and play a game in Cheyenne, Wyo., that night. …That is the common practice to save hotel bills."[8]

He recalled his second encounter with the reserve clause, when he was back with Sioux Falls after the war and attending Augustana College there in the offseasons. The parent Chicago Cubs ordered him to move to another Class C farm club in Hutchinson, Kansas. He refused to go, and the Cubs suspended him. After two weeks with no income, he agreed to report, but it cost him. He had to rent a hotel room in Hutchinson while continuing to pay for his room at the Sioux Falls YMCA "so that when I came back in the fall I would have a place to live, to go to college."

Horning said the reserve clause was part of baseball's "mercantile theory of economics, whereby each major league club has little colonies all over the United States, and the primary purpose of these colonies or minor league clubs is to produce players for the parent club."[9] (He certainly didn't talk like a ballplayer.) "It is

difficult to see how 16 owners should have complete control of America's national game."[10]

He attacked the owners' central argument that the reserve clause was needed to ensure fair competition between rich and poor teams. On the contrary, he said, benchwarmers on rich clubs could help weaker teams if they were free to choose where to play. "If there were no reserve clause, then [a team] could say to a man on the bench of the wealthy team, 'You can play regular with us.'…He would rather play, surely."[11]

Horning pointed out that a minor leaguer could be released with no notice and no severance pay, not even bus fare home. "Imagine that Ted Williams was hitting .200 on the first of July. He would never lose his job. He would never be fired. He would always receive his year's contract.

"That is not true in the minor league case. If a man was hitting .200, he would probably lose his job on July 2."[12]

Horning continued: "The contract is binding on only one party. There is no binding factor as far as the club is concerned. …If you live to be 75, you cannot play for any other baseball team than the owner says— unless you get an absolute release, that is. You have no choice."[13]

Under questioning, Horning acknowledged that he had no specific ideas on how to replace the reserve clause. "Not every ballplayer is a major league ballplayer or ever will be a major league ballplayer," he concluded. "But I feel they have a right to play where they want to and work where they want to, and to feel that a contract is binding upon the other party as well as upon themselves. That is my entire interest in being here."[14]

THE SALESMAN

Seymour "Cy" Block was never shy about speaking up for himself. When he thought he had been wronged, which was often, he went straight to the top. At different times he confronted Commissioner Kenesaw Mountain Landis, National League President Ford Frick, and Dodgers President Larry MacPhail over his disputes with baseball management. All his appeals failed.[15]

As a 21-year-old in 1940, the Brooklyn boy told a sportswriter, "There's no room for sissies in the minors today." He had his own horror stories of overnight bus rides: "We sit up all night, sing songs I can't repeat, drink a million cokes and when we get out our fannies are as flat as a phonograph record."

"You can't stand the food and the bus rides unless you are young and strong and always have before you the picture of yourself in a big league uniform," he added. "I'll make the Big Top some day. You wait and see."[16]

He made it, but only for a short cup of coffee with the Chicago Cubs. He totaled 17 games in three trials before and after wartime Coast Guard service, and had a Moonlight Graham moment in the 1945 World Series as a pinch-runner who never took the field or came to bat. In 10 years in the minors, the "peppery second baseman," as *The Sporting News* called him, won a Most Valuable Player award and batted over .300 six times.[17] He had been released by Triple-A Buffalo in April 1951 and was now selling insurance.

Block had written to Celler, his hometown congressman, volunteering to testify.[18] Appearing on October 15, he asserted that he was speaking for most minor leaguers, who didn't dare complain "because they would be blacklisted."[19]

"Actually, the reserve clause is just the final breaking point of a number of grievances that have been building up for years among ballplayers," he said as he reeled off a litany of injustices inflicted on players in the minors.[20]

- "In your major league contract, you have a minimum salary of $5,000 and no maximum. You can go as high as the sky, which is fine. On the other hand, in your minor league contract you have no minimum. There is no minimum in any league, but you have a maximum. Outside of a very few ballplayers, the maximum salary you can attain in the minor leagues is about $6,000."

- "In your major leagues, if you get a release, if they release you, you are entitled to 1 month's pay. … In the minor leagues, you could be playing in Podunk and get released in 24 hours, without pay, and you are stuck."

- "In the major leagues, if you are injured you are paid for the season. In the minor leagues they are only liable for two weeks' salary."[21]

- "In the major league contract, when the season ends, they pay your way home. In the minor league, you can live in New York and play in California, and when it ends, you have to pay your own way home."[22]

- A minor leaguer's pay was cut when he was demoted to a lower level. "That is not fair, because when you sign a contract you figure that is the

Brooklynite Cy Block had presented various grievances to no avail during his mostly minor-league career, and contacted Chairman Celler volunteering to testify during the hearings.

salary you're going to get."[23] Unlike the majors, minor leaguers received no moving expenses, no expense money during spring training, and no pension plan.

Block's personal grievance concerned the waiver process, "the farce in baseball."[24] He believed he had been cheated out of a fair shot in the majors because the Cubs had put him on waivers, then refused to sell him when the Phillies and Pirates expressed interest. He thought the Cubs had invoked a "gentlemen's agreement" to send him down to Double A in violation of the rules.

After unloading that barrage, Block insisted that his objection to the reserve clause was limited to its impact on minor leaguers. Major league players, he said, "are really well taken care of."[25]

SIGNIFYING NOTHING
The tame sporting press largely ignored or ridiculed the minor leaguers. Block appeared on the same day as Clark Griffith, ancient owner of the Washington Nationals, who dominated news coverage. Horning may have wished he had passed unnoticed as well.

"Ross Horning's record indicates he can't hit a lick and has no chance to move up in baseball," sneered Francis Stann of the *Washington Evening Star*. Never mind that Horning had no desire to move up in baseball. *Seattle Times* columnist Eugene Russell dismissed him as a "bush leaguer" who was biting the hand that had paid him enough to fund his college education.[26]

In the days following Block's testimony, several active major-league stars parroted the owners' line, exhibiting a kind of Stockholm Syndrome. Detroit pitcher Fred Hutchinson—the American League player representative, no less—pronounced the reserve clause necessary and reasonable. So did Red Sox shortstop Lou Boudreau. "Without the reserve clause, I don't think that baseball could operate," said Dodgers shortstop and captain Pee Wee Reese.[27]

After 16 days of hearings, 33 witnesses, and 1,643 pages of transcript, the subcommittee decided to do nothing. Its final report recommended that Congress take no action on baseball's antitrust exemption because the issue was before the courts.[28] Eight lawsuits challenging the exemption were pending.

In 1953 the US Supreme Court rejected an appeal by former Yankees farmhand George Toolson. "We think that, if there are evils in this field [baseball] which now warrant application to it of the antitrust laws, it should be by legislation," the court majority said.[29] Ballplayers were trapped in a Catch-22: Congress left it up to the courts, and the Supreme Court left it up to Congress.

DIFFERENT BALLGAMES

Ross Horning and Cy Block were born 17 months and 1,400 miles apart, Block in Brooklyn in 1919 and Horning in Watertown, South Dakota, in 1920. They died six months apart in 2004 and 2005. They never met, as far as is known. The two men followed different paths after baseball and achieved more success than they ever had on the diamond.

Block exuded salesmanship. Less than a decade after he began selling life insurance, he was his company's top performer in the country. He rented a 40-foot-tall billboard overlooking Times Square in New York, with his photo in his Cubs uniform and the slogan, "Cy Block Says life insurance is the home run investment. With it you can't strike out."[30]

Eventually he went out on his own to sell insurance and pension plans, and his CB Planning firm topped $100 million in annual sales. Cy and Harriet Block were generous supporters of Jewish charities in the United States and Israel. "Maybe God looked down and said, 'Block, you know, you should have been a helluva ballplayer,'" he said, "and he waved his hand, and whatever I was supposed to do in baseball happened to me in insurance."[31]

Ross Horning completed his Ph.D. at George Washington while playing in independent leagues during several summers. He found that he could make more money in semipro ball than in Class C. He could choose where he played and enjoy a pleasant vacation with his wife, Maxine. After studying in India as a Fulbright Scholar, he became a professor of history at Creighton University in Omaha.

Dr. Horning taught the history of Russia, India, Ireland, Scotland, and Canada, spicing his lectures with corny humor and occasional juggling of tennis balls. He served three terms as faculty president, headed the university's athletic committee, and put in time on practically every other committee on campus. He fed his competitive fire by playing intramural softball and pickup basketball with students into his 70s, even after a hip replacement. Upon his death at 84, Creighton established a scholarship and an annual history lecture in his name.

Horning revisited the plight of minor leaguers in 2000 for an essay in SABR's *The National Pastime*. While major leaguers had won free agency and fabulous salaries, he wrote that the minor-league contract had actually become more oppressive. True, it granted a player free agency after six years—for the few who lasted that long—but he could still be sold or released without notice. In addition, the new contract gave the team year-round call on his services, so he could be prohibited from getting an offseason job to supplement his poverty-level income or, like Horning, going to school.

That was the nature of professional baseball, Horning wrote: "a wonderful, enjoyable sport that is also very cruel."[32]

EPILOGUE

Minor leaguers were still second-class citizens in 2018. A group of players had filed suit seeking to be paid the federal minimum wage, $7.25 per hour, with overtime for working more than 40 hours a week. This time Congress had no hesitation about interfering with the courts. In March 2018 Congress passed and President Trump signed legislation that exempted baseball players from federal overtime laws. The provision, pushed by lobbyists for major- and minor-league baseball, was inserted in a 2,232-page government funding bill, even though Congress had never held hearings or debated the issue.[33]

Garrett Broshuis, a former minor-league pitcher who is the lead attorney for the players, was trying to keep the lawsuit alive by seeking overtime pay under the various state minimum wage laws. The suit was pending as this issue of *Baseball Research Journal* went to press. ■

Acknowledgments

Cindy Workman of Creighton University contributed information about Ross Horning. The research staff of the Library of Congress led me to the transcript of the Celler hearings. Judith Adkins of the National Archives Center for Legislative Archives provided the monopoly subcommittee's files. Attorney Garrett Broshuis briefed me on his lawsuit on behalf of minor leaguers.

Notes

1. *Study of Monopoly Power, Hearings Before the Subcommittee on Study of Monopoly Power of the House Committee on the Judiciary*, 82nd Congress, First Session, Serial No. 1, Part 6: Organized Baseball, 372 (1952). Hereafter cited as "Hearings."
2. "Truman Approves Baseball Reserve Clause Investigation," *Washington Post*, July 19, 1951.
3. Hearings, 30.
4. A note on terminology. While the "reserve clause" itself had been replaced by that point, several provisions in the contract added up to the same effect and were referred to collectively as "the reserve clause." The Celler hearings used that terminology throughout. All baseball witnesses used the term "reserve clause" to describe the contract provisions that bound a player to his team, including the team's right to trade or sell the contract.
5. "Ross Horning: Scholar, wit, and athlete," *Creighton University Colleague*, July 1985: 8; "Younger Shackles Duluth Team, 8–0," *Sioux Falls Argus-Leader* (South Dakota), July 9, 1942. Horning was sold because the Sioux Falls owner needed fast cash to pay expenses for the road trip.
6. Hearings, 352.
7. Ross C. Horning to Representative Cellar [sic], May 14, 1951, "Correspondence A–H," Papers of the House Subcommittee on the Study of Monopoly Power of the Committee on the Judiciary from the 82nd Congress, National Archives Center for Legislative Archives. Hereafter cited as "subcommittee papers."
8. Hearings, 348–9.
9. Hearings, 359.
10. Hearings, 374.
11. Hearings, 374.
12. Hearings, 372.
13. Hearings, 393–4.
14. Hearings, 396.
15. Cy Block, as told to Leonard Lewin, *So You Want to Be a Major Leaguer?* (Privately published, 1964). Block's memoir of his baseball career was a promotional pamphlet for his insurance business.
16. Jimmy Powers, "Minor Leaguer's Grief and Hopes," *New York Daily News*, reprinted in *The Sporting News*, November 14, 1940.
17. "Texas League," *The Sporting News*, June 25, 1942.
18. Cy Block to Hon. Emanuel Celler, July 23, 1951, in subcommittee papers.
19. Hearings, 587.
20. Hearings, 582.
21. Hearings, 583.
22. Hearings, 589.
23. Hearings, 586.
24. Hearings, 589.
25. Hearings, 590.
26. Francis Stann, "Win, Lose, or Draw," *Washington Evening Star*, August 8, 1951; Eugene H. Russell, "Bush Leaguer Talks," *Seattle Times*, August 8, 1951.
27. Hearings, 852. Subcommittee records indicate that the three major leaguers did not volunteer to testify. They were summoned by Chairman Celler, probably at the suggestion of baseball's lobbyist, Washington attorney Paul Porter, because they were considered friendly to the owners' position.
28. *Organized Baseball, Report of the House Subcommittee on Study of Monopoly Power of the Committee on the Judiciary*, 82nd Congress, 232 (1952).
29. Toolson v. New York Yankees, Inc., 346 US 356 (1953), 346.
30. Block, *So You Want to Be a Major Leaguer?* Photo inside back cover.
31. Peter Ephross and Martin Abramowitz, *Jewish Major Leaguers in Their Own Words* (Jefferson, NC: McFarland, 2012), 68.
32. Ross Horning, "Minor League Player," *The National Pastime 20* (SABR, 2000), 104.
33. Bill Shaikin, "Minor Leaguers Could Be Paid Minimum Wage—and No More," *Los Angeles Times*, March 23, 2018.

Revisiting the Origin of the Infield Fly Rule

Richard Hershberger

What is a catch? A player grasps the ball. At some instant the catch is completed. If the player drops the ball before this instant, a catch has not occurred. If he drops the ball after this instant, this does not change the fact of the catch. Determining when this critical moment takes place is important in many sports.

The NFL puts the problem on weekly display. Did the receiver catch the ball before stepping out of bounds or landing on the turf? Viewers and officials study high definition slow motion footage from multiple angles, watching for any movement of the ball that might indicate something less than full control by the receiver. This exercise proves unsatisfactory for everyone. Baseball is spared this, to its great benefit. The closest thing is when a fielder fumbles the transfer from the glove to the throwing hand. In practice this is rarely a problem. The situation arises infrequently, and arouses controversy even less often.

What is a catch? Baseball was not always free of this question. Consider the following scenario: There are runners on first and second with fewer than two outs. The batter hits a fly ball to the shortstop. In the ordinary course of events, the shortstop will take the easy catch, putting the batter out. The runners, expecting this, will remain cautiously close to their bases. But suppose the shortstop instead lets the ball drop to the ground. This is now a force play, with the runners so out of position that the shortstop can pick up the ball and throw it to third base, and the third baseman can relay it to second, resulting in a double play. If the infield fly was a high pop up, the shortstop may be able to let it fall untouched in front of him and catch it on the bounce. More often, however, he will have to direct its fall. He will place his hands in position to catch the ball, but will instead of completing the catch, will drop the ball in front of himself, so that he can pick it up and make his throw to third.

This can be called the "infield fly play." The point of the infield fly play is that the fielder can convert a double play on an easy fly ball. The problem with the infield fly play is that it allows into the Garden of Eden the question of what is a catch. The play depends on the fielder not catching the ball, while still controlling it. How long can his hands be in contact with the ball before it is a catch? How is the umpire to make this determination? How is baseball to avoid endless arguments and, in the modern era, video replays?

The solution is the infield fly rule. If the circumstances are right for the infield fly play, the batter is simply declared out, without reference to the actions of the fielder. This removes the force, and play proceeds naturally from there.

This is not the usual account of the infield fly rule. The typical explanation of its purpose focuses on the baserunner's dilemma. *The Dickson Baseball Dictionary*, for example, begins the entry on the infield fly rule: "A special rule to protect the baserunners."[1] The baserunner's dilemma is that he has, in the infield fly play, no correct course of action.

There are many plays in which the runner has no good course of action, but there is nevertheless a correct, least bad choice. Consider a runner on first with fewer than two outs, and the batter hits a routine ground ball to the shortstop. The correct play is to run hard for second base. This puts him in position to take advantage of a defensive misplay, or failing this he might be able to prevent the second baseman from turning the double play. An aggressive runner can help his team's chances, if only slightly. The runner's prospects are grim, but there is no dilemma.

In the infield fly play, on the other hand, the correct course of action for the runners depends on the action of the fielder, but the runners must commit before the fielder, who can be verbally assisted by his teammates about whether to catch or drop the ball. The baserunner's dilemma is unique, and seems unfair.

Another account of the rule, complementing the baserunner's dilemma, is the perverse incentive the infield fly play gives to the fielder. In the ordinary course of play the fielder's goal is to catch a fly ball. (It is not quite true that this is always the case, even apart from the infield fly play. Consider a tie game in the bottom of the ninth inning with a runner on third base and fewer than two outs, when the batter hits a long fly ball that is foul but within the field of play. Catching the ball would allow the runner to tag up and score, winning the game. The outfielder should instead let the ball fall. Such situations are, however, rare.) The infield fly play gives the fielder the incentive, against all normal practice, to intentionally fail to catch the ball. This was characterized by Harold Seymour and Dorothy Seymour Mills in their seminal work *Baseball: The Early Years* as the defense making a double play "by subterfuge, at a time when the offense is helpless to prevent it, rather than by skill or speed."[2] This account proved attractive to the legal mind, resulting in a decades-long series of seriocomic law review articles.[3]

The baserunner's dilemma and the fielder's perverse incentive in combination provide a satisfying explanation for the infield fly rule. This can be reinforced by the observation that the rule developed in the 1890s, concurrently with the widespread adoption of fielders' gloves. This suggests a further elaboration that the timing of the adoption of the rule was influenced by improved fielding, with gloves making easy what had been, in the barehanded days, a difficult play.

The author long accepted this account of the infield fly rule. It is coherent and plausible. Only recently has closer examination of the antecedents to the rule shown that the actual reason for it is the problem of distinguishing what is and is not a catch. This is an extraordinary claim, and the bulk of what follows will be a defense of it. To be clear, this is a historical rather than a philosophical argument: a historical account of how and why the infield fly rule was developed; not a philosophical discussion of its implications. This does not affect the validity of discussions of the baserunner's dilemma or the fielder's perverse incentive, except to the extent that they claim to describe the historical development of the rule.

The infield fly play first became possible in 1859, the year the tagging up rule was instituted. The tagging up rule set up the play by forcing the runners to linger near their bases in anticipation of the ball being caught. This implication was worked out quickly. It already was an established play in 1863, as this game report makes clear:

[Atlantics v. Mutuals 8/3/1863] [Atlantics at bat, Ticknor on first base, A. Smith on third:] Start hit a high ball for [second baseman] Brown to take on the fly.... Ticknor, who runs the bases well, watched Brown closely, and running the chances of his dropping the ball and picking it up on the bound, which Brown often does to get two outs

instead of one, ran for his second, and was close to it, when Brown missed the ball not only on the fly but on the bound too. Had A. Smith been quicker, he might have got home in the excitement, but in this match Smith made several errors in running his bases, thereby losing the reward of several good hits that he made.[4]

The problem of determining what is a catch arose soon thereafter:

[National vs. Louisville 7/17/1867] In the sixth innings a very peculiar double play was made by the Nationals, and the noise of the crowd cost the Louisvilles an out in this instance. It occurred in this way: L. Robinson was on his first when A. Robinson hit a high ball to Fox, who was playing at second.... Fox held the ball on the fly, but in turning to throw it he dropped it. The umpire called "out on the fly," but the yells of the crowd were so deafening when Fox dropped it that L. Robinson did not hear the cry of the umpire, and seeing the ball dropped, ran for his second. Fox made no effort to pass the ball to Parker at second as he knew he had caught the ball, but leisurely passed it to Fletcher [the first baseman]. An appeal being made, the umpire called "time," and stated to the Louisville players that he could not proceed unless better order was observed.... If a fly ball is held if but for a second or two, unless it plainly rebounds from the hand, it should be considered a catch, and when an umpires sees a ball dropped purposely for a double play, he should decide the ball dropped as a fair catch.[5]

It is not clear whether Fox was actually attempting the infield fly play or if the double play was merely opportunistic, but the editorial comment about what constitutes a catch clearly has the infield fly play in mind. The opinion that the ball is caught if held "but for a second or two" was not generally heeded, and the infield fly play was an established technique. Here is an example from later in the same season where the runner got caught up trying to guess what the fielder would do:

[Mutuals vs. Atlantics 8/12/1867] [Bearman at first:] McMahon then hit a high one...which was falling nicely into [second baseman] Smith's hands, and Bearman stopped at his base; but McMahon, thinking Charley [Smith] would drop it for a double play, called to Bearman to run for

The Mutuals (above) and Atlantics (below) were early teams involved with the infield fly play.

second, and as Smith held the ball and then passed it to [first baseman] Start before Bearman could get back, the result was a double play, and the closing of the innings for a blank score, a round of Atlantic applause greeting the good fielding.[6]

The infield fly play invited controversy about whether the ball was caught:

[Cincinnatis vs. Mutuals 6/15/1869] Eggler popped up a high ball for Waterman to take, and, as it looked like a sure catch, Swandell and Mills kept their places on the second and first bases, seeing which Waterman let the ball drop from his hands, stepped on third-base, promptly sent the ball to second, and the result was that Swandell and Mills were both out, Eggler getting his base on the dropped ball…. The point played

by Waterman, though apparently simple, is really one of the most difficult plays to be made in the position he occupied. In the first place, to drop a ball and avoid a catch, and yet manage to have the ball drop dead in readiness to be quickly picked up again, is very difficult to do, and Waterman failed to legally accomplish the feat. Secondly, the ball, when thus purposely missed must not be held for a second, or it becomes a catch. In this instance the ball seemed to us to have been caught—that is, it was settled in Waterman's hands sufficiently to constitute a catch. The umpire, however, gave the field the benefit of the doubt—for there was barely a doubt—and decided both were out.[7]

A different reporter, discussing the same play, puts the problem in a nutshell:

There was some little uncertainty as to whether the point was properly made; whether Waterman did not actually hold the ball. Here is a nut for the expounders of the law to break their teeth on. How long must the ball be held? However, both men were declared out and the sharp play was well applauded.[8]

This was something of a leitmotif. No one really knew what a catch was, giving endless potential for second-guessing. The matter came to a head in 1872:

[Troy vs. Athletic 5/13/1872] [bases loaded, McBride on third:] Fisler popped one up that dropped directly into [shortstop] Force's hands, and then out again, being purposely missed by that individual in order to make a double play. McBride, of course being under the impression that he was forced off third-base, attempted to run home, and amidst a scene of undescribable confusion, the Umpire decided that Fisler was also out, "caught on the fly" by Force, but on what rule he based that decision, we confess that we are at a loss to know, as the ball just momentarily touched Force's hands and was not held long enough to constitute a catch. The innings closed.[9]

This particular game mattered because of the identity of the umpire. Umpires came and went at a furious rate in the 1870s, so questionable decisions are to be expected. Here, however, the umpire is Nicholas Young, then the secretary of the National Association and later the secretary, then president, of the National League. Young had gravitas. His opinion on what was and was not a catch commanded respect, if not necessarily agreement.

Here the umpire makes the opposite call:

[Mutual vs. Boston 5/11/1872] In the game…a precisely similar point to that of Force's, in the Athletic-Troy, was played by Geo. Wright, but the umpire in this case made a correct decision. Hicks and McMullin were on the first and second bases, when Hatfield popped up a fly that landed into Geo. Wright's hands and then fell out. Quickly fielding it to Schafer, Hicks was put out by being forced by McMullin, who in turn was forced out at second. This play occasioned some talk between the umpire and the captains of the rival nines, but it was allowed, of course, to pass as a muffed fly.[10]

The umpire here was one Moses Chandler, who umpired a total of six professional games between 1872 and 1877. The reporter's opinion notwithstanding, Young's opinion would prevail. The reporter did make his point in one respect: In his criticism of Young's call he noted that Force held the ball but "momentarily." Two years later, in 1874, this was adopted as the standard for a catch, at least in an infield fly play situation. The 1873 rule read:

Rule IV Sec. 7. In the case of a fair hit ball on the fly, the player running the bases shall not be entitled to any base touched after the ball has been hit, and before the catch has been made.

This was revised for 1874, reading:

Rule VI Sec. 11. No base shall be run, or run scored, when a fair ball has been caught, or momentarily held before touching the ground, unless the base held when the ball was hit is re-touched by the base-runner after the ball has been so caught or held by the fielder. But after the ball has been so caught or held, the base-runner shall be privileged to attempt to make a base or score a run. He shall not, however, be entitled to any base touched after the ball has been hit and before the catch is made.

The 1874 revision is mostly expanded language for clarity, making the requirements for tagging up explicit. The new part was the addition of the words

"momentarily held." This was a ratification of Young's call two seasons previous. The reporter may have been correct that the ball had been held only momentarily, but that was all that was needed. While the language seems at face value to present two possibilities, that the fielder might either catch the ball or momentarily hold it, in reality these were two statements of the same thing. Since the runners were prohibited from running prior to the fielder catching or holding the ball, it followed that they weren't forced off their bases, which in turn only worked if the batter were out, regardless of whether the ball were caught or merely momentarily held. The two meant the same thing.

Next, compare this with the following excerpt from the 1874 rules, which specifies how the batter is put out:

Rule V Sec. 14. The batsman shall be declared out by the umpire…if a fair ball be caught before touching the ground, no matter how held by the fielder catching it, or whether the ball first touches the person of another fielder or not, provided it be not caught by the cap.

There is no mention of the batter being out if the ball is held "momentarily." In combination, these two rules are confusing, if not outright contradictory. Does the "momentarily held" standard apply to all situations? If so, then why is it stated only in relation to baserunners? Or are there two different definitions of a catch, depending on the presence or absence of baserunners?

The answer in practice was the latter. The "momentarily held" standard was only applied when an infield fly play situation existed. The incompatible rules were an oversight, resulting from the failure to notice that the one fix would logically affect the other rule, but this wasn't a problem, as everyone knew what was meant.

With this we have many of the elements of the modern infield fly rule. Just as with the modern rule, there is an expansion of how the batter can be put out in an infield fly situation. Just as with the modern rule, an infield fly is treated as if it were caught, even in situations where it isn't really. And just as with the modern rule, the practical effect for the runners is usually to remain at their bases, as if the ball were caught. One difference is that the 1874 rule is not expressly limited to infield flies, but there are no known game accounts of the "momentarily held" standard being applied in this era to a fly ball to an outfielder, and it is likely that it never occurred to anyone that it would.

A substantive element of the modern infield fly rule absent from the 1874 rule is that the earlier rule only applies when the fielder actually fields the ball, while the modern rule applies even if the ball reaches the ground untouched. The 1874 rule allows the infield fly double play in the case of the high pop-up that drops in front of the fielder.

The untouched fly ball will be addressed, but first we will consider why the rule was designed to treat the momentarily held ball as a catch rather than as a muffed ball. If the point is to clarify marginal catches, it would appear at first look that the rule could have gone the other direction, and defined such plays as dropped balls, and this would seem the more natural ruling. This turns out on closer examination not to solve any of the problems. As the rule was enacted, once the ball was dropped, this phase of the play was over and the umpire could declare the ball effectively caught. Had the rule declared such a ball dropped, this would have merely extended the question of how long the fielder can hold the ball before dropping it. He could catch the ball cleanly, observe that the runners had returned to their bases, then drop the ball at his leisure, reopening the force play for the easy double play. The problem would remain of ruling when the catch had truly occurred.

The overall rules were reformatted in 1880. Under the new format, the batter became a runner upon hitting the ball in fair territory. The rule for a fielder catching a fair fly ball was therefore moved to the rule on how the baserunner was put out. The "momentarily held" language was placed here, in Rule 46(1). The baserunner is out

if, having made a fair hit while Batsman, such fair hit ball be momentarily held by a Fielder, before touching the ground or any object other than a Fielder, provided it be not caught in the Fielder's hat or cap.

The language for tagging up came in a later paragraph, in Rule 46(10). The baserunner is out

if, when a Fair or Foul Hit ball is legally caught by a Fielder before it touches the ground, such ball is legally held by a Fielder on the base occupied by the Base-Runner when such ball was struck (or the Base-Runner be touched with the ball in the hand of a Fielder), before he retouches said base after such Fair or Foul Hit Ball was so caught…

This would seem to say that the "momentarily held" standard now applied to all fair balls, and not merely in infield fly play situations. It was not understood that way. There are no game accounts, outside of infield fly situations, of batters being called out on seemingly muffed balls. The "momentarily held" standard only applied in practice to Rule 46 (10), by reference to the ball being "legally held." This was a clumsy attempt to combine these incompatible rules in the new format. It was neither intended nor understood to be a substantive change.

This was not the only problem of rules draftsmanship. The rule simply was not well written. The "momentarily held" standard was too vague to be satisfactory. It authorized the umpire to declare the ball caught, but it provided little guidance about when he should do this. The arguments therefore continued:

Farrell purposely missed an easy catch in the fourth, when men were on first and second bases, and made a brilliant triple-play, which elicited round after round of applause.[11]

While the home crowd applauded the play, the Clevelands played the rest of the game under protest.[12]

The general response from league officials was to try to strengthen the rule. After the 1882 season, the American Association defined "momentarily held" as

making a catch of the ball if it be grasped by the fielder but for an instant. Under this ruling, therefore, a fielder desiring to make a double play must let the ball drop to the ground and catch it on the rebound close to the ground in order to effect it.[13]

The same year, the Spalding baseball guide included a discussion of definitions, including:

In regard to the definition of the words "momentarily held" as applicable to the catching of the ball, it should be understood that a catch is legitimately made when the fielder catching it has a fair opportunity afforded him for making the catch, and purposely fails to hold the ball after stopping it with his hands. In playing the point of refusing to accept a chance for a catch in order to make a double play, the only method officially regarded as legal is to allow the ball to fall to the ground and then to catch it on the bound, or to pick it up at once. If an easy chance is offered to make the catch, and the ball is allowed to drop from the hands of the fielder, the Umpire should regard such stopped ball as "momentarily held," and decide the striker out on the catch.[14]

This was not merely journalistic opinion. Nicholas Young, in his position as National League secretary, restated the position in his official instructions to NL umpires:

> The umpires' instructions on this question are such as to defeat almost any play of the kind that can be attempted. They are required to rule that if a fielder even stops the force of the fly ball, with the object of effecting a double play, the ball shall be decided as having been caught and held. If a fielder were to put up his open hands and bounce the ball off them to the ground it would be ruled a catch, and a runner having left a base on such a play may be put out by return of the ball to the base.[15]

Young would repeat this instruction regularly over the ensuing years, but these exhortations were not followed consistently. Fielders continued to make the play while touching the ball. Here is an example from a game in 1885 between Chicago and St. Louis:

> Pfeffer did a pretty piece of work in the ninth inning by which he recorded a double play for himself and drew forth much applause from the audience. Shafer had taken his base on Anson's error, and had reached second on McKinnon's base hit. Glasscock then knocked a fly to Pfeffer, which the latter dropped. Glasscock reached first, but Shafer and McKinnon, thinking that Pfeffer had held the ball, stood their bases, and Pfeffer, running to second, touched Shafer, who should have run to third, and then put out McKinnon by touching the second base with the ball.[16]

The state of affairs eventually reached the point that in 1893 a sportswriter responded to a report of Young's instructions with incredulity:

> President Young, in his instructions to the league umpires, in regard to the interpretation he gives to section 2 of rule 47, is evidently in error. The rule in question states that the base runner is out "if, having made a fair hit while batsman, such fair hit ball be momentarily held by a fielder before touching the ground." Mr. Young,

Nicholas Young, the first secretary of the National League from 1876 and both president and secretary of the NL until his retirement in 1902. He propounded the earliest version of the infield fly rule, to avoid controversy over what was and was not a catch.

> in his instructions to umpires interprets the words "momentarily held," in the case of a fly ball hit to the infield and simply touched by the fielder, as a catch; while if a fly ball to the outfield be similarly touched by an outfielder it is to be scored as not a catch but an error. Most assuredly if it be a catch in the infield it must be a catch in the outfield. The cause of the forced interpretation thus give the rule is to prevent a force out play, from an intentionally dropped fly ball in the infield. But this can only be done by adding a new clause to the rule making a force out play from a dropped fly ball inoperative in the case of an infield hit and then only.... As it is now an interpretation is given the rule which applies to the infield, but not the outfield, and this the president of the league has no legal right to do.[17]

This brings us to the 1890 Players League. Its rules included a few changes from the existing set of the National League and American Association. One of them was a new section added to the rule on how the batter could be put out:

> Rule 41 Sec. 9. The Batsman is out...if, where there is a Base Runner on the First Base and less than two players on the side at bat have been put out in the inning then being played, the Batsman make a fair hit so that the ball falls within the infield, and the ball touches any Fielder whether held by him or not before it touches the ground.

This is sometimes said to be the first Infield Fly Rule.[18] In reality, it is a restatement of the 1874 rule, as interpreted by both the NL and AA. It is credited as the first because it takes a more recognizable form. Where the old inscrutable "momentarily held" language is overlooked, the PL rule says the same thing, but more clearly.

The Players League lasted just the one season. The older leagues felt no urge to borrow any ideas from it. Their rules kept the old language, retaining the old confusion. The Cleveland Leader complained about this in 1892:

The differences of opinion as to what constitutes a muffed infield fly are annoying. Each umpire is disposed to rule upon it his own way. At the next annual meeting of the League the committee upon rules should settle the matter so there will be no further mistakes.[19]

The National League finally addressed the problem in 1894. A new section was added to the rule on how batters are put out:

Rule 45 Sec. 9. The Batsman is out...if he hits a fly ball that can be handled by an infielder while first base is occupied with only one out.

The rule was written carelessly. It should apply only when both first and second bases (and optionally third) are occupied. (If the batter is the second out on this play, he wasn't running very hard.) The language of "with only one out" nonsensically suggests that the rule doesn't apply with no outs. These points were fixed over the next few years. The 1895 rules required that both first and second (and optionally third) bases be occupied for the rule to apply. Not until 1901 was the rule changed to apply "unless two hands are out." It never made any sense to apply the rule only when there was one out. It is possible that umpires had been enforcing it that way all along.

The 1894 rule had one novelty. The rule now applied whether or not the fielder even touched the ball. Holding the ball, momentarily or longer, no longer entered into the matter. The batter was out regardless of the actions of the fielders. This, it was soon realized, allowed the umpire to call the out while the ball was still in the air. The 1897 rules codified this practice, mandating that the umpire "shall, as soon as the ball is hit, declare an infield or an outfield hit," meaning that he inform the runners whether the batter was out or play was to continue as normal. This was changed

in 1931 to the modern rule, with the umpire declaring only the infield fly, leaving an outfield fly unremarked. Several 1931 revisions brought the rules in line with actual practice. This may have been such a revision, with umpires only calling infield, and not outfield, flies all along.

The new rule removed the fielder's actions, much less his intent, from the decision to call the batter out. The discussions behind this were held in private, so we can only speculate as to the motivation. A plausible explanation is that by rendering the actions of the fielder irrelevant, he couldn't game the play and arguments would be avoided. The old standard, even when enforced, could still lead to arguments. Sportswriter Jacob Morse wrote in late 1893 of the proposed rule as being designed

to stop the double play on a fly ball hit to the infield whether the ball touches the infielder's hands at all or is trapped. I have seen infielders trap the ball and yet the umpires would not allow the play. There is a great deal more disappointment on the part of the spectators when such a double play is allowed than over any other point of the play. The base runners are perfectly helpless in such emergencies. It would help run getting immensely if this change were made.[20]

Here, finally, we come to discussions of the baserunner's dilemma. Several discussions around the 1894 rule included this feature. Sportswriter O.P. Caylor in 1894 offered this explanation:

This new rule was aimed particularly at McPhee of the Cincinnatis and Fred Pfeffer of the Louisvilles, who, to use the language of the boys on the sun seats, "had de play down fine as silk and made suckers outen de guys on the de bases. See?" When an infield fly went to either of those two players, men on bases were 'twixt his satanic majesty and the fathomless ocean. If they stood still, the fly would be dropped, and they would be forced; if they ran, the fly would be caught, and so the magnates found it necessary to legislate against those two great players.[21]

The new, stronger form of the rule, removing entirely the infielder's actions from consideration, may have been motivated by the baserunner's dilemma. The idea was in the air. It came from the abolition of a play involving the dropped third strike, with its similar incentives to the infield fly play. In its original form, the dropped third strike rule applied regardless of the situation. So, for example, with the bases loaded and fewer than two outs, the catcher could intentionally drop the third strike, pick up the ball, tag home plate for the force out, and throw the ball to first base for the second out. The two plays presented similar difficulties for the umpire, and the same standard of "momentarily held" was applied. The dropped third strike presented the additional challenge that the single umpire positioned behind the catcher was peculiarly ill-positioned to see whether the catcher held the ball, even momentarily.[22] For this reason, the rule was changed for 1887 to the modern form, where the dropped third strike rule does not apply if first base is occupied with fewer than two outs. The *Detroit Free Press*, for one, approved of the change:

> Heretofore the rule declaring a batter out "if the ball be momentarily held," has led to a vast amount of wrangling among opposing players, dissatisfaction to spectators, and yowling at the umpire. This new rule is intended to put a stop to all this disgusting confusion. When there is a man on first and no more than one man out…what has been the point of sharp play by the catcher? To purposely muff the third strike, force both men to run, and then, by throwing to second, to make a double play. This he can no longer do, the batter being out upon the fourth missed strike [four strikes being required for an out in 1887], no matter whether the ball is caught or not.[23]

The dropped third strike play presented a baserunner's dilemma similar to that of the infield fly play, where a runner would find himself forced off his base in a situation where ordinarily the correct play would be to stay in place. This wasn't why the dropped third strike rule was changed, but an urban legend arose that it had been. This in turn gave rise to the idea that the infield fly rule served the same purpose. In 1893 Washington manager Gus Schmelz tied the two together:

> No double playing should be allowed on a trapped ball when there is more than one man on a base. If the play can be made when first base alone is occupied, through the carelessness of the batsman in not running out his hit, all well and good, but in every other case where a double is possible the batsman should be given out when the ball is hit up over the infield. The catcher was stopped from making a double by dropping the third strike when first base was occupied, because it made a monkey out of the base runner. The trapped ball should go for the same reason.[24]

With the 1894 infield fly rule, the "momentarily held" language was now obsolete, but in a characteristically sloppy piece of legal draftsmanship, it remained on the books. Its purpose was soon forgotten. The rule was rarely cited, and even more rarely under happy circumstances. This report of a Pirates-Giants game in 1914 is one example:

> When is a ball "momentarily held," is a question which Umpire Mal Eason decides one way, and Umpire Bill Klem another. In Wednesday's game at the Polo Grounds, Mike Mowrey hit a line drive to left field which Burns got under at the fence, juggled the ball, collided with the stand and then dropped the ball.

> "You are out!" yelled Eason to Mowrey, who had rounded second. "He dropped that ball," came back Mowrey. "He momentarily held it," said Eason with the entire Pirate squad surrounding him.

> In yesterday's game at Brooklyn, Eddie Collins, in the eighth inning, after a hard run, caught a fly hit by Cutshaw. The youngster couldn't stop and after carrying the ball fully five yards it dropped out of his hands. Klem declared Cutshaw, who reached second, safe, and when Clarke and Wagner insisted Collins had momentarily held the ball, Klem waved them away and declared, "There ain't no such thing."[25]

Here Thomas Holmes of the *Brooklyn Eagle*, writing in 1928, takes a cynical view of the rule, that it served mainly to let umpires justify blown calls:

> There is something in the rules saying that a thrown or batted ball to be caught must be "momentarily held," and apart from providing umpires with an easy alibi, it doesn't mean a thing. This rule gives a mistaken umpire a great break. If he calls one too soon or calls one obviously wrong, he can sometimes get out of the jam with honor intact by saying: "Well, the ball was momentarily held, wasn't it?" and who can say him nay? For any ball that hits in the pocket of a player's glove is momentarily held.

The interpretation of this vague and unnecessary phrase narrows down to a question of how long is a moment. The answer of that is largely a matter of what the umpire had for lunch and whether it agreed with him.[26]

Not until 1931 was the "momentarily held" language finally cleansed from the rules.

The infield fly rule is occasionally criticized today, usually in two forms. The first is to criticize borderline (or perceived borderline) infield fly calls and suggest that these could be avoided by doing away with the rule. The prominent recent example is the 2012 NL wild-card game between the Cardinals and the Braves. With runners at first and second and one out—the classic infield fly situation—Braves batter Andrelton Simmons popped a ball into shallow left field. Cardinals shortstop Pete Kozma was in position to catch the ball, then moved away, apparently to cede the play to left fielder Matt Holliday. The ball dropped. This initially seemed to result in the bases being loaded, but umpire Sam Holbrook had called an infield fly. The result was runners on second and third—having advanced as with any uncaught fair ball—with two outs. Regardless of the correctness of the call itself, the play shows the intrinsic problem of the borderline infield fly. In practice, however, this occurs very rarely. The 2012 game resulted in a flurry of debate, which rapidly disappeared.[27]

The second critique is more substantial: The infield fly rule rewards failure. Where the baserunner's dilemma looks at the play from the baserunner's perspective, and the fielder's perverse incentive to drop the ball looks at it from the fielder's, this critique looks at the play from the point of view of the batter. Whatever he was trying to achieve, an infield fly was not it. So why is he protected from a double play? A sharp ground ball to the shortstop or a line drive at the first baseman would most likely have resulted in a double play and no one would suggest that this was anything less than fair. So why should an infield fly be any different? The response to the baserunner's dilemma and the fielder's perverse incentive in this critique is "So what?" It has a point.

What is a catch? This question rebuts the critiques. Imagine watching ultra-slow-motion replay from various angles: Did the shortstop's glove close around the ball just enough that the ball was caught? Did the ball move around in the glove enough that it was never secured? This would, absent the infield fly rule, be the world we lived in. It's a world no one wants. ■

Notes

1. Paul Dickson, *The Dickson Baseball Dictionary*, 3rd ed. (New York: W.W. Norton & Co., 2009), 451.
2. Harold Seymour and Dorothy Seymour Mills, *Baseball: The Early Years* (New York: Oxford University Press, 1960), 276.
3. The first was "Aside: The Common Law Origins of the Infield Fly Rule." 1975. *University of Pennsylvania Law Review* 123 (6): 1474. The unsigned article was by William S. Stevens, then a student at the University of Pennsylvania Law School. Recent examinations of the idea, and riffs on Stevens's article, include Andrew J. Guilford & Joel Mallord, "A Step Aside: Time to Drop the Infield Fly Rule and End a Common Law Anomaly." 2015. *University of Pennsylvania Law Review* 164 (1): 281; and Howard M. Wasserman, "Just a Bit Aside: Perverse Incentives, Cost-Benefit Imbalances, and the Infield Fly Rule." 2016. *University of Pennsylvania Law Review* 164 (1): 145.
4. "Sports and Pastimes," *New York Sunday Mercury*, August 9, 1863.
5. "The Nationals at Louisville," *Ball Players Chronicle*, July 25, 1867.
6. "Grand Club Match in Brooklyn," *Ball Players Chronicle*, August 15, 1867.
7. "Sports and Pastimes," *New York Sunday Mercury*, June 20, 1869.
8. "The National Game," *New York Herald*, June 16, 1869.
9. "Base Ball," *Evening City Item* (Philadelphia), May 14, 1872. This account is unclear about the third out, but another account of the same game states that Force relayed the ball to the third baseman, intending for a force play on the runner from second but credited per Umpire Young's decision as putting out the runner from third, who failed to tag up. "Athletic vs. Troy," *Philadelphia Sunday Mercury*, May 19, 1872.
10. "Base Ball," *Evening City Item* (Philadelphia), May 16, 1872.
11. "Providence vs. Cleveland," *New York Clipper*, August 14, 1880.
12. "In and Out-Door Sports," *Cleveland Plain Dealer*, August 6, 1880.
13. "Good Boys," *Cincinnati Enquirer*, December 14, 1882.
14. *Spalding's Base Ball Guide: Official League Book for 1883* (Chicago: A.G. Spalding & Bros., 1883), 28-29. The same language is in the 1884 edition, but the entire section omitted thereafter.
15. "Instructions of League Umpires," *Sporting Life*, June 3, 1883.
16. "Sporting Matters," *Chicago Tribune*, June 10, 1885.
17. "Praying Hard for Rain," *Brooklyn Eagle*, May 17, 1893.
18. Peter Morris, *A Game of Inches*, 2nd ed. (Chicago: Ivan R. Dee 2010), 164.
19. "March On, March On," *Cleveland Leader*, August 18, 1892.
20. Jacob C. Morse, "Hub Happenings," *Sporting Life*, November 4, 1893.
21. O.P. Caylor, "The Baseball Outlook," *Daily Illinois State Journal*, March 11, 1894.
22. For a longer discussion of the history of the dropped third strike rule, see Richard Hershberger, "The Dropped Third Strike: The Life and Times of a Rule," *Baseball Research Journal*, vol. 44, no. 1, Spring 2015.
23. "Ciphers for Memphis," *Detroit Free Press*, April 10, 1887.
24. "Schmelz's Idea," *Sporting Life*, November 4, 1893.
25. "Conferences of Pittsburg Club Officials May Mean More Pirate Deals," *Pittsburgh Press*, August 1, 1914.
26. Thomas Holmes, "Umpires Make a Joke out of the Old 'Momentarily Held' Rule," *Brooklyn Eagle*, July 13, 1928.
27. The call clearly was correct. The fielders were not attempting to turn a double play, and the ball dropping uncaught was inadvertent. Intent is not, however, a consideration in the rule. The ball could have been caught by an infielder with ordinary effort. That the fielder did not make that ordinary effort is irrelevant, and that he would not was unknowable to the umpire when he had to make the call. More abstractly, were there no infield fly rule, the shortstop could have turned an infield fly double play on that ball.

The Rise and Fall of the Deadball Era

Dr. David J. Gordon

If a modern fan could be transported back to a baseball game in 1908, to the strains of the new tune "Take Me out to the Ball Game," he or she would feel right at home. The rules, the two major leagues, and many of the teams were similar then to what they are today. However, 1908 was also the offensive nadir of what is now popularly called the Deadball Era, a two-decade period of depressed run-scoring between 1901 (when the elevation of the American League to major league status doubled the number of major-league teams from eight to 16) and 1919 (the year Babe Ruth started hitting home runs in bunches).[1] This was a period when all major-league teams combined to hit .254/.316/.332 (batting average/on-base average/slugging average), and the average game featured only 3.9 runs, 8.4 hits, and 0.15 home runs per team.[2]

The popular narrative attributes the dearth of offensive production during this period largely to the properties of the ball (hence "Deadball"), pointing to the change from a rubber center to cork in 1910, the abolition of the spitball and other ball-doctoring techniques in 1920, and a policy mandating the removal of dirty and damaged balls from the game (inspired by the death of Cleveland shortstop Ray Chapman, who was hit in the head by an errant Carl Mays fastball that he could not see in August 1920).[3] But I believe this is an incomplete and overly simplistic narrative. While ball-centered theories help explain the end of the Deadball Era, they cannot explain why it began in the first place, since the ball was no "livelier" only seven years earlier (when scoring was at an all-time high) than it was in 1901.

I propose here a more holistic narrative to describe the rise and fall of the Deadball Era. I will describe how conditions in the 1870s, when major-league baseball began, favored a contact-oriented approach to hitting and produced an entertaining, high-scoring game; how changes in the rules governing pitchers, the adoption of fielding gloves, and the evolution and refinement of fielding gradually tipped the balance toward defense; how rule changes—designed mostly to favor hitters—helped ward off the inexorable decline of scoring in the 1880s and 1890s; how the advent of power pitchers in the late 1890s and the foul-strike rule in 1901–03 finally overwhelmed these measures and brought about the Deadball Era; and how the arrival of Ruth (and his imitators) led to the obsolescence of the "scientific" contact-oriented strategies in favor of a new hitting paradigm based on power and a free-swinging approach.

While it is impossible to completely sort out cause and effect in the many trends that shaped the game in its first 50 years, I believe this narrative fits the historic data far better than the simplistic dead ball/live ball dichotomy.

SPECIALIZED STATISTICS

In addition to the conventional stats, I have devised a statistic called Defensive Efficiency (DE), closely related to batting average on balls in play (BABIP). DE quantifies the percentage of balls in play that result in the batter being retired without reaching base safely, and counts reaching base on an error as equivalent to a hit. Specifically,

$$DE = 1 - (H + ROE - OPHR) / (AB - OPHR - SO + SH)$$

where H = hits, ROE = reached base on an error, OPHR = out-of-the-park home runs, AB = at-bats, SO = strikeouts, SH = sacrifice hits. Data for sacrifice hits are imperfect, since sacrifice bunts were not tracked until 1894 and sacrifice flies were not broken out as a separate category until 1954, but SH are only a minor component of this calculation. Data for inside-the-park home runs (IPHR) and OPHR, and for ROE and errors that only allow existing baserunners to take an extra base were obtained from Baseball-Reference.com's Play Index tool, which contains tabulations of IPHR and ROE based on play-by-play data going back to 1925.[4] Note that the data are 100% complete going back to 1974, 97% complete from 1950–73, but only 64–90% complete from 1925–49. The percentage of errors resulting in a baserunner ROE is quite constant over time, so I have simply multiplied total errors per game by 63.3%, the average of the 1974–2017 percentages, to determine ROE for each season. For HR, which has a strong decreasing temporal trend, I divided the 1925–73 IPHR totals by the percent coverage to correct for missing data (which assumes that IPHR/HR is the similar for the missing and covered data). For 1871–1924, I assumed that the percentage of home runs that were IPHR in each time period were as follows:

Years	IPHR %
Before 1880	99
1880–92	90
1893–1900	50
1901–08	35
1909–19	25
1920–25	10

Even though a high proportion of HR before 1900 did not leave the ballpark, IPHR were never sufficiently frequent to have much impact on the calculation of DE.

I have also used a stat called BIP%, the percentage of plate appearances on which a ball is put in play. Specifically,

$$BIP\% = 100\%*(PA - BB - SO - OPHR - HBP) / PA$$

where BB = bases on balls and HBP = hit batsmen. This stat is basically one minus "three true outcomes" (TTO), with the slight correction that IPHR are counted as balls in play.[5]

IN THE BEGINNING

When the National Association of Professional Base Ball Players was established in 1871, the rules were very different from what they are today or what they were during the Deadball Era.[6] Pitchers delivered the ball from anywhere within a 6-by-6-foot pitcher's box whose front edge was only 45 feet from the batter. The pitcher could take a short running start but was required to pitch underhanded. The batter could ask for a pitch to be high or low, and when the batter did not offer at a pitch, the umpire generally called "no pitch" unless the ball was where the batter asked for it (a strike) or the pitcher threw the ball in the dirt or behind the batter or persistently out of the strike zone (a ball). The first pitch was never called. The batter received a free base after three balls were called, but walks, like strikeouts, were rare. The real action took place after the ball was hit.

Many games were played in open fields or with distant fences, so there was no great incentive for a batter to hit the ball far, so long as he hit it hard and in play. Fielders played bare-handed and errors were common. The result was a highly entertaining but inelegant game, with lots of errors and lots of runs, mostly unearned. Despite the fact that the ball itself was similar to the ones used 30 years later in the Deadball Era, it is safe to say that no one who watched baseball in the 1870s would have dreamed of using the epithet deadball to describe what they saw.

So how did this free-wheeling, high-scoring game turn into the tight, low-scoring chess-matches of the Deadball Era? The answer is to be found not in the ball itself, but in two significant historic trends.

1. The development and popularization of fielding gloves, which improved DE and made it harder to reach base by merely putting the ball in play.

2. A series of rule changes that shifted power from soft-tossing pitchers who relied heavily on deception and finesse to bigger pitchers who could throw hard enough to succeed from 60 feet away.

Pud Gavin

In Table 1, I have summarized key rule changes that contributed most to the long-term decline in run-scoring and the evolution of the Deadball Era. The most important of these changes were probably the removal of restrictions on a pitcher's delivery and the batter's ability to call for a high or low pitch in the mid-1880s, and the addition in the early 1900s of the foul-ball strike, which accelerated the scoring decline that was already well underway. Rule-makers tried to mitigate this trend by making it easier to walk hitters and by increasing the pitcher-batter distance—most successfully in 1893, when they set the distance at 60.5 feet and eliminated the pitcher's box, setting off a brief but spectacular scoring explosion in the mid-1890s. But eventually, the scoring decline won out and would persist until 1920.

Let us pause for a moment to think about the profound implications of the changes in pitching distance.[8] The three staples of pitching are velocity, command, and deception. Although we know that the top pitchers in the nineteenth century were masters of command and deception, there were no radar guns to tell us how hard they threw. However, what matters to a batter is not velocity per se, but how much time he has to react to a pitch, which is a function not only of velocity but the distance the ball travels to reach him. Mathematically, reaction time equals 0.682 times distance divided by velocity (where $0.682 = 60 * 60/5280$ is the conversion factor from feet per second to miles per hour). So, in terms of batter reaction times (Table 2), a change in pitching distance from 55.5 to 60.5 feet is equivalent to nearly a 10 percent drop in velocity.

For example, a 100-mph fastball thrown from the post-1892 distance of 60.5 feet takes 0.41 seconds to reach the batter—similar to a 91.7-mph fastball thrown from 55.5 feet, an 82.6-mph fastball thrown from 50 feet, or a 74.4-mph fastball thrown from 45 feet. Given how difficult it is for modern hitters to catch up to a 100-mph fastball and the rarity of strikeouts in the nineteenth century, one does not need a radar gun to infer that 19th century pitchers generally did not exceed these velocities. For simplicity, I have ignored air drag and the length of a pitcher's stride from these calculations.

Now, let us examine four simple graphs tracking the trends in scoring, fielding, home runs, and strikeouts from 1871–2017. While this article will focus primarily on trends in baseball's first five decades, the subsequent decades provide a useful context and perspective.

Table 1. Key nineteenth- and early twentieth-century changes in official rules[7]

Pitching Distance

1871–73	45' (pitcher's line)
1874–78, 80	45' (Front line at 45'; back line at 51')
1879	45' (Front line at 45'; back line at 49')
1881–85	50' (Front line at 50'; back line at 56')
1886	50' (Front line at 50'; back line at 57')
1887–92	55.5' (Front line at 50'; back line at 55.5'). Pitcher began delivery from back line.
1893–	60.5' (hard rubber slab—no box)

Pitching Delivery

1879–82	Arm must be below waist
1883	Arm can be above waist
1884–1919	No restrictions
1920–	Spitball outlawed (but 17 practitioners grandfathered)

Strike Zone

1871–86	Batter can call for high or low pitch
1887–	Pitcher can throw anywhere in the strike zone.

Base on Balls Definition

1871–78	3 balls (but balls only called on pitches in dirt, behind batter, etc.)
1879	9 balls (but every pitch must be called a ball, strike, or foul)
1880–83	8 balls
1884–86	6 balls
1887–88	5 balls, batters awarded 1B on hit by pitch
1889–	4 balls, batters awarded 1B on hit by pitch

Strikeout Definition

1871–86	3 strikes
1887	4 strikes
1888–1902	3 strikes

Foul Balls

1871–82	Not counted as strikes. But batter is retired on foul balls caught on the fly or on one bounce
1883–93	Not counted as strikes. Batter only retired on foul balls caught before hitting ground.
1894–1900	Foul bunts counted as strikes
1901–1902	Other foul balls counted as strikes unless the batter already had 2 strikes (NL)
1903–	Other foul balls counted as strikes unless the batter already had 2 strikes (AL and NL)

The Bat

1871–84	Must be round
1885–92	One side may be flat
1893–	Must be round

The Ball

1871–1909	Hard rubber core, balls replaced infrequently
1910–1919	Lighter cork core, balls replaced infrequently
1920–	Lighter cork core, dirty or damaged balls replaced

Table 2. Impact of distance and velocity on time (in seconds) from pitcher's hand to batter

Velocity in mph	100	95	90	85	80	75	70	65
Velocity in ft/sec	146.67	139.33	132.00	124.67	117.33	110.00	102.67	95.33
Distance (ft)								
60.5	0.41	0.43	0.46	0.49	0.52	0.55	0.59	0.63
55.5	0.38	0.40	0.42	0.45	0.47	0.50	0.54	0.58
50	0.34	0.36	0.38	0.40	0.43	0.45	0.49	0.52
45	0.31	0.32	0.34	0.36	0.38	0.41	0.44	0.47

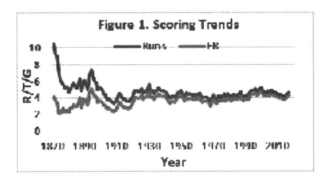

Figure 1. Scoring Trends

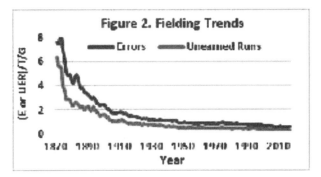

Figure 2. Fielding Trends

Figure 3. Home Run Trends

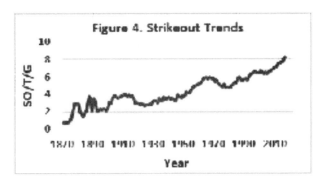

Figure 4. Strikeout Trends

Scoring fluctuated wildly in baseball's first half-century and has been relatively flat ever since (Figure 1). Perturbations like the scoring drought of 1963–72 and the high scoring of the steroid years seem small by comparison. There was also a steep downward trend in errors and unearned runs between 1870 and 1910, reflecting the development, popularization, and improvement of fielding gloves and increasing consciousness of the importance of defense (Figure 2). Fielding gloves had been used as early as 1869 by some catchers and first basemen to protect their hands from injury; they chose flesh colors for camouflage to avoid ridicule, since the use of such gloves was widely considered to be unmanly.[9] As the frequency of games increased in the late 1870s and '80s, and as the daily pounding to their hands became more painful, more padding was added. By the mid-1880s, gloves began to catch on, as other position players followed suit. By 1895, everyone wore a fielder's glove. Most of the early gloves were pretty crude and lacked sufficient flexibility to do much more than knock down hard-hit balls and hope that a play could be made. It was only in 1920, when the Rawlings company created the Bill Doak glove with a web between the thumb and forefinger, that the glove began to be viewed as a defensive as well as a protective accessory.[10] Fielding and fielding gloves have continued to improve since then.

Home runs were relatively scarce in baseball's first five decades but took off in 1920, and have been increasing in fits and starts ever since (Figure 3). The discernible peak in the steroid years is not the only one. Finally, strikeouts fluctuated in the 1880s, went up temporarily during the Deadball years with the implementation of the foul-strike rule, dropped in the 1920s and '30s, then took off in the 1950s and are still rising today (Figure 4). While I will focus in this article on analyzing the trends in baseball's first 50 years, the subsequent trends provide a useful context and perspective.

In Table 3, I have selected a one-season snapshot from each decade of the nineteenth century (1873, 1888, and 1894), the Deadball Era (1908 and 1917), and the beginning of the post-Deadball Era (1922), and compared them to baseball in 2017. In choosing these seasons, I have avoided atypical years like 1884, 1890, and 1915–16, when MLB lost players to the Union Association, Players League, and Federal League respectively, and 1918, when many players served in World War I. The italicized numbers represent estimates of data that were not tracked contemporaneously.

THE NATIONAL ASSOCIATION (1873)

In 1873, baseball bore little resemblance to the modern game (Table 3). In addition to the rules differences summarized in Table 1, teams played only 44 games, and most teams used the same pitcher to start every game. Teams usually employed one or two backup pitchers (who usually played other positions as well), but pitchers finished what they started 91 percent of the time. Pitchers threw underhand and tended to rely more on deception than velocity; hitters put the ball in play in 96 percent of plate appearances despite standing only 45 feet away from the pitcher. Walks (0.84 per team per game) and strikeouts (0.70 per team per game) were exceedingly rare, since batters were permitted to call for a low or high pitch and umpires most often called "no pitch" on balls out of the requested zone.

Fielding was abysmal in 1873, largely because fielders eschewed gloves. In the average game, the two teams would combine to make 16 errors and allow 11 unearned runs (out of 18 total runs); by contrast, a typical 2017 game featured only 9.3 runs, of which only 0.7 were unearned. Indeed, teams scored almost a full earned run more per game in 2017 than in 1873. DE in 1873 was only 58 percent (compared to 69 percent today). In other words, any hitter who could put the ball in play in 1873 had a 42 percent chance to reach base safely. With those odds, it would be foolish for a batter to take big swings and risk striking out, especially in ballparks where the odds of an OPHR were limited by distant or non-existent fences.

In this environment, a contact-oriented, "scientific" approach to hitting flourished. Even big, strong players like Chicago White Stockings star Cap Anson, who stood 6'0" and weighed well over 200 pounds, choked up on his bat and half-swung, using his wrists to generate line drives.[11] No exit velocities and launch angles for him! This style became the model for most players and produced a very lively, high-scoring (albeit sloppy) brand of baseball.

Table 3: Changes in Key Stats over 5 Decades

Stat	1873	1888	1894	1908	1917	1922	2017
Number of Teams (Tms)	9	16	12	16	16	16	30
Games per Team (G)	44.22	136.50	133.17	155.50	155.88	154.75	162.00
AtBats + Sacrifice Hits (AB+SH)	*42.61*	*34.54*	36.75	33.73	34.13	35.66	34.50
Runs per Team per game (R/G)	8.99	4.87	7.38	3.38	3.59	4.87	4.65
Earned (ER)	3.40	2.89	5.12	2.36	2.68	4.03	4.31
Unearned (UER)	5.59	1.98	2.26	1.02	0.91	0.84	0.34
Hits per team per Game (H)	12.38	8.24	11.14	7.75	8.18	9.94	8.69
Walks per team per game (BB)	0.84	2.16	3.67	2.36	2.77	2.93	3.26
Strikeouts per team per game (SO)	0.70	3.76	2.09	3.65	3.48	2.81	8.25
Errors per team per game	7.93	3.44	3.04	1.71	1.50	1.30	0.58
Reached base on error (ROE)	*5.02*	*2.18*	*1.92*	*1.08*	*0.95*	0.82	0.36
Advanced on error (AOE)	*2.91*	*1.26*	*1.12*	*0.63*	*0.55*	0.48	0.22
Baserunners per team per game (BR)	18.24	12.58	16.73	11.19	11.90	13.69	12.31
Home runs per team per game (HR)	0.12	0.24	0.39	0.11	0.13	0.43	1.26
Left the field (OPHR)	*0.001*	*0.02*	*0.19*	*0.07*	*0.10*	0.39	1.26
Inside the Park (IPHR)	*0.12*	*0.22*	*0.20*	*0.04*	*0.03*	0.04	0.004
Balls in Play % (BIP)	96%	83%	84%	82%	82%	84%	66%
Defensive Efficiency (DE)*	58%	66%	63%	71%	70%	68%	69%
Modified On-Base Percentage (OBPm)**	0.4198	0.3495	0.4195	0.3161	0.3262	0.3585	0.3323
Slugging Average (SLG)	.357	.320	.435	.305	.324	.401	.426

* Defined as 1-(H+ROE-OPHR)/(AB-OPHR-SO+SH)
** Defined as (H+BB+HBP)/(PA+HBP+SH+SF)

THE 1880s: A DECADE OF CHANGE (1888)

The 1880s were a decade of constant tinkering with the rules (Table 1). By 1888, most of these changes were already in effect, although it still took five balls for a walk and pitchers still threw from 55.5 feet from home plate. With teams now averaging 136 games per season, most employed two principal starting pitchers to share the workload. However, pitchers still completed 96 percent of the games they started and racked up workloads of 500 innings or more—unheard of before or since. The frequency of walks and strikeouts increased, since umpires called every pitch and only five balls were needed for a walk. Therefore, the percentage of balls put in play fell from 96 percent to 83 percent of plate appearances. Crude fielding gloves were in widespread (but not universal) use by 1888. Thus, the frequency of errors had fallen by more than half (from 7.93 to 3.44 per team per game) and unearned runs had fallen correspondingly, from 5.59 to 1.98 per team per game.

Although DE increased from 58 percent in 1873 to 66 percent in 1888, a contact-oriented approach still made sense, since walks remained less frequent than errors and OPHR were still uncommon. Players could still reach base 33.8 percent of the time by putting the ball in play, and that is exactly what most of the powerful sluggers did. Four exemplars of this approach were Anson, who was still going strong at age 37, 6' 0" Dan Brouthers, 6' 2" Sam Thompson, and 6' 3", 220-pound "giant" (for his time) Roger Connor, who with 138 home runs was baseball's career leader until Ruth came along, and whose impressive bulk inspired sportswriters to dub his team the Giants. Anson, Brouthers, Thompson, and Connor rarely struck out, with career strikeout rates ranging from Brouthers's 3.1 percent to Connor's 5.1.

THE ROARING '90s (1894)

If one considers only earned runs, the highest scoring season in MLB history was not 1930, when the entire NL batted .303, nor at any time during the steroid era, but in 1894, a mere seven years before the start of the Deadball Era, with the same ball and mostly (with one key exception) the same playing rules (Table 1). A year earlier, MLB had increased the pitching distance from 55.5 to 60.5 feet and had replaced the pitcher's box with a rubber slab in order to boost offense, which succeeded far beyond anyone's wildest dreams. This was a major disruptive change and raised the leaguewide ERA from 3.28 in 1892 to 4.66 in 1893 and to 5.33 in 1894. Many of the small, wily pitchers who thrived in the 1880s could re-calibrate their breaking pitches to the new distance, but there was nothing they could do to compensate for the 10% increase in the time it took their fastballs to reach home plate. This extra time for a batter to react demotes a plus fastball to adequate and an adequate fastball to batting practice. Most pitchers simply could not adapt to this loss of effective velocity. For example, the 32-year-old, 5' 9" Bill Hutchinson, who was among the NL Top 10

Dan Brouthers

Cap Anson

in ERA at 2.76 in 1892 (and had a 2.81 ERA in 1891), immediately saw his ERA balloon to 4.75 in 1893 and 6.03 in 1894. Similarly, Hall of Famer John Clarkson, who stood 5'10" and turned 31 in 1892, saw his ERA, which had been 2.79 in 1891 and 2.48 in 1892, jump to 4.45 in 1893 and 4.42 in 1894. He promptly retired.

Younger players were not exempt. Diminutive (5' 7") rookie Nig Cuppy, who debuted with a 2.51 ERA in 1892 at age 22, saw his ERA rise to 4.47 in 1893 and 4.56 in 1894, although he went on to have a fine career. Other pitchers 25 years old or younger (like George Davies, Gus Weyhing, Harry Staley, and George Haddock) who populated the lists of ERA leaders in 1891–92 were less fortunate and never again posted an ERA under 4; all but Weyhing quickly fell out of the league. Bigger pitchers, like 25-year-old 6' 2" Cy Young and 21-year-old, 6' 1" fireballer Amos Rusie (as well as 5' 10", 22-year-old Kid Nichols), tended to fare better, but none escaped the league-wide rise in ERA in 1893–94. Indeed, all but Rusie saw at least a one-run increase in ERA.

The drastic change in pitching conditions continued to propel this high-scoring version of baseball up to the turn of the century. Although fielding gloves had now become almost universal, fielding had not improved all that much since 1888, perhaps because more balls were hit hard. There were still six errors and 4.5 unearned runs by the two teams in the average game, but walks were now more frequent than errors. The frequency of HR also increased from 0.24 per team per game in 1888 to 0.39 in 1894, a fact that is often overlooked and is probably attributable to the decimation of top pitchers. (The proportion of HR that left the park is not really known; the numbers in Table 3 are "guestimates.") It was still unusual for any single player to hit 20 or more HR. Still, 84 percent of all PA resulted in balls in play, and defenses converted only 63 percent of these plays to outs. Hall of Fame outfielder Willie Keeler of the 1890s Baltimore Orioles, who stood only 5' 4", weighed only 140 pounds, and struck out only 136 times in 8,591 AB in his career (best ratio by far of any player ever), famously explained his success by claiming that he "hit 'em where they ain't."[12] Actually, the secret to his success was to put the ball in play; the fielders did the rest. Few pitchers in the 1890s could stop him.

LOW EBB (1908)

With scoring at an all-time high in 1894, the gradual scoring decline throughout the rest of the 1890s was barely noticeable at first—6.58 runs per team per game in 1895 to 6.04 in 1896 to 5.88 in 1897 to 4.96 in 1898. But after a small uptick in 1899–1900, the scoring

decline picked up steam, falling below 4.5 in 1902–03, below 4 in 1904–07 and reaching an all-time low of 3.38 in 1908. The Deadball Era had taken hold.

So, how did that happen? First, a new rule counting foul balls as strikes was adopted in 1901 in the NL and 1903 in the AL (Table 1). Strikeout rates per nine innings immediately jumped by more than 50 percent in each league—from 2.45 in 1900 to 3.83 in 1901 in the NL and from 2.54 in 1902 to 3.86 in 1903 in the AL. Scoring had already been in decline before 1901, but this new rule almost certainly helped accelerate the trend. Second, fielding had taken a leap forward, as errors fell from 3.04 per team per game in 1894 to 1.71 in 1908. Batters continued to put the ball in play 82 percent of the time, but fielders now converted 71 percent of these balls into outs and allowed only one unearned run per team per game. Finally, a new generation of pitchers stepped into the breech: Christy Mathewson, Ed Walsh, Eddie Plank, Rube Waddell, and others. Some of them threw hard and others were armed with new pitches like the fadeaway, the spitball, and the knuckleball. It is also noteworthy that teams began to carry more pitchers and share the workload. In 1908, Walsh was the last pitcher to work more than 400 innings in a season.

Table 4 lists all of the Hall of Fame pitchers who enjoyed their career peaks in 1871–92, 1893–1900, and 1901–19 in descending order of Wins Above Replacement (WAR).[13] Pitchers were clearly bigger after 1892.

Rube Waddell

Table 4. Evolution of Pitching from 1971–20 [14]

Pre-1920

Hall of Fame Pitchers	Years	Height	Weight	ERA	Wins	SO / 9 IP	WAR
Peaked in 1871–92							
Tim Keefe	1880–93	5'10"	185	2.63	342	4.6	86.5
John Clarkson	1882–94	5'10"	155	2.81	328	3.9	84.0
Old Hoss Radbourn	1880–91	5'9"	168	2.68	309	3.6	75.3
Pud Galvin	1875–92	5'8"	190	2.85	365	2.7	73.5
Mickey Welch	1880–92	5'8"	160	2.71	307	3.5	63.1
John Montgomery Ward*	1878–84	5'9"	165	2.10	164	3.4	28.1
Peaked in 1893–1900							
Cy Young	1890–1908	6'2"	210	2.63	511	3.4	168.0
Kid Nichols	1890–1906	5'10"	175	2.96	361	3.3	116.1
Amos Rusie	1889–1901	6'1"	200	3.07	246	4.6	69.3
Peaked in 1901–19							
Walter Johnson	1907–27	6'1"	200	2.17	417	5.3	165.2
Grover Alexander	1911–30	6'1"	185	2.56	373	3.8	120.2
Christy Mathewson	1900–16	6'1"	195	2.13	373	4.7	104.0
Eddie Plank	1901–17	5'11"	175	2.35	326	4.5	81.9
Ed Walsh	1904–17	6'1"	193	1.82	195	5.3	66.0
Vic Willis	1898–1910	6'2"	185	2.63	249	3.7	63.7
Rube Waddell	1897–1910	6'1"	196	2.16	193	7.0	58.3
Mordecai Brown	1903–16	5'10"	175	2.06	239	3.9	58.3
Joe McGinnity	1899–1908	5'11"	206	2.66	246	2.8	57.6
Chief Bender	1903–25	6'2"	185	2.46	212	5.1	48.2
Addy Joss	1902–10	6'3"	185	1.89	160	3.6	44.2
Jack Chesbro	1899–1909	5'9"	180	2.68	198	3.9	42.1
Rube Marquard	1908–25	6'3"	180	3.08	201	4.3	32.1

* Played primaily at SS from 1884-92, earning 29.7 WAR, after injuring his throwing arm.

Among the six pre-1893 pitchers who were selected for the Hall of Fame as players, none stood taller than 5'10", and only one, Tim Keefe, who packed 185 pounds on his 5'10" frame, struck out more than 4 batters per nine innings pitched (IP). The 16 Hall of Fame pitchers of 1893–1919 had a decidedly different look; 11 stood more than 6'1" and only one (Jack Chesbro) stood 5'9" or less. While most were not power pitchers by modern standards, Waddell averaged a previously unheard of 7 SO per 9 IP, and Walter Johnson, spitballer Walsh, and Chief Bender each averaged more than 5 SO per 9 IP.

Instead of looking for new strategies to generate more runs to counter the falloff in offense, managers doubled down on the old small-ball strategies, treating every run as precious. If their teams couldn't score a lot, they would use every trick in the book to capitalize on their scoring opportunities and to deny runs to the opposing team. Pitching, fielding, and speed took on new importance. Bunts, hit-and-run plays, and stolen bases moved to the fore, and power took a

backseat. Home run rates fell by two-thirds (to 0.11 per team per game) from 1894 to 1908. The best position players following the turn of the century were Honus Wagner and Nap Lajoie, who hit for high average and excelled on defense as well. In 1906, a Chicago White Sox team nicknamed the "Hitless Wonders" upset the 116-win Chicago Cubs in the World Series after hitting only .230/.301/.286 during the season.[15] But a closer inspection reveals that the Cubs only hit .262/.328/.339 that year—better than the Sox, to be sure, yet not exactly "Murderers' Row."

THE TWILIGHT OF DEADBALL (1917)

The next decade saw the peaks of all-time great hitters like Ty Cobb, Tris Speaker, Eddie Collins, and Shoeless Joe Jackson—who (in the mold of Wagner and Lajoie) excelled in all aspects of the game except power—and the arrival of all-time pitching greats like Walter Johnson and Grover Alexander. The introduction of a new livelier ball with a cork center in 1910 barely moved the needle.[16] Runs (3.59 per team per game), baserunners (11.90 per team per game), and home runs (0.13 per team per game) ticked up slightly from 1908, but contact-oriented one-run strategies continued to prevail. The percentage of balls put in play (82) and DE (70) did not budge at all.

By 1917, most teams used four-man rotations, allowing pitchers to rest more between starts. Also, relief pitchers were used more often, and the percentage of complete games fell from 88 percent in 1904 to 67 percent in 1908 and to 55 percent in 1917. However, the top pitchers of 1917 (Johnson, Alexander, Ruth) still completed more than 80 percent of their starts. Finally, errors and unearned runs continued to decline, to 1.5 and 0.9 per team per game respectively, cutting into the small increase in earned runs from 2.36 to 2.68 per team per game.

BABE RUTH AND THE PARADIGM SHIFT (1922)

By the early 1920s many of the elements for improved scoring were in place—a lighter, livelier ball, the phasing out of the spitball, and a new policy removing damaged balls from the game more frequently. But it would take the example of an extraordinary talent, ex-pitcher Babe Ruth, who became a full-time outfielder in 1919, to change the landscape. Rather than use the "scientific approach" championed by old school stars like Ty Cobb, who thrived in the Deadball Era by perfecting the art of using his contact skills, speed, and sheer meanness to extract every advantage from his prodigious talent, Ruth worried about nothing but swinging the bat as hard as he could and sending balls flying over the fence.[17] Ned Williamson, who hit a flukish 27 HR for the Chicago White Stockings in 1884 when they changed the ground rules of their home field, White Stocking Park (186' in LF, 300' in CF, 196' in RF), for a single season to allow balls hit over the fences to be called HR instead of doubles, held the record until Ruth broke it with 29 in 1919.[18] At first, Ruth stood alone, outhomering his nearest competitor 29–12 in 1919, 54–19 in 1920, and 59–24 in 1921. But in 1922, imitators started crashing the party. Rogers Hornsby, a player in the Cobb mold who had played since 1915 without hitting more than nine homers in a season, suddenly hit 21 in 1921 and an MLB-leading 42 in 1922. The 30-home-run club would add 19 more hitters by 1930.[19]

But how could a single player, no matter how special, overturn a paradigm that had been in place for 50 years? To put it simply, the new paradigm worked. Ruth and Lou Gehrig anchored a powerful Yankees lineup that won six pennants and three World Series between 1921 and '28. When they were finally displaced, it was by the Philadelphia Athletics, another powerhouse, who featured sluggers like Jimmie Foxx and Al Simmons. Every team wanted one or two of these guys and every player with the requisite size and strength wanted to be one. Baseball has always been a game of adjustments and imitation. When something works, it is quickly adopted by opponents.

On a more abstract level, small ball may have been the most effective run-scoring strategy under the conditions that prevailed in the nineteenth century, but it is an inefficient scoring strategy in an environment where fielders convert 70 percent of balls in play into outs. In just five years between 1917 and 1922, scoring increased by 36 percent, from 3.6 to 4.9 runs per team per game, despite continuing declines in errors and unearned runs. Perhaps surprisingly, strikeouts decreased in the 1920s, and more balls were put in play (84 percent) despite the tripling of the HR rate from 0.13 to 0.43 per team per game and a slight increase in walks. I attribute the small decline in DE (70 to 68 percent) to the fact that more balls in play were being hit hard. Viewed through a historical lens, the surprise is not that this paradigm shift took place, but that it took so long.

To be sure, the aforementioned ball-related changes laid the groundwork for the paradigm shift embodied by Ruth. But the chronology doesn't fit so neatly:

1. Ruth's first monster season in 1920 (when he hit 54 HR) came a decade after the cork core was introduced to make the ball lighter and livelier. What took so long?

2. Ruth's 54-HR season also pre-dated Chapman's fatal beaning and was accomplished before the new policy on replacing dirty and scuffed baseballs took full effect.

3. When the spitball and similar pitches were phased out in 1920, only 17 pitchers threw the pitch regularly. These 17 pitchers were grandfathered and continued to use the pitch legally until they retired; the last one was Burleigh Grimes, who retired in 1934. Of course, anyone who knows anything about Gaylord Perry understands that the practice of deliberately defacing or applying foreign substances to the ball to get extra movement did not end in 1934.[20] It seems implausible that such a small and gradual change could have changed baseball so quickly and profoundly.

However, whatever role these ball-related changes may have played in ending the Deadball Era, one thing is certain. These changes had nothing to do with how the Deadball Era started in the first place.

THE MODERN GAME: FAST FORWARD (2017)

The changes Ruth set in motion in 1919 have grown more extreme in the ensuing century. Most strikingly, HR rates have nearly tripled from 0.43 to 1.26 per team per game between 1922 and 2017 (Table 3), and strike-outs have skyrocketed from 2.81 to 8.25 per team per game (Table 3). The average pitching staff today has more SO per 9 IP than Waddell, the top strikeout pitcher of baseball's first half century! A detailed analysis of this trend is beyond the scope of this essay, but it surely must have a lot to do with 13-man pitching staffs and the rise of the relief pitcher. The concomitant rise in bases on balls to 3.26 per team per game is less dramatic. As gloves have improved and fielders become more athletic, error rates have continued to fall to where they now reside at 0.58 per team per game (less than half the 1922 rate), with unearned runs down by 60 percent to 0.34 per team per game (Figure 2). Baseball has increasingly become a game of the "three true outcomes" (walks, strikeouts, and home runs), with only 66 percent of plate appearances ending in balls put in play, but DE has held steady at 69 percent. Finally, scoring has had ups (the steroid era) and downs (the late 1960s), but has mostly remained between 4 and 5 runs per team per game (Figure 1).

Now, in 2018, MLB may be in a place similar to where it was at the end of the nineteenth century, ex-cept that now baseball is stuck in a long-ball paradigm that is beginning to show cracks. The decline of balls in play has made it harder to string together hits and productive outs, and has thereby produced a game full of long dead patches punctuated by staccato bursts of scoring, often driven by home runs. The 2014–15 Kansas City Royals bucked this trend, but only briefly. Since walks and strikeouts typically consume more pitches per batter than balls put in play, and frequent pitching changes (accompanied by breaks for TV com-mercials) are time-consuming, games have become longer. Modern analytics have brought us extreme de-fensive shifts to further enhance defensive efficiency, and hitters, instead of bunting and hitting to the op-posite field to counter these shifts, have doubled down on long-ball strategies to try to yank the ball over the shifts. According to the late Orioles manager Earl Weaver, "Pitching keeps you in the game. Home runs win the game."[21] That aphorism may still be apt, but one wonders if hordes of smoke-throwing relief pitch-ers shuttling to and from the minors daily, fortified by defensive shifts that batters are too stubborn to break, will soon bring the game to a tipping point similar to the Deadball Era.

CONCLUSIONS

"Deadball" is largely a misnomer. The ball was no "deader" than it had been when offenses were riding high a few years earlier. Moreover, the many devoted fans of the aggressive and closely contested games of 1901–19 found the games to be anything but "dead." The process leading to "deadball" was set in motion 30 years earlier by rules and conditions that incentivized contact over power and produced plenty of baserun-ners and scoring. But when fielding improved and the restrictions on pitchers' deliveries were removed, it became increasingly difficult to string hits together into runs. Baseball rule-makers repeatedly tinkered with the rules to curb this trend, but these efforts were of no lasting avail. Even in 1893, when the pitcher's box was replaced by a more distant pitching rubber, the resulting scoring explosion petered out before the end of the decade, as bigger, harder-throwing pitchers replaced the old ones. Rather than devising strategies to open up scoring, managers doubled down on the old strategies and emphasized run prevention and squeezing the most out of their own scoring opportu-nities. While this led to some good, exciting baseball, these old tried-and-true strategies were suboptimal for scoring runs in an environment where defenses con-verted 70 percent of balls in play into outs.

When Babe Ruth started breaking home run records in 1919, the paradigm shifted dramatically. The success of Ruth's Yankees in the 1920s spawned imi-tators who swung for the fences, even at the risk of whiffing or popping the ball up. The bottom line is that teams that adopted the new paradigm scored more runs. Baseball's evolution has continued to move inexorably from small ball to long ball since the 1920s. We are now in an environment where the long-ball paradigm may be reaching its natural limit, as strike-outs skyrocket and balls in play decline. Another adjustment or recalibration may loom ahead: perhaps the resurgence of some small-ball strategies, perhaps enforcement of limits on the seemingly endless sup-ply of hard-throwing relievers, or perhaps something entirely new. ∎

Notes

1. "Deadball Era," Baseball-Reference.com, https://www.baseball-reference.com/bullpen/Deadball_Era.
2. All player and MLB average statistics are taken from Baseball-Reference.com, https://www.baseball-reference.com.
3. Zachary D. Rymer, "The Evolution of the Baseball From the Dead-Ball Era Through Today," Bleacher Report, June 18, 2013, https://bleacherreport.com/articles/1676509-the-evolution-of-the-baseball-from-the-dead-ball-era-through-today; "Spitball," Wikipedia, https://en.wikipedia.org/wiki/Spitball, accessed September 11, 2018; Don Jensen, "Ray Chapman," SABR Biography Project, https://sabr.org/bioproj/person/c2ed02f9.
4. Play Index, Baseball-Reference.com, https://www.baseball-reference.com/play-index/
   Queries: IPHR: https://www.baseball-reference.com/tiny/UuJct
       IPHR-8: to_Location_IPHR%408; locat&criteria139=hit_location
       IPHR-7: to_Location_IPHR%407; locat&criteria140=hit_location
       IPHR-9: to_Location_IPHR%409; locat&criteria141=hit_location
       ROE: https://www.baseball-reference.com/tiny/mKfqM
5. Diane Firstman, "The Growth of 'Three True Outcomes': From Usenet Joke to Baseball Flashpoint," *Baseball Research Journal* 47, no. 1 (Spring 2018), https://sabr.org/research/growth-three-true-outcomes-usenet-joke-baseball-flashpoint#_edn1.
6. Bill James, *The New Bill James Historical Baseball Abstract* (New York: Free Press, 2001), 8–12.
7. "Baseball Rule Change Timeline," Baseball Almanac, http://www.baseball-almanac.com/rulechng.shtml. Accessed September 11, 2018.
8. Eric Miklich, "The Pitchers Area," 19th Century Baseball, http://www.19cbaseball.com/field-8.html.
9. egdcltd, "Baseball Glove History and Evolution," InfoBarrel Sports, December 21, 2011, http://www.infobarrel.com/Baseball_Glove_History__Evolution.
10. John Thorn, "Why Did the Baseball Glove Evolve So Slowly?" Our Game, June 9, 2014, https://ourgame.mlblogs.com/why-did-the-baseball-glove-evolve-so-slowly-bff30f33737a.
11. David Fleitz, "Cap Anson," SABR Biography Project, https://sabr.org/bioproj/person/9b42f875.
12. Doug Skipper, "Willie Keeler," SABR Biography Project, https://sabr.org/bioproj/person/074d42fd.
13. "WAR Explained," Baseball-Reference.com, https://www.baseball-reference.com/about/war_explained.shtml.
14. "Hall of Fame Explorer," National Baseball Hall of Fame, https://baseballhall.org/explorer. Accessed September 11, 2018.
15. "1906: The Hitless Wonders," This Great Game, http://www.thisgreatgame.com/1906-baseball-history.html.
16. Rymer, "The Evolution of the Baseball."
17. Allen Wood, "Babe Ruth," SABR Biography Project, https://sabr.org/bioproj/person/9dcdd01c.
18. Leonard Koppett, *Koppett's Concise History of Major League Baseball* (New York: Carroll & Graf, 2004), 49.
19. "Year-by-Year Top-Tens Leaders and Records for Home Runs," Baseball-Reference.com, https://www.baseball-reference.com/leaders/HR_top_ten.shtml. Accessed September 11, 2018.
20. Mark Armour, "Gaylord Perry," SABR Biography Project, https://sabr.org/bioproj/person/f7cb0d3e.
21. Warren Corbett, "Earl Weaver," SABR Biography Project, https://sabr.org/bioproj/person/0cfc37e3.

1908's Forgotten Team

The Pittsburgh Pirates

Steve Steinberg

The 1908 National League race is best remembered for the "Merkle game" between the New York Giants and the Chicago Cubs, who were in a dead heat for first place at the end of the season. The clubs met to replay that tie game. The Cubs won and went on to beat the Detroit Tigers in the World Series for the second year in a row. But there was a third team in that season-long struggle, a team that, like the Giants after the replayed game, finished just a game out of first place, the Pittsburgh Pirates. Here are the final 1908 National League standings:

Team	Wins	Losses	Avg.	GB
Cubs	99	55	.643	–
Giants	98	56	.636	1
Pirates	98	56	.636	1

The Pirates' season and place in the race has largely been forgotten—partly because New York and Chicago were larger media centers, partly because managers John McGraw of the Giants and Frank Chance of the Cubs were such dominant personalities, and partly because the fierce Giants-Cubs rivalry came together in the Merkle controversy. In her book *Crazy '08*, Cait Murphy wrote, "In this triangular pennant race, Pittsburgh is clearly the short side in terms of attention. New York and Chicago, the nation's two biggest cities, have a rivalry that goes deeper than baseball, and their fans are more passionate. Looked at strictly in baseball terms, though, Pittsburgh is no also-ran. … This is a good team having a very good year."[1]

Both McGraw and Chance saw each other's team as their key competitor in 1908; they were not concerned about the Pirates. Early in the season, McGraw said, "The Giants have just one team to beat, the Chicago Cubs."[2] In early August, Christy Mathewson explained why his focus and concern was on the Cubs: "Chicago, in my mind, is the one team we have to beat. I figure the Cubs stronger than the Pirates because of the experience of Frank Chance's men and the confidence that the successes of two consecutive years have engendered."[3] While McGraw seemed to ignore the Pirates, Chance put them down. In May he said, "They [the Pirates] are pretty sure to blow before the season is half over."[4]

Each of these three teams had a pitching great; all three men would be elected to the Hall of Fame. Mathewson would have perhaps his greatest season in '08, going 37–11 with a 1.43 ERA, and the highest WAR of his career, 11.7. Mordecai Brown of the Cubs would post a 29–9 mark with a 1.47 ERA; his WAR of 9.5 was second only to his 1909 mark of 9.6. Vic Willis of the Pirates, far less known than the other two, would have a 23–11 record with a 2.07 ERA. His WAR of 4.7 lagged behind that of the other two aces and was considerably below that of his best seasons (he had four with a WAR of more than 8.0).

If the Pirates had the league's third-best pitching ace, they had by far the league's best everyday player, shortstop Honus Wagner. The 34-year-old star had an arthritic shoulder and was talking of retiring before the season began. But when Pirates owner Barney Dreyfuss doubled his annual salary to $10,000, he reported to the team. He would bat .354 in 1908, with a career second-best OPS of .957. His WAR of 11.5 was his best ever, and he also had 20 more extra-base hits than his nearest competitor. Giants pitcher Hooks Wiltse, who would win 23 games in 1908, felt the Pirates were more dangerous than the Cubs. "The Pirates. Ah, there's the dig. Pittsburgh may be a one-man team, but that one man is a 'dilly.'"[5]

While the Cubs did not have a big hitting star in 1908, the Giants had one in outfielder Mike Donlin. While it seems surprising today, more than 100 years later, Donlin was considered not far behind Wagner in hitting ability at the time. Donlin hit .351 in 1903, only to be edged for the batting title by Wagner's .355. Two years later, he hit .356, yet Wagner edged him again with a .363 mark (while Cy Seymour led with .377). Donlin missed most of the 1906 season with a broken leg and did not play at all in 1907, when he joined his famous wife, Mabel Hite, on the vaudeville circuit.[6]

His battle with Wagner in '08 would be one of the season's leading stories.

	June 30	July 31	August 31	Final
Wagner	.314	.331	.340	.354
Donlin	.351	.339	.330	.334

Donlin's enormous popularity among New York fans in 1908, exceeding that of the beloved Mathewson, seems surprising today. A *New York Evening Mail* reporter wrote on August 1, "Mike Donlin, one of the best ball players who ever graced a New York uniform, and without a doubt the most popular player the city has ever had, will make his debut as an actor. ... He wants to quit at the height of his popularity and will go out of the National League in a blaze of glory."[7] Just a few days later a *New York World* sportswriter wrote, "Mike Donlin's admirers—and no man that ever wore the uniform of the Giants was more popular in this city than Turkey Donlin—claim he is handicapped by his position in right field. Otherwise no one would dispute that he is Wagner's equal."[8]

The home-road splits of the three teams in 1908 were significant:

	Home	Road
Cubs	47–30, .610	52–25, .675
Giants	52–25, .675	46–31, .597
Pirates	42–35, .545	56–21, .727

The Giants' home record could be explained at least in part by their intimidation of umpires, according to sportswriter James Crusinberry: "On the Polo Grounds in New York, where policemen dare not tread and visiting players and umpires are in danger of their lives, victories have been comparatively easy for the Giants."[9]

The Pirates had the worst home record of the three clubs, and as the season drew to a close, their player-manager, Fred Clarke, suggested the club's support could have been better. "The fans of Pittsburg have not supported us as they might have done," he said. "Any glory that might accrue to the city from the way we finish the season belongs to the players and not to the people....The boys did not depend on the plaudits of the multitude, and they paid no attention to the smears and criticisms that were hurled at them."[10]

Clarke's approach was quite different from that of McGraw in dealing with umpires. He said, "There's nothing to be gained by paying attention to the umpires, but it may mean a big loss when men get put out of the game."[11]

Wagner was a thorn against the Giants all season long. He almost singlehandedly beat them on both May 11 and June 11, by identical scores of 5–2. In the first game, the opener of a three-game series in Pittsburgh, his triple was the key blow, but not the only one. The *Pittsburg Leader* reporter wrote, "The performance and achievements of the big German in the opening contest against the Giants truly beggar description. He was in the main responsible for each of the five runs the locals secured and played perfectly in the field."[12] On June 11 in New York, his home run off Mathewson helped them win, 5–2. Wagner was also a force in the field. "The wonderful Teuton was everywhere, choking off sure hits and encouraging his comrades," wrote William Kirk. "His large paws, the fingers of which seemed like tentacles of a devil fish, raked in everything that came within a mile of them. Oh, Honus, how could you do it?"[13]

At the end of June, the three clubs were within three games of each other:

Team	Wins	Losses	Avg.	GB
Pirates	40	24	.625	–
Cubs	37	23	.617	1
Giants	37	27	.578	3

The most significant run that month was made by the Pirates, who had been just 15–15 on May 29.

Mordecai Brown shut out the Pirates on July 2 and again on July 4, on one day's rest. His record that season against the other two teams was impressive: 6–3 vs. New York and 6–1 vs. Pittsburgh. Mathewson,

COURTESY OF THE DENNIS GOLDSTEIN COLLECTION

Mordecai Brown won 29 games in 1908. His performance in the season's final week propelled the Cubs to the pennant.

on the other hand, had a .500 record against both clubs, and Willis went 4–3 against Chicago and 3–2 against New York. The scrappy Pirates bounced back with a dramatic 7–6 win over the Giants on July 10 on Tommy Leach's inside-the-park home run.

"Though Mike Donlin pursued the ball with the speed of a greyhound," wrote a New York reporter, "he could not get it to [catcher Roger] Bresnahan in time to head off the wee whaler."[14]

On July 25, Wagner went 5-for-5 with four hits off Mathewson in a 7–2 Pittsburgh win at the Polo Grounds, and the New York papers saluted the mighty slugger. "Wagner's ability to do almost anything at any time gives the Pittsburg infield a wonderful lot of confidence," was a typical comment.[15] After the game, Polo Grounds fans tried to carry the Pirate shortstop on their shoulders, but he "escaped" with the help of his teammates.

Perhaps because of his greatness and perhaps because of his modesty, Wagner had enormous fan support in New York. The *New York Tribune* noted, "Such mighty swatting against a pitcher of Mathewson's caliber is seldom seen and was worth the price of admission alone."[16] Ralph Davis, who covered the Pirates for *The Sporting News*, noted how unusual such recognition for a visiting player was. "It is seldom, indeed, that New Yorkers can see any good in anything that does not bear the Gotham trademark, but Wagner's play was so great as to demand recognition anywhere."[17]

One feature of the pennant race was the huge crowds all three teams drew, none more so than in New York. "The largest crowd ever" was reported more than once after Polo Grounds games in 1908. Fans on the field were not uncommon when the Giants hosted both the Pirates and the Cubs, as well as in Pittsburgh's Exposition Park and Chicago's West Side Grounds.

And especially in New York, these fans were not simply behind ropes in the outfield. They were everywhere. Here was one description of that July 25 crowd, reported to be 30,000. "Swung around the field on the grass and in double phalanx were spectators who filled all but about thirty of the 360 degrees of the far-flung circle." In the ninth inning, the crowd "edged forward and penned the Pittsburg outfield to a pretty small playing space.... The Pittsburg outfielders couldn't have gone back a yard for a fly ball without bumping into somebody." Circus seats strung around the field "were intended to sit on but were used to stand on. It was a case of the survival of the tallest."[18] The *New York Times* described McGraw taking a bat to the fans

Pirates ace Vic Willis was not as well known as Christy Mathewson or Mordecai Brown, but 1908 was his seventh 20-win season.

who kept surging onto the field.[19] The *Times* writer used more words to describe the crowd than the game itself that day. "What may have been aisles on Friday were people on Saturday, and if you weren't there with a [boxer Jim] Jeffries punch, you looked like a long shot," he wrote.[20]

After the Pirates won two games in that series and the Giants won only one (a fourth game was a 16-inning tie), Joe Vila wrote in *The Sporting News*, "There is no doubt that of the 70,000 persons who saw the four Pittsburg games, a large majority came to the conclusion the Giants were outclassed." The month of July, in which all three teams did not play much over .500 ball, ended with the Pirates holding onto first place:

Team	Wins	Losses	Avg.	GB
Pirates	56	36	.609	–
Cubs	55	36	.604	½
Giants	53	37	.589	2

On August 24, the Giants arrived in Pittsburgh for a four-game series. While the Pirates were still in first, the Giants had gone on a 15-5 run to draw close:

Team	Wins	Losses	Avg.	GB
Pirates	66	42	.611	–
Giants	65	42	.607	½
Cubs	64	47	.577	3½

The Giants continued their hot streak as they stunned the Pirates by sweeping the series. After New

York won a doubleheader before a capacity crowd of 16,440, only 4,429 fans turned out for the third game.

Mathewson allowed one run for his 26th win in the second game. Veteran sportswriter and former ballplayer Sam Crane wrote, "Mathewson's pitching was simply up to his class, which is the top notch of them all. He lighted up when forced to do so and showed how he is the peer of any twirler in the business. You can't beat him—that's all, and the game never saw his equal."[22] At a dramatic point in the game, Donlin's celebrity wife rose and shouted, "Mike, dear, if you don't make a hit, I will never speak to you again, and you can take back your old bracelet."[23]

In the ninth inning of the final game, Donlin turned to acknowledge Mabel's words of encouragement, smiled, and singled in the tying run in a game Mathewson won in relief.[24]

With the sweep, it appeared that the Giants had taken control of the pennant race, and the Pirates, if not the Cubs, were done. After the doubleheader win, the reporter for the *Times* wrote, "Consensus of opinion is that if the NY team plays as good ball as they did today from now to the end of the League race, they will have no trouble winning the pennant."[25] C.B. Power of the *Pittsburg Dispatch* wrote of "the dejection that pulsated through and oozed out of the pores of Pittsburg fandom."[26]

But the Pirates were not finished. On September 4, they edged the Cubs in 10 innings, 1–0. Chief Wilson got the game-winning hit, but when Pirate Warren Gill, who was on first base, did not touch second, Chicago second baseman Jack Evers insisted to umpire Hank O'Day that the run therefore did not count. O'Day did not agree. The Cubs protested. Chicago sportswriter I.E. Sanborn wrote that the protest had grown "out of Jack Evers' ability to think faster than one bush league player and one veteran major league umpire, to wit: Pirate Gill and Hank O'Day."[27] The protest was not upheld; Vic Willis had his 18th win and Mordecai Brown was denied his 21st. The Pirates remained one-half game behind the Giants, with the Cubs now two games back.

On September 16, in a win over the St. Louis Cardinals, O'Day ejected Donlin for arguing that he was safe at first base. One New York sportswriter suggested that the club's captain was willing to be tossed because "Donlin is sore because he wants to fatten his batting average."[28] It was his sixth ejection of the season, and ex-ballplayer Crane called him out in the *New York Evening Journal*: "Hank O'Day is one of the very real umpires, and as such he should be appreciated by Mike Donlin.... Umpire O'Day should be nursed, not

trampled upon.... I have played ball with him and against him, and I can say that no squarer man lived."[29]

Mathewson saw O'Day's stubbornness more than his fairness. In his book, *Pitching in a Pinch*, he wrote of the umpire, "It is dangerous to argue with him as it is to try and ascertain how much gasoline is in the tank of an automobile by sticking down the lighted end of a cigar or cigarette."[30]

The Pirates came to New York for a four-game series starting on September 18. The standings that morning revealed the torrid pace of all three teams since late August.

Team	Wins	Losses	Avg.	GB	Since August 26
Giants	85	46	.649	–	16–4, .800
Cubs	85	52	.620	3	18–5, .783
Pirates	85	52	.620	3	19–6, .760

The series was played under an eerie and premature twilight, as smoke from upstate forest fires in the Catskills and Adirondacks had drifted down to the city.[31]

Once again, the series began with a doubleheader, and once again, the Giants swept. Mathewson won his 33rd game with a 7–0 shutout, and Hooks Wiltse won his 22nd. The *New York Tribune* saluted "the greatest pitcher in the world." Mathewson "was master of the situation at every moment of the first game. He pitched with that beautiful precision and judgment...and it was absolutely impossible to rattle him."[32]

The Pirates fell five games back, and the pennant seemed to be slipping away. New York newspapers celebrated the expected title. The *New York Press* gloated, "The Galloping Giants made secure their grasp on the National League pennant and put out of the running the Pesky Pittsburg Pirates," who "now may be considered out of the race."[33]

When Donlin's three-run home run settled matters in the first game, "the greatest crowd that ever saw a baseball game," in the words of the *Tribune*, made the winning of the pennant "a foregone conclusion."[34] Even the Pittsburgh papers felt the chance had slipped away from their city's team. "The Giants are joyous tonight because they realize it will be next to impossible for any club to snatch the pennant from their grasp," declared one.[35]

There was an ugly scene during the afternoon when Donlin went into the New York crowd and brutally beat up a fan who was razzing him. It took more than one policeman to pull him off the fan, which probably saved the fan from damage.[36] To the credit of the Giants' fans, many booed and hissed at Donlin

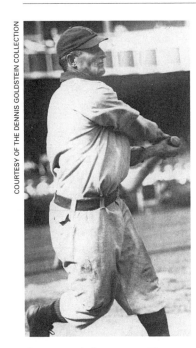

COURTESY OF THE DENNIS GOLDSTEIN COLLECTION

Honus Wagner was a one-man wrecking crew against the Giants in 1908. He won his sixth batting title that season with a .354 average.

the rest of the game. Yet one New York sportswriter almost justified Donlin's attack. He wrote that while "it was denied Donlin had attacked a fan," he "had reason to retaliate because some chap insulted him villainously."[37]

O'Day, who seems to show up in Forrest Gump-like fashion at many key games during this season, did not eject Donlin. Ralph Davis of *The Sporting News* saw this inaction as another example of the Giants' intimidation of foes and arbiters alike at the Polo Grounds: "The New York Players appear to have the umpires bluffed to a standstill and are getting away with all sorts of tricks that would never be tolerated for a moment by any other aggregation. Last Friday Mike Donlin attacked one of the spectators with his fists, and it required three policemen to separate the belligerents, yet Hank O'Day lacked the nerve to even put Mike out of the game."[38] Davis went still further. "The conduct of McGraw recently has been most reprehensible.... The opinion is general among the base ball writers that the sooner the National League decides it can get along without McGraw and his hoodlumism, the sooner will the ideal state of affairs be realized."[39]

After the doubleheader, the league's standings confirmed the Pirates' predicament. After play on Friday, September 18, with the Giants having completed a 26–4 run, the standings looked like this:

Team	Wins	Losses	Avg.	GB
Giants	87	46	.654	–
Cubs	85	53	.616	4½
Pirates	85	54	.612	5

But the Pirates steadied and took the next two games in New York. They snapped the Giants' 11-game win streak on Saturday with a 10-inning victory, 6–2. After an off day on Sunday, Mathewson again started for New York, but lost to Willis, 2–1. The *New York Sun* wrote of the pitchers' duel in which both men "made the ball talk and in a language that was Greek to most of the batters."[40]

Pittsburgh scored both of its runs in the third inning, a rally started by a close call at first base, when O'Day called the Pirates' Chief Wilson safe. McGraw argued strenuously and earned his eighth ejection of the season.[41] While the *New York American* described O'Day's call as "one of the worst ever seen on the grounds," the *Times* again defended the umpire.[42] It called O'Day "the best umpire in the game" and bemoaned "the clamor of those who are always ready to condemn the umpire should a decision go against the home team." The writer concluded, "Perhaps he [O'Day] was right; perhaps he was wrong. Anyway, he was right on top of the play, and had a closer and better view of it than the crowd."[43]

As the Pirates left New York, they had stayed relevant, if not close, for a while longer. The standings after play on September 21:

Team	Wins	Losses	Avg.	GB
Giants	87	48	.644	–
Cubs	88	53	.624	2
Pirates	87	54	.617	3

The next day, the Giants dropped a doubleheader to the Cubs, and the day after that they played the famous Merkle game, ruled a tie. After they split four games against the Reds, the Giants had eight games with the Phillies. Rookie Phils pitcher Harry Coveleski beat them three times in the space of just five days.[44] After he beat Mathewson 3–2 on October 3, the *New York Press* wrote, "The agonizing defeat...will go down in baseball history as one of the most nerve-racking games in the most desperate struggle in years for a National League pennant. Coveleski, a raw-boned coal miner...has done more to put the Giants out of the race than any of the veteran league stars."[45] A Pittsburgh paper hailed the pitcher who had risen "from the depths of oblivion" and added, "The name of Covaleskie will go down in history, and right here in Pittsburg the lad will be as revered as he is despised in New York."[46] After sweeping the Pirates on September 18, the Giants had gone 8–9 down the stretch, with three rainout makeup games remaining against Boston, known at the time as the Doves.

After leaving New York, the Pirates went on an 11–1 run, including a six-game home-and-away sweep of the Cardinals. As they headed to Chicago for the final game of the season, the Pirates were very much back in the race. On the morning of Sunday, October 4, here were the standings:

Team	Wins	Losses	Avg.	GB	Since August 26
Pirates	98	55	.641	–	32–9, .780
Cubs	97	55	.638	½	30–8, .789
Giants	95	55	.633	1½	26–13, .667

Mike Donlin, the immensely popular Giants' outfielder, was considered a legitimate rival to the Pirates' Honus Wagner for the 1908 National League batting title.

COURTESY OF THE STEVE STEINBERG COLLECTION

If the Pirates could beat the Cubs that day, the 1908 pennant would seem to be theirs. National League President Harry Pulliam had upheld the umpires' ruling that the Merkle game was a tie, and the National League Board of Directors, due to review that ruling later in the week, was unlikely to overrule its own president. The Pirates seemed to be under the impression—widely shared among sportswriters as well—that the board would not order the Merkle game replayed, in which case the Giants would not have been able to match Pittsburgh's 99 wins.

With their excellent road record and a well-rested Vic Willis (he had last pitched on September 30, throwing only three innings), the Pirates felt confident. But so were the Cubs, especially with Mordecai Brown pitching. "The composite mental attitude of the vast assemblage was quiet confidence, so great was the faith in Brown," wrote one New York reporter.[47] Sportswriter Hugh Fullerton wrote that the strain of the pennant race did not seem to show on the Chicago players. "They feel that tomorrow's game already is won, and with Brown pitching, Pittsburgh cannot win except by accident."[48] This, despite the fact that Brown had pitched twice in the previous five days.

New York sports fans were in the strange position of rooting for the Cubs, to keep their pennant hopes alive. Huge crowds gathered in front of electronic scoreboards that some midtown Manhattan New York newspapers had set up, which followed every pitch. The Polo Grounds also had large boards, what *The New York Times* called "monster imitation baseball diamonds."[49] The Giants opened the ballpark, and thousands of people paid the 25-cent entrance fee. Among the attendees were members of both the Giants and the Doves. Fifty-thousand Pirates fans followed the game outside two Pittsburgh newspaper offices.

The enormous crowd, reported as 30,247, was declared a new baseball record, but it was destined to be a record for only 96 hours.[50] "This fringe of humanity was ten or fifteen deep in the outfield," in the words of the *Chicago Daily News*, "while on foul ground, running in one thick compact mass from third to first base and behind the catcher was another jam ten or fifteen deep."[51] Fullerton wrote of "two of the gamest clubs in the league locked in the death combat."[52]

Even the great ones have bad days. Wagner's throwing error in the fifth inning led to the Cubs' second run and a 2–0 Chicago lead. The Pirates star helped tie the score in the next inning, as his double knocked in a run and he later scored. But Chicago took the lead back in the bottom of the sixth when Brown hit a two-out single after the Pirates had walked the dangerous Johnny Kling intentionally. The Cubs scored again in the seventh, with a rally that began when Wagner fumbled a routine ground ball and let it get between his legs.

With the Cubs up 5–2 going into the ninth, Pittsburgh generated drama and controversy. After a leadoff single by Wagner, Ed Abbaticchio hit a drive down the right-field line. O'Day was the umpire behind home plate, and he called the ball foul. "At first, umpire O'Day seemed to wave the runners on to their bases," wrote the *Chicago American*.[53] The Pirates thought it was a fair ball and quickly rushed to encircle O'Day, who held his ground. They then appealed to the other umpire, Cy Rigler. The *Pittsburg Post* writer said that Rigler first told "Abby" that the ball was fair.[54]

Rigler was almost certainly standing near second base, the proper position of the second man in a two-umpire team, and would have had a poor angle on the ball. But the reality was even more problematic. With fans on the field, the foul line was likely obscured. "The ball went into the crowd on the line," said the account in the *Examiner*.[55] Rigler eventually upheld O'Day's call, Abby struck out, and the Pirates went quietly.

For the same reasons the Pirates and others thought a win would guarantee them the pennant, it was widely accepted that the loss had eliminated them.

Without a makeup of the Merkle game, they would finish a half-game behind the Cubs. The standings at the end of the day:

Team	Wins	Losses	Avg.	GB
Cubs	98	55	.641	–
Pirates	98	56	.636	½
Giants	95	55	.633	1½

Wagner was disconsolate; he said he would have traded his personal achievements for a pennant. *The New York Times* headline read, "Hans Wagner Heartbroken; Will Kill 10,000 Birds This Winter Trying to Forget Pirates Defeat." The team dispersed, their season, they believed, at an end. Pirates owner Barney Dreyfuss went into the Chicago clubhouse, congratulated the Cubs, and added that somebody had to lose. "You are a better loser than I am…You are the best loser in the league," Chicago owner Charles Murphy sarcastically replied.[56] Pittsburgh player-manager Clarke said to Chance, "I want to congratulate you, Frank. It was a great game…. We'll be back at you next year."[57] The Cubs would improve to 104 wins in 1909, but the race would not be close, as Clarke's Pirates would win 110.

The Giants had three games remaining with the Doves, starting Monday, October 5. The league's directors still had to rule on the Merkle game, which their president had ruled a tie. Chance expressed confidence the pennant would belong to his club, but so did John McGraw. If his Giants would not be awarded the tie game, they would beat Chicago "in the playoff, whether it be one game or three," he said.[58]

Most fans of baseball history know that the Giants did go on to sweep Boston, only to lose a replay of the Merkle game—and the pennant—to the Cubs. But overlooked in the story is the strange and confounding situation that could have developed.

First, had the National League Board of Directors overruled President Pulliam and awarded the Merkle

National League President Harry Pulliam played a key role in the outcome of the 1908 season. His decision to replay the Merkle game, upheld by the league's directors, had an overlooked aspect that could have resulted in postseason chaos.

game to the Giants, and had the Giants won two of three against the Doves, the final league standings would have looked like this:

Team	Wins	Losses	Avg.	GB
Cubs	98	56	.636	–
Pirates	98	56	.636	–
Giants	98	56	.636	–

On Tuesday afternoon, October 6, the Board of Directors of the National League upheld Pulliam's ruling (which upheld the umpires) that the Merkle game was indeed a tie and announced that the game would be replayed at the end of the season—even if the Giants lost a game to the Doves and finished the season a game behind Chicago.

The ruling declared, "We realize the great importance that the game in question may be in determining the winner of the championship in the National League."[59] It also stated, "We hold that the New York club should, in all justice and fairness, under these conditions be given the opportunity to play off the game in question."[60] The National League's owners had ruled that the Giants deserved a chance to replay the Merkle game.

While the Giants would sweep the Doves (the author delivered a paper at the 2012 SABR national convention that raised questions about the legitimacy of that series), the chronology is significant. While New York won the first game on Monday, they were leading by only a 1–0 score in Tuesday's game. With a 3:30 start time for games at the Polo Grounds, the afternoon ruling was handed down when the game was very much in doubt, if not before it had begun. And Wednesday's game saw the Giants fall behind 2–0 early.

Only some observers and reporters realized that the ruling could cause "an awful muddle," in the words of one Pittsburgh paper.[61] The possibility of a three-way tie for the pennant was a distinct possibility. One New York paper grasped the implications of the ruling and explained it well:

By making it mandatory to play the game tomorrow, the Giants have a better chance than if the contest had been decided a tie, and the controversy closed…. A defeat by Boston now will not affect the New York-Chicago game, which must be replayed.

New York now has two chances to win the pennant, where formerly they had only one. If the

Giants beat Boston today, they will tie Chicago.... The winner of tomorrow's game will then be champions of the National League. Should, however, New York lose the remaining game with Boston, the Chicago contest will follow. If the Giants should prove successful against the Cubs after losing to Boston, a three-cornered tie would result.[62]

Had the Giants dropped a game against the Doves, the standings at the end of play on Wednesday, October 7, would have looked like this:

Team	Wins	Losses	Avg.	GB
Cubs	98	55	.641	–
Pirates	98	56	.636	½
Giants	97	56	.634	1

The Merkle game would still have been replayed, and had the Giants beaten the Cubs in that game on Thursday, the standings would have been the three-way tie at 98–56 referenced above.

The headline in Monday's *Pittsburg Leader*, reflecting this possibility, read, "One Faint Last Hope." Wednesday's *Pittsburg Dispatch* noted the possibility of that tie and declared, "Well, the Pittsburg Club has disbanded, and it is hard to tell what we would be able to do."[63] Even if they could regroup, league rules required three best two-of-three playoffs. In a round-robin, each of the three teams could have won three games and lost three.

After the fact, *The Sporting News* railed against the ruling, arguing in an October 15 editorial that the board had "exceeded its authority in ordering a championship game to be played off after the close of the regular race to settle a tie for first place. The [National League] constitution imposes on the directors the duty of arranging a special series of three games between the tied teams."[64]

The following spring, the *1909 Spalding Baseball Guide* stated, "There was still another embarrassing feature to the order to play one game to settle the New York and Chicago tie. That was, that if the Giants should have happened to have lost one game in Boston, and then should have beaten Chicago, there would have been a three-cornered tie for the championship between New York, Pittsburg, and Chicago. That was feared in some quarters but did not materialize."[65] Sportswriter Fred Lieb confirmed this possibility in his history of the Pirates.[66]

The ruling had given the Pirates a lifeline, but Dreyfuss did not seize it. The Pirates' owner was not allowed to vote in the Board of Directors meeting (just as John Brush of the Giants and Charles Murphy of the Cubs were excluded) because he had a direct interest in the outcome. Yet he said that had he been able to vote, he would have voted that the Merkle game be awarded to the Cubs, which would have given them the pennant. Dreyfuss had an intense dislike of McGraw and called the board's ruling "a sickening case of 'straddling' and trying to avoid the issue."[67] He even said the Cubs should refuse to play the replay of the Merkle game.

Fortunately for the National League, the Giants swept the Doves, the possibility of a three-way tie was averted, and the Pirates were eliminated—again. So why did the league risk such chaos and give the Giants two opportunities to win the pennant? Neither Pulliam nor the team owners explained the ruling, and Pulliam took his own life less than 10 months later, at least in part over the stress of the Merkle game controversy. "No one can tell precisely how much all these vicissitudes had to do with Pulliam's suicide the following July," wrote Harold Seymour and Dorothy Seymour Mills, "although undoubtedly they played their part."[68] Perhaps Pulliam tilted toward the Giants to avert or at least minimize the explosive reaction of McGraw and Brush, should their Giants fall short of the pennant. ∎

Notes
1. Cait N. Murphy. *Crazy '08: How a Cast of Cranks, Rogues, Boneheads, and Magnates Created the Greatest Year in Baseball* (New York: HarperCollins, 2009), 245.
2. *New York Sun*, April 12, 1908, as quoted in G. H. Fleming, *The Unforgettable Season* (New York: Penguin Books, 1982).
3. Christy Mathewson, *New York American*, August 9, 1908, as quoted in Fleming, 161–62.
4. David W. Anderson. *More than Merkle: A History of the Best and Most Exciting Baseball Season in Human History* (Lincoln: University of Nebraska Press, 2000), 120.
5. Craig R. Wright and Tom House. *The Diamond Appraised* (New York: Fireside, 1989), 389.
6. Michael Betzold and Rob Edelman, "Mike Donlin," SABR BioProject, https://sabr.org/bioproj/person/3b51e847. See also Charles C. Alexander, *John McGraw* (New York: Viking, 1988), 124–25.
7. *New York Evening Mail*, August 1, 1908, as quoted in Fleming, 147.
8. *New York World*, August 9, 1908, as quoted in Fleming, 161.
9. James Crusinberry, *St. Louis Post-Dispatch*, August 17, 1908, as quoted in Fleming, 172.
10. Ralph S. Davis, "Fought to Finish," *The Sporting News*, October 8, 1908. At the time, the official spelling of Pittsburgh omitted the final h.
11. *Sporting Life*, July 18, 1908.
12. "Wagner's Wonderful Work Won Game for Pittsburg," *Pittsburg Leader*, May 12, 1908.
13. William F. Kirk, *New York American*, June 12, 1908, as quoted in Dennis and Jeanne DeValeria. *Honus Wagner, A Biography* (New York: Henry Holt, 1998), 180.
14. "Leach's Home Run Wins for Pirates," *New York Press*, July 11, 1908.
15. "Mathewson is Knocked Out of Box," *New York Evening Telegram*, July 26, 1908. Wagner hit three singles and two doubles.
16. "Great Crowd Sees New York Lose," *New York Tribune*, July 26, 1908.

17. Davis, "Two Series Over," *The Sporting News*, August 6, 1908.
18. "Pirates Drub the New Yorks," *New York Sun*, July 26, 1908.
19. W.W. Aulick, "Record Crowd Sees Giants Routed," *The New York Times*, July 26, 1908.
20. Aulick.
21. Joe Vila, "Beat Weak Teams," *The Sporting News*, August 6, 1908.
22. Sam Crane, *New York Evening Journal*, August 25, 1908, as quoted in Fleming, 183.
23. Crane.
24. "Brilliant Finish Wins for Giants," *The New York Times*, August 27, 1908.
25. "Giants Now Lead for the Pennant," *The New York Times*, August 25, 1908.
26. C.B. Power, "Giants Make It Four Straight, Winning in the Ninth Inning," *Pittsburg Dispatch*, August 27, 1908.
27. I.E. Sanborn, "Cubs Will File Protest," *Chicago Tribune*, September 5, 1908. Gill played only 27 games in his major-league career.
28. "Giants Drive New Pitcher to Bench," *The New York Times*, September 17, 1908. O'Day ejected 13 men that season.
29. Crane, *New York Evening Journal*, September 17, as quoted in Fleming, 222–23.
30. Christy Mathewson. *Pitching in a Pinch: Baseball from the Inside* (Lincoln: Bison Books, 1994), 175.
31. "Pirates Turn Tables on the Giants," *New York Tribune*, September 20, 1908.
32. "Giants Pennant Bound," *New York Tribune*, September 19, 1908.
33. "29,000 Persons See Giants Rout Pittsburg Twice," *New York Press*, September 19, 1908.
34. "Giants Pennant Bound."
35. "Crowd Numbering 32,000 Sees Pittsburg Team Practically Lose the Pennant," *Pittsburg Post*, September 19, 1908.
36. "Giants' Bats Crush Pittsburg Team," *The New York Times*, September 19, 1908. The *Times* has a vivid description of Donlin's attack.
37. *New York Evening Telegram*, September 19, 1908.
38. Davis, "Played Poor Ball," *The Sporting News*, September 24, 1908.
39. Davis, "Hard Trip Ahead," *The Sporting News*, September 17, 1908.
40. "Willis Trips New York," *New York Sun*, September 22, 1908.
41. Retrosheet currently has McGraw with 118 ejections as a manager. This number may grow as more box scores are added to the database.
42. William F. Kirk, *New York American*, September 22, 1908, as quoted in Fleming, 237. It is odd that McGraw was ejected by home-plate umpire Bill Klem, and not by O'Day. But the writer for the Pittsburg Dispatch, C.B. Power, explained that after McGraw made "some awfully hateful remark" about O'Day to Klem, the latter stood up for his fellow umpire and ejected McGraw.
43. "Pirates Beat Giants," *The New York Times*, September 22, 1908.
44. Coveleski appeared in four games in 1907 and six in 1908. Besides his three victories over the Giants, he won only one other game that year. His only decision in 1907 had come against the Giants.
45. "Giants Lose Grip on Pennant when Mathewson Fails to Check Phillies," *New York Press*, October 4, 1908.
46. Ernest E. Mooar, "Pirates are Favorites in Remarkable Fight for National Pennant," *Pittsburg Leader*, October 4, 1908.
47. "Cubs, by Beating Pirates, Now Lead National League," *New York Press*, October 5, 1908.
48. Hugh Fullerton, "The Pirates in Battle for Pennant Today," *Chicago Examiner*, October 4, 1908.
49. "Fans at the Polo Grounds," *The New York Times*, October 5, 1908.
50. The replay of the Merkle game drew around 40,000 fans. The attendance for the October 4 game broke the West Side Grounds record by around 6,000. The first game of the 1907 World Series drew 24,377 fans.
51. *Chicago Daily News*, October 5, 1908.
52. Fullerton, "Brown Leads Champions in Thrilling Climax of Season," *Chicago Examiner*, October 5, 1908.
53. *Chicago American*, October 5, 1908.
54. "Buccaneers are Welcomed Home," *Pittsburg Post*, October 6, 1908.
55. "Story of Cub Triumph over Pittsburg Told Play by Play," *Pittsburg Examiner*, October 5, 1908. The *Chicago American* stated that Rigler was "working on the foul line right back of first base."
56. DeValeria, *Honus Wagner*, 196.
57. Harvey T. Woodruff, "Cubs Jump to Top, Beating Pirates," *Chicago Tribune*, October 6, 1908. The Giants would finish 18½ games back. Perhaps because they were not in the race, John McGraw argued less with umpires than in previous seasons, with only three ejections.
58. "Doves Out to Help the Cubs Win Pennant," *Chicago American*, October 5, 1908.
59. "Must Play Off Tie," *Chicago Tribune*, October 7, 1908.
60. "Pulliam's Tie Game Decision Upheld," *The New York Times*, October 7, 1908.
61. "Monster Baseball Muddle Confronts National League," *Pittsburg Leader*, October 7, 1908. See also "Race Undecided at Season's End," *Pittsburg Chronicle-Telegram*, October 7, 1908.
62. "Pulliam's Tie Game Decision Upheld," *The New York Times*, October 7, 1908.
63. "Giants and Cubs Ordered to Play Off Tie Game," *Pittsburg Dispatch*, October 7, 1908.
64. Editorial, *The Sporting News*, October 15, 1908.
65. John B. Foster, editor, *Spalding Baseball Guide 1909*, 111.
66. Frederick G. Lieb. *The Pittsburgh Pirates* (Carbondale: University of Southern Illinois Press, 2003), 128.
67. Power, "Giants and Cubs Ordered to Play Off Tie Game," *Pittsburg Dispatch*, October 7, 1908.
68. Harold Seymour and Dorothy Seymour Mills, *Baseball: The Golden Age* (New York: Oxford University Press, 1971), 27.

Becoming a Contract Jumper

Deacon Jim McGuire's 1902 Decision

James K. Flack

In the first years of the American League, its eight clubs added to their ranks by drawing away players from the older National League. Baseball had been slumping, a situation stemming from the country's economic depression and the failed leadership of team owners. Attempting to snap out if it, the NL magnates had pared down their monopoly—"the great circuit reduction of the spring of 1900"—from 12 teams to eight, thus rendering surplus talent available. But the American League owners wanted popular veterans, not merely whoever was on hand. This meant luring players to jump contracts binding them to clubs in perpetuity.

Since 1883, baseball's owners had steadily strengthened their "reserve system" so that all but a few players on each roster were held by the club that originally signed them until they were transferred or released. Consequently, players were prevented from negotiating for their services. The American League, as Harold Seymour has written, ignored the repressive contract clause, and players in demand were quick to realize that the situation could be worked to boost their salaries as well as enhance their dignity. Seizing new opportunities, National League contract jumpers soon filled more than half of American League rosters. One of them was Deacon Jim McGuire.[1]

The Brooklyn catcher was beginning his 18th major-league season. After an 1884 rookie year with Toledo, there were stops at Detroit, Philadelphia, Cleveland, Rochester, and Washington, interrupted by a couple of minor-league stints.[2] The first of these made him Detroit property and, in the process, introduced him to the business maneuverings of big-league baseball.

In 1885, McGuire was playing in the financially wobbly Western League for Indianapolis. On June 13, he doubled and caught the Hoosiers' 2–1 home win against Kansas City. After the next game, the league folded. (Soon it would become the American League under President Ban Johnson.) At the time it lost its affiliation, Indianapolis occupied first place and was picked to win the championship. Detroit had finished last in 1884 and started the 1885 season 5–25, so the

club was determined to rebuild by whatever means necessary. In order to capture the disbanded league's top talent, Detroit's directors moved boldly: They went to Indianapolis and bought the franchise for $5,000—with payment contingent upon players signing Detroit contracts. All but four Wolverines were replaced, making McGuire and nine other ex-Hoosiers, plus skipper Bill "Wattie" Watkins, the core of Detroit's suddenly formidable club. *Sporting Life* editor Francis C. Richter wrote: "They are, as a whole, a much stronger playing team…and the Detroit public may look forward to some excellent work in the near future in this new aggregation."[3]

Pulling this off required creative machinations. Teams technically were not allowed to bargain with released players until after a 10-day waiting period; but the likelihood of surreptitious bidders for McGuire and his teammates had to be thwarted. "As managers began to put in an appearance and tempt players to jump their obligation," reported the *Detroit Free Press*, "it was deemed best to remove them from outside influence, and the entire team came to this city yesterday morning with the Detroit directors. From Detroit they proceeded by rail to Toronto and will there take a steamer for a pleasure trip down the St. Lawrence to the Thousand Islands."[4] After it was safe to dock and to sign contracts, the new players had a dramatic impact. The Wolverines finished June with an 8–33 record, but in early July, a week after the arrival of the new players, they began a streak of 12 wins in 13 games, and were roughly a .500 team from the consolidation to the end of the season.[5] Deacon Jim was again a big-leaguer, following an unusual journey that must have taught the 21-year-old a lesson about wily magnates.

Certainly his half-season with Detroit was a learning process. Charlie Bennett, the Wolverines' number one catcher, furnished exceptional instruction for continued improvement at the position. McGuire's apprenticeship coincided with overhand pitching. As pitchers threw harder, catchers began using heavier padded gloves, catching the ball primarily in the

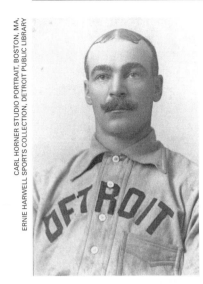

Deacon Jim McGuire, 1902

pocket, rather than wearing thin leather gloves with the fingers cut off and grabbing the ball with both hands. The earliest citation for the word "receiver" meaning catcher comes from 1885, and Bennett exemplified the position's changes.[6] His understudy that year fit in well. As a local account put it: McGuire was "a fellow with abundance of nerve, cool head and a fine thrower to bases. He promises to make a valuable relief for Bennett, our inimitable catcher."[7]

Additionally, he no doubt got Bennett's advice about what to expect from employers. Bennett could reference his recent experience based on "baseball's first real case of contract litigation."[8] Toward the end of the 1882 season, he had signed a preliminary agreement with the Alleghenys of the American Association for his personal services for the next year. But then he had a change of heart, chose to stay in Detroit, and refused to sign the 1883 contract. The Alleghenys' principal owner, Harmar Denny McKnight, sued, seeking a federal court injunction compelling Bennett to sign a formal contract and restraining him from playing for Detroit. The court dismissed the charge, deciding in Bennett's favor that a preliminary arrangement did not amount to a final agreement; and, furthermore, the contract that was presented for signature lacked mutually equitable terms between club ownership and the ballplayer. Bennett's case was "one of the first attacks on the legality of the reserve clause."[9] McGuire's would mirror it two decades later.

McGuire's disposition to resist the magnates' absolute authority had to have been affected by Detroit's team captain, center fielder Ned Hanlon. Captains at that time took responsibility for on-field decisions, and Hanlon was on his way to becoming a savvy practitioner of "inside," or "scientific" baseball, which relied on pitching, tight fielding, and aggressive baserunning.

He also was a vital organizer of the Brotherhood of Professional Base Ball Players, formalized in 1885 by John M. Ward, New York's shortstop and captain who had graduated from the Columbia Law School.[10] Chapters emerged throughout the league. Detroit, with Hanlon and Bennett, was the second to join, in May 1886. McGuire, who was then Philadelphia property, joined two months later.[11]

The Brotherhood's aims evolved from encouraging better player deportment to asserting players' basic rights. In 1887, Hanlon and others appeared at the National League winter meetings seeking recognition of their organization, modifications to the standard contract, and elimination of the reserve system. The club owners responded by recognizing the Brotherhood and granting a few contract concessions pertaining to blacklisting and suspensions, but refused to get rid of the National Agreement clause, which now bound 14 rather than 11 men to their employers. A year later they introduced a five-tiered rating scheme for all major-leaguers: Players would be categorized according to "habits, earnestness, and special qualifications" and paid between $1,500 and $2,500 depending on how they were graded.[12]

There was some sentiment for a strike, but Ward counseled otherwise. The membership voted it down, opting instead to launch a separate Players League. Its eight teams were run cooperatively, with profit-sharing and personnel decisions arrived at by joint consent. Ward and Hanlon were player-managers of the 1890 Brooklyns and Pittsburghs, respectively. The league lasted for only one season. Attendance lagged, financial backers reneged, most clubs crumbled, and the Brotherhood collapsed.[13]

Yet the Brotherhood of Professional Base Ball Players occupies an enduring place in late-nineteenth-century US history. As the major leagues' first union, it derived its ideas from trade associations, producers' cooperatives, and an array of wage-earners' organizations. It channeled those impulses into progressive acts resisting complete domination by the magnates and collective efforts to reform its small sphere of industrial society. "To be sure," historian Peter Levine writes, "the struggle between competing groups of capitalists for baseball's marketplace, the demands of ballplayers and the risks they undertook to achieve them, and the ultimate triumph of the better organized and better financed side hardly matched the stakes or costs of workers or entrepreneurs in other industries. When major league ballplayers bolted their clubs to form their own league, however, they set the stage for events that announced, if less grandiosely, these significant themes."[14] Ned Hanlon's prominent role in the union surely influenced Jim McGuire's viewpoint toward management in the years ahead.

For the time being, his development as a complete player was shaped by Philadelphia's Harry Wright, one of professional baseball's founding fathers and its foremost early manager. Wright's reputation had been growing since 1869, when he built the first openly professional team, the Cincinnati Red Stockings. It was not just that his club was "better trained and more practiced," as Henry Chadwick wrote.[16] In a deeper sense, Wright's teams were guided by their leader's benevolent paternalism, maintaining discipline over his players—both in and out of uniform—for their own good. How did McGuire, under Wright's tutelage between 1886 and 1888, respond to this parent-like authority? His own father, born in Ireland, had died before the future big-leaguer turned seven. Were Wright's British-accented words of wisdom heard with special meaning? Was the void left by his father, George McGuire, filled in some manner by Harry Wright?[17] As his career advanced, Deacon Jim, as he came to be known, would emulate Wright's ethos of respecting the game whether he happened to be on a winning or losing team.

The Washington Senators, the team McGuire played for throughout most of the 1890s, fell into the latter category. During his eight and one-half seasons with them, they never finished close to .500; they finished in the lower third of the 12-team National League every year except 1897, when they managed a 61–71 record and a sixth-place tie with Brooklyn. Washington's won-lost record may have been woeful, but the decade yielded less quantifiable aspects that kept local interest alive. In 1892, McGuire's club began playing at Boundary Field—later the location of Griffith Stadium—where President Benjamin Harrison became the first sitting chief executive to watch a major-league game (the Senators lost to Cincinnati 7–4, in 11 innings). Beyond the left-field fence, team owner Jacob Earl Wagner pastured his horse, Phil. Home fans considered it an auspicious omen if Phil faced the diamond when a comeback was needed, calling him the "Rally Horse." "Reliable Jim McGuire behind the bat" provided another hopeful sign, as told by one Frederic Tyler, a die-hard follower of those perennial "disappointments."[18] In 1895, McGuire's reliability was manifest when he caught in every one of his team's games, a record that will never be broken.

Fifty-five games into the 1898 season, he became Washington's player-manager, taking over from first baseman Dirty Jack Doyle. The new skipper had scarcely settled in when Wagner began encroaching on his prerogatives. "I will suggest certain ideas and exchange views with McGuire as to points of play," the boss said in early July, "such as the selection of certain pitchers to work against certain clubs and other details involved in the conduct of a team."[19] That arrangement produced a 21–47 record and, with the Senators in 11th place and only a couple of dozen games left on the schedule, McGuire resigned. His popularity, however, did not suffer. At the home opener the following season, it was reported that "McGuire's reception indicated his hold on local fans."[20] Nonetheless, his situation with another owner had been adversarial.

Deacon Jim's exit from Washington brought him back together with Ned Hanlon, who had become a part-owner of Brooklyn, along with Charles Ebbets and others, as well as the club's manager. In 1899, "Foxy Ned" sought to solidify his catching position by trading for Washington's Duke Farrell and McGuire.[21]

McGuire no doubt had mixed feelings. Though the Senators were pathetic, his long service with them— 900 games played, including almost 800 caught—and professionalism had earned him the admiration of his peers. Brooklyn's Superbas, on the other hand, held out the promise of finally being on a first-place club. The closest he had come had been in 1887, when Harry Wright's Phillies were runners-up to the Wolverines, finishing three and one-half games behind. Now in his 15th major-league season and approaching age 36, McGuire had a chance to put years of frustration behind him. As a Superbas booster confidently rhymed:

And let me emphasize the fact, and say it once again,
That we're bound ter[sic] win the Pennant with Hanlon and his men.[22]

Thanks to Hanlon, McGuire joined these men in July. And win they did, finishing first in 1899 and 1900, then capping their repeat by garnering a post-season win. For four years during the mid-'90s, the top two teams had played-off, with Hanlon's Baltimore Orioles being involved each time. After a two-season hiatus, the *Pittsburgh Chronicle-Telegraph* donated a handsome silver and gold punch bowl bearing the inscription "Presented to the Winner of the World's Championship of Base Ball [best-of-five series]."[23] Brooklyn took the trophy three games to one in 1900, Manager Hanlon racking up another title and McGuire, in baseball parlance, going from the outhouse to the penthouse.

1895 Washington Senators, McGuire top row, far right.

Yet the celebrations were somewhat muted by financial and personnel concerns. The Brooklyn club was less profitable in 1900 than it had been the prior year due to smaller home attendance, thus shrinking rewards for the winning Superbas. According to McGuire's recollection of how players expected increased bonuses: "We were drawing bigger [away] crowds than the season before so naturally we thought we would draw a bigger stake than we received for copping the first one, but when we finished, instead of a cash donation, each player received a pair of gold cuff links."

He said this with a chuckle.[24] But the American League was no laughing matter for team management. At the same time Brooklyn was wrapping up its championship in Pittsburgh, plans for a revamped circuit were being finalized in Chicago. Following the series, Joe McGinnity jumped to the American League's new Baltimore Orioles—the National League version of the team having been one of the four shut down in 1900. After the next season, his former batterymate did the same in favor of American League Detroit.

"McGuire was long noted as a big league catcher, serving with the Brooklyn National club in the zenith of his career."[25] This 1911 newspaper description archived at the Hall of Fame has gained twenty-first century credibility through Stats Inc. rating him the 1901 National League All-Star backstop. The Superbas' best years, by contrast, were behind them. After their championship season, they dropped to third, below Philadelphia and the pennant-winning Pirates; in 1902, Pittsburgh won again, finishing 27½ games ahead of the second-place Superbas. A few members of Hanlon's club who had brought the *Chronicle-Telegraph* trophy back to Brooklyn remained, but decline was reflected in the shrinking number of Brooklyn All-Stars between 1901, when there were five (Tom Daly, Bill Donovan, Joe Kelley, Jimmy

Sheckard, and McGuire), and the club's lone All-Star in 1902 (Bill Dahlen).[26]

Ebbets had underestimated the impact of the American League, as well as a new players organization, the Protective Association of Professional Baseball Players, which came together in June 1900 with delegates from every National League team. Its purpose was to improve the terms and conditions of employment, particularly the length of time that a player could be reserved. The emergent American League seemed prepared to accept most of its demands, but entrenched National League owners stood adamantly opposed. Any compromise with the upstarts was out of the question, insisted Ebbets: "They're only bluffing.... The demands of these fellows are simply preposterous."[27]

On September 25, 1901, McGuire re-signed with Brooklyn. According to the standard Articles of Agreement, his contractual obligations would run from April 15 until October 15, 1902, with the club's option to renew for 1903 at a salary of $2,600. Just before the contract was to take effect, on March 14, 1902, he signed American League Articles of Agreement with Detroit for two years, from March 20, 1902, until October 5, 1903, which would pay him $3,500 per season.[28]

Not only were Detroit's contract terms considerably better, but the team's third-place finish in 1901 promised a brighter immediate future than Brooklyn's. The Superbas' roster was decimated; the Tigers had a solid core of veterans and prospects. These were practical considerations. Comparing contracts, sizing up rosters, and doping out how teams were likely to perform in the next few years called for businesslike calculations.

Personal factors probably further motivated McGuire. For one thing, going to Detroit would put him close to home. Albion, Michigan, where he had resided since boyhood, was only a two and a half-hour train trip away. Not that he would be able to chug back and forth on the Michigan Central Railroad very often during the season, but proud local citizens could come to see him. The industrial town of slightly over 4,500 people in 1900 also counted among its population his wife, May, as well as George and Lizzie McGuire, his older brother and sister-in-law. The two families were immediate neighbors and the brothers jointly owned a main-street tavern. (At the beginning of 1901, the *Pittsburgh Chronicle-Telegraph* [McGinnity] Cup was displayed at McGuire Bros. where an enlarged portrait of Deacon Jim, wearing his 1885 Detroit uniform, hung above the bar.) Albionites cheered their hometown hero

McGuire below Ebbets and Hanlon, a Superba for the time being.

wherever he played, but their chests would puff out especially if he came to the Tigers.[29]

Getting to play at Bennett Park must also have impacted his decision. Formed as he had been by Charlie Bennett, being able to compete on the grounds named for his original mentor would hold special meaning. (Not all of Detroit's home games were at Bennett Park because Sunday baseball was prohibited, so the Tigers had to use a park outside of the city limits, near Dearborn.) Bennett Park was located at the corner of Michigan and Trumbull Avenues—a hallowed site in the making—and honored the fan favorite whose career ended abruptly in 1894 when he lost his left foot and right leg below the knee in a freak off-season railroad accident. Two years later, Bennett caught the ceremonial first pitch, personifying the positive attitude McGuire shared.[30]

His other important 1885 Detroit teammate did not seem so admirable. Since acquiring a financial interest in Brooklyn, it looked like Ned Hanlon had joined with the conniving owners. Once instrumental in the Brotherhood of Professional Base Ball Players—as well as a director of the cooperative Pittsburgh Players League team—he now epitomized syndicate maneuverings. To boot, he and Ebbets were both angling to get the better of each other. And, worst of all, respect for him as a manager had diminished. Years later, Sam Crawford related how Hanlon would "start telling some of those old-timers [former National League Orioles who had been transferred to Brooklyn] what to do. They'd look at him and say, 'For Christ's sake, just keep quiet and leave us alone. We'll win the ball game if only you shut up.'"[31] After 1900, Hanlon never won another pennant. He did enter the Hall of Fame posthumously, though, in 1996, upon the vote of the Committee on Veterans.

The clubhouse at Washington Park in South Brooklyn hardly overflowed with feelings of loyalty toward management. Only a few Superbas showed up at the October 25, 1900, testimonial dinner at the exclusive men's Carleton Club in Park Slope, sponsored by boosters, honoring the championship team. "Many of the leading citizens of the Borough have subscribed for the event," the Brooklyn Daily Eagle reported. "The pennant of 1900 will occupy the prominent place...and the World's Championship Cup... will grace the occasion. ...A vaudeville entertainment has been arranged, and the Twenty-Third Regiment Band in full uniform will serenade the players." For the finale, "gold sleeve buttons would be presented to the players."[32] Except only Willie Keeler and pitcher Harry Howell were there.

This was the second display of disregard for the organization in a week. On the previous Friday, when the Chronicle-Telegraph trophy was presented by Pittsburgh Mayor William J. Diehl, there had been no-shows. Joe Kelley, Brooklyn's captain, received the cup with: "Ladies and gentlemen, I beg that you will pardon the absence of some of our members," conspicuously among them McGinnity and McGuire. His conclusion—"I also ask your indulgence for our hasty departure. We are about to start for Cuba and the time of preparation is short"—indicated another situation that would not redound to the advantage of the Superbas.[33]

Their postseason trip—Kelley did not go—lacked total team support. Club secretary Tommy Simpson arranged for players from Brooklyn and the New York Giants to play eight exhibitions against each other in Cuba during November 1900; games against Cuban teams were scheduled for off days. Simpson's National League contingent arrived to find preparations somewhat lacking, and in mid-month 10 of his group hastily returned to New York. That left barely enough men to take on Cuban and US military teams. Nonetheless, "The net result of the Cuban trip [was] a pleasant time and valuable experience, but no financial profit," Sporting Life reported. Others agreed with Keeler: "The next time that I go to Cuba, I am going with a party of excursionists."[34]

One can imagine McGuire perusing news reports from Havana as he was readying his Albion tavern to exhibit the championship trophy. Something that would have grabbed his attention concerned Brooklyn's first baseman and the secretary of the Protective Association: "[Hughie] Jennings from far off Cuba has written his associates not to do business for 1901 before December 10 when he will be back."[35] This, of course, pertained to teammates who were considering various bids. Jennings' status was uncertain (Hanlon would sell him to the Phillies six months later). Another Superba on Simpson's trip was right-hander Harry Howell, soon to jump to the American League's Orioles. Fielder Jones signed that winter with the Chicago White Sox, Lafayette Cross jumped to the Philadelphia Athletics, and McGinnity refused more money offered by Ebbets so that he could reunite with John McGraw in Baltimore. While admiring the McGinnity Cup, and mulling over the Superbas' questionable state, other options surely crossed Deacon Jim's mind.

At present he belonged to Brooklyn, but 1901 would turn out to be his last year in the National League. McGuire's decision to breach his contract mingled pragmatic considerations and personal interests. By early 1902, tough-minded thinking and responses to sentiment convinced him that the time was right.

His start in Detroit was complicated by *Brooklyn Base Ball Club v. James T. McGuire*. On May 26, the club asked the Philadelphia Court of Common Pleas to enjoin its catcher "from playing base ball with or giving his services as a ball player for the season of 1902 to any other club or organization." The complaint averred that because Brooklyn's ballclub was a corporation

which has elevated the game...to high standards of respectability, integrity and popularity [through] securing and maintaining a team of skillful players to compete [in] popular exhibitions. ...That if the Defendant be permitted to... give his services...to a rival organization...it will not only result...in the withdrawal of a large portion of...customers...it will also cause great deterioration in the combined..."team work" of...other skillful players. [Moreover], the Defendant was and is a very expert, experienced and skillful player [contractually bound to fulfill his obligation and...prohibited] from performing such duties for any other party.[36]

A bill for injunction was served on May 28 notifying McGuire that he had 15 days to enter an appearance in court and answer charges, or the bill would be "taken pro confesso."[37]

The time and place of Brooklyn's filing reflected considered calculation. Less than a month earlier the Pennsylvania Supreme Court had ruled in favor of a club that had brought suit against a jumper. That was when the Phillies stopped Napoleon Lajoie (and

others) from playing for the Athletics and sought his return. Litigation in that case also had begun in the Court of Common Pleas. The arguments were basically the same as those used against McGuire, and Colonel John I. Rogers (co-owner of the Phillies and the National League's lawyer) represented the plaintiff in both proceedings.[38] William Jay Turner was the defendant's counsel for each case; his handling of McGuire's would prove most effective.

If Rogers' strategy was to take advantage of the recent high-profile outcome in the Pennsylvania state court system, he was several steps behind Turner and his associate, William Y.C. Anderson. First, McGuire's attorneys successfully petitioned for the case to be removed to federal court on the grounds that the civil suit involved citizens of different states.[39] Then they countered Rogers' argument that the plaintiff's player had irreplaceable skills and that losing him would cause irreparable harm to Brooklyn.

On Monday June 23, 1902, at 10 o'clock in the morning, the United States Circuit Court for the Eastern District of Pennsylvania began its examinations of the complainant and the respondent, Judge George M. Dallas presiding. It was immediately clear that Rogers would stress the jumper's extraordinary playing ability and turnstile appeal, as he had done in winning the Lajoie case.

> **Q. [Rogers]** Kindly state, as Mr. McGuire has been a player since 1899, what kind of a player, as to his skill.

> **A. [Ebbets]**... a very skillful player.... He did not have any one [sic] to excel him.... It is impossible almost to replace him.

> **Q. [Rogers]** What is the extent of your financial loss owing to the withdrawal of Mr. McGuire from your team?

> **A. [Ebbets]**...unless you have first class attractions...they [the public] do not turn out to attend your games the way they otherwise would.

Hanlon's testimony underscored McGuire's reputation as being "one of the best we have in the game," and there was no catcher "not under contract with another club who could be secured to replace him."[40]

Turner voiced objections and raised cross examination questions. Then he and Anderson read 10 remarkable affidavits sworn to the effect that "There were numerous other catchers...who were the equals of Mr. McGuire, if not his superior."[41] These statements had been written only three days before the hearing, when Boston arrived in Detroit for a weekend series. Five Bostons (including Cy Young, his batterymate Lou Criger, and third baseman-manager Jimmy Collins) and five Tigers (including manager Frank Dwyer and pitcher Win Mercer) affirmed that the defendant was not exceptional at his position. Mercer added that Brooklyn's drawing power would not be impaired by McGuire's absence.[42] Such downgrading of McGuire would seem absurd—especially in light of him later being ranked the National League's best catcher the year before. Judge Dallas (without the benefit of SABR's Deadball Era Committee's research) found it persuasive, though, and the counter affidavits submitted by Turner and Anderson informed his decision.

On June 25, the court denied Brooklyn's motion for a preliminary injunction. Judge Dallas ruled that the club had not suffered injury due to McGuire's jumping: "The evidence adduced is by no means conclusive upon the question whether the services which the defendant contracted to render were so unique and peculiar that they could not be performed, and substantially as well, by others engaged in professional base ball playing, who might be easily obtained to take his place."[43] A more significant issue in the decision was that the National League's contract lacked mutuality, thus making it unenforceable. The plaintiff could terminate its obligations upon giving the defendant 10 days' notice, whereas the defendant's obligations remained in effect at the plaintiff's discretion.[44] *Brooklyn Base Ball Club v. James T. McGuire* had national scope in its application.

Afterward, Rogers spoke respectfully of the judge and his ruling. Although sweeping, it failed to mention the Lajoie case, "completely ignoring the unanimous decision of the Supreme Court of Pennsylvania."[45] He was silent on the question of whether there would be an appeal to the US Supreme Court.

That definitely would have added a special feature to this study of McGuire the contract jumper. But it would not answer deep-seated questions concerning how and why his court case came about. Viewed historically, McGuire's 1902 decision stemmed from a multitude of events over the course of 17 big-league seasons. Some of them were instrumental in shaping his outlook and actions. Moreover, these personal experiences and influences provided him with an abundance of firsthand anecdotes for telling as he grew older. After retiring to his home in Michigan—with 26 seasons of major league service, the all-time

record for catchers—venerable Deacon Jim coached the Albion College team. Think of the baseball stories those young men must have heard. ■

Notes

1. Harold Seymour and Dorothy Seymour Mills, *Baseball: The Early Years* (New York: Oxford University Press, 1960), 104–15, 305; David Quentin Voigt, *American Baseball: From Gentleman's Sport to the Commissioner System* (University Park, PA: Pennsylvania State University Press, 1983), 168, 225–40, 306–308; Benjamin G. Rader, *Baseball: A History of America's Game* (Urbana, IL: University of Illinois Press, 1994), 70–79; Patrick K. Thornton, *Legal Decisions that Shaped Modern Baseball* (Jefferson, NC: McFarland, 2012), 44.

2. *Major League Baseball Profiles, 1871–1900, Volume 1: The Ballplayers Who Built the Game* (Lincoln, NE: University of Nebraska Press, 2011), 255–57; Robert W. Bigelow, "Deacon McGuire," SABR Biography Project, http://sabr.org/ bioproj/person/62d7cf30.

3. *Sporting Life*, June 24, 1885; June 17, 1885; *Detroit Free Press*, June 16, 1885; June 23, 1885.

4. *Detroit Free Press*, June 17, 1885; Seymour and Mills, *Baseball*, 110. Watkins' role in the Indianapolis part of this deal, which "demonstrated both his ingenuity and the traits that would make him one of the most despised NL managers in the nineteenth century," is discussed in: Nemec, comp. and ed., *Major League Baseball Profiles, 1871–1900, Volume 2: The Hall of Famers and Memorable Personalities Who Shaped the Game* (Lincoln, NE: University of Nebraska Press, 2011), 149.

5. "The 1885 Detroit Wolverines Regular Season Game Log," Retrosheet, https:// www.retrosheet.org/boxesetc/1885/VDTN01885.htm.

6. Peter Morris, *Catcher: How the Man Behind the Plate Became an American Hero* (Chicago: Ivan R. Dee, 2009), 327; David Nemec, *The Rules of Baseball: An Anecdotal Look at the Rules of Baseball and How They Came to Be* (New York: Lyons & Burford, 1994), 152; John Richmond Husman, "Charles Wesley Bennett," in *Nineteenth Century Stars*, ed. Robert L. Tiemann and Mark Rucker (Kansas City: Society for American Baseball Research, 1989), 12.

7. *Sporting Life*, July 8, 1885.

8. Thornton, *Legal Decisions*, 33; *Allegheny Base Ball Club v. Bennett*, 14 F.257 (W.D. Pa., 1882), https://law.resource.org/pub/us/case/reporter/F/0014/0014.f.0257.pdf.

9. Voigt, *American Baseball*, 155; Seymour and Mills, *Baseball: The Early Years*, 142. At the end of the 1885 season, the magnates cut salaries to $2,000 maximum and increased the number of scheduled games from 112 in 1885 to 126 in 1886. David Stevens, *Baseball's Radical for All Seasons: A Biography of John Montgomery Ward* (Lanham, MD: Scarecrow Press, 1998), 42.

10. David Quentin Voigt, *Baseball: An Illustrated History* (University Park, PA: Pennsylvania State University Press, 1987), 137; Voigt, *American Baseball*, 113; Nemec, *Profiles*, vol. 2, 34; Stevens, *Baseball's Radical for All Seasons*, 42–43; Bill Lamb, "John Montgomery Ward," SABR Biography Project, https://sabr.org/bioproj/person/2de3f6ef.

11. *Players' National League Base Ball Guide* (1890), 8, courtesy of Matt Rothenberg, Giamatti Research Center, National Baseball Hall of Fame (hereafter cited as HOF).

12. Seymour and Mills, *Baseball: The Early 12 Years*, 129–32, 224–25. The categories were lettered A through E in descending order and class E men were tasked with sweeping ballparks after games. Stevens, *Baseball's Radical*, 79.

13. Stevens, 89.

14. Peter Levine, A.G. *Spalding and the Rise of Baseball: The Promise of American Sport* (New York: Oxford University Press, 1985), 58–59.

15. Andrew J. Schiff, *"The Father of Baseball:" A Biography of Henry Chadwick* (Jefferson, NC: McFarland, 2008), 6, 115–23; Warren Goldstein, *Playing for Keeps: A History of Early Baseball* (Ithaca, NY: Cornell University Press, 1989), 113–14, 151–52.

16. Voigt, *American Baseball*, 26.

17. Eighth Census of the United States: 1860—Population, Aurora, OH, M653_1025, image 33; and 1870—Population, Youngstown, OH, M593_1239, image 602, National Archives Building; Schiff, *Father of Baseball*, 184; "Wright, a native of Sheffield, England, spoke with a British accent," Lee Allen, *Cooperstown Corner: Columns from the Sporting News* 1902–69 (Cleveland: Society for American Baseball Research, n.d.), 88; Jerrold Casway, "A Monument for Harry Wright," *The National Pastime*, no. 17 (1997): 35–37.

18. Jonathan Fraser Light, *The Cultural Encyclopedia of Baseball* (Jefferson, NC: McFarland, 1997), 586; Kevin and Karen Flynn, "The 1897 Ladies Day Riot," *Nats News*, no. 59 (July 2012): 13; Frederick S. Tyler, "Fifty-five Years of Local Baseball, 1893-1947," read before the Society, October 21, 1947, *Records of the Columbia Historical Society of Washington, D.C.*, 1946–47, (1949): 265–67.

19. Rich Eldred, "Umpiring in the 1890s," *Baseball Research Journal*, no. 18 (1989): 75; Shirley Povich, *The Washington Senators* (New York: G.P. Putnam's Sons, 1954), 26.

20. *Washington Evening Star*, April 19, 1899

21. Zack Triscuit, "Edward Hugh Hanlon, [Brooklyn] Manager 1899–1905," in *Deadball Stars of the National League*, written by the Deadball Committee of the Society for American Baseball Research, ed. Tom Simon (Cleveland: Society for American Baseball Research, 2004), 273; John Saccoman, "Charles Hercules Ebbets, [Brooklyn] Owner 1898–1925," in *Deadball Stars of the National League*, 271; Voigt, American Baseball, 267–68.

22. Lawrence William Westholm, "Our Base Ball Winners," *Brooklyn Daily Eagle*, April 23, 1899.

23. *Brooklyn Daily Eagle*, October 11, 1900. In 1965, the Hall of Fame accessioned the *Pittsburgh Chronicle-Telegraph* Cup (also known as the McGinnity Cup), describing it as "a missing link between the Temple Cup and and the modern World Series." *Twenty-Sixth Annual Program* (Cooperstown), July 26, 1965.

24. *Brooklyn Daily Eagle*, October 13, 1900; Guy M[clIvaine] Smith, "He Could Catch Anything and Anybody," photocopy of an undated typescript, HOF; Don Doxie, *Iron Man McGinnity: A Baseball Biography* (Jefferson, NC: McFarland, 2009), 55. Smith (1872-1950) was a Danville, Illinois, baseball writer and *Sporting News* correspondent who apparently interviewed McGuire in the early 1930s.

25. Photocopy of an untitled newspaper clipping, May 8, 1911, HOF.

26. *Deadball Stars of the National League*, 17.

27. Seymour and Mills, *Baseball: The Early Years*, 311. "The Players' Association has achieved all it set out to do," concluded Francis C. Richter, *Sporting Life*, April 20, 1901.

28. *Brooklyn Base Ball Club v. James T. McGuire*, 116 F.782 (3d Cir. 1902), case file scans from the National Archives at Philadelphia (hereafter cited as Brooklyn v. McGuire, NAP); "a renewal clause (reserve)" had been part of the revised contract for 10 years, Seymour and Mills, *Baseball: The Early Years*, 256.

29. George J. and James T. McGuire were born in Youngstown, Ohio, in 1858 and 1863 respectively, and settled in Albion, where the latter apprenticed as an iron molder; the *Albion Recorder*, January 10, 1901, reported that the championship trophy was on exhibit, which was also documented in an undated photograph, Frank Passic, "McGuire Brothers," pt. 3 (1995), http://www.albionmich.com/history/histor_notebook/950730.shtml.

30. Michael Betzold and Ethan Casey, *Queen of Diamonds: The Tiger Stadium Story* (West Bloomfield, MI: A&M Publishing, 1992), 29–30, 32; Philip J. Lowry, Green Cathedrals (Cooperstown, NY: Society for American Baseball Research, 1986), 51; Ron Selter, "A History of Bennett Park—Detroit's First Major League Ballpark," pt. 1, *Inside Game* 5, no. 4 (November 2005): 2–3; pt. 2, 6, no. 1 (February 2006): 3, 7.

31. Lawrence S. Ritter, *The Glory of Their Times: The Story of the Early Days of Baseball Told by the Men Who Played It* (New York: Macmillan, 1960), 52–53.

32. *Brooklyn Daily Eagle*, October 25, 1900; Ebbets mailed these "tokens of the rooters' esteem to the men who found it impossible to attend," however some Superbas "were told by Ebbets that they were not entitled to them," *Brooklyn Daily Eagle*, October 29, 1900; December 4, 1900.

33. *Brooklyn Daily Eagle*, October 20, 1900.

34. *Sporting Life*, December 8, 1900; November 24, 1900.

35. *Sporting Life*, December 8, 1900, after he got back, Jennings resumed his law studies and baseball coaching at Cornell University, to the displeasure of Ebbets and Hanlon, C. Paul Rogers III, "Hughie Jennings," SABR Biography Project, http://sabr.org/bioproj/person/c9d82d83.

36. Exemplification of Record No. 4265, docket entries, Court of Common Pleas No. 1 for the County of Philadelphia, State of Pennsylvania, May 26, 1902, *Brooklyn v. McGuire, NAP*.

37. Exemplification of Record No. 4265.

38. The relevant cases of Lajoie (1901–02)—the first court-ordered injunction enforcing a sports contract—and of John Ward (1890), too technically detailed for discussion here, are elaborated in, Thornton, *Legal Decisions*, 21–40, 51–57, Robert Berry and Glenn Wong, *Law and Business of the Sports Industries*, vol. 1 (Dover, MA: Auburn House, 1986), 71–73, and Richard L. Irwin, "A Historical Review of Litigation in Baseball," Marquette Sports Law Review, 1 (Spring 1991): 283–88, http://scholarship.law.marquette.edu/sportslaw/vol1/ iss2/6; in something of a twist, Ward—who 15 years earlier likened the reserve rule to a "fugitive slave law"—assisted Rogers in the McGuire case, "ironically, hypocritically, he argued on the side of management," Bryan DiSalvatore, *A Clever Base Ballist: The Life and Times of John Montgomery Ward* (New York: Pantheon Books, 1999), 372–73.

39. Petition for Removal of Case No. 4265, Court of Common Pleas No. 1, to United States Circuit Court in and for the Eastern District of Pennsylvania, May 29, 1902, *Brooklyn v. McGuire, NAP*.

40. Motion for Preliminary Injunction, U.S.C.C., E.D. of PA., June 23, 1902, 4–5, 14–15, *Brooklyn v. McGuire, NAP*.

41. *Sporting Life*, July 5, 1902.

42. Counter Affidavits on Behalf of Defendant sur Application for Special Injunction, Wayne County, Michigan, June 20, 1902, *Brooklyn v. McGuire, NAP*.

43. Opinion Denying Motion for Preliminary Injunction, June 25, 1902, *Brooklyn v. McGuire, NAP*.

44. Gary D. Hailey and Douglas R. Pappas, "Baseball and the Law," in *Total Baseball*, ed. John Thorn, Pete Palmer, Michael Gershman, and David Pietrusza, 5th ed. (New York: Viking Books, 1997), 495.

45. *Sporting Life*, July 5, 1902.

Ties in Baseball (and Beyond)

Erik M. Jensen

It's often said that there are no ties in baseball. If a game is deadlocked after nine innings,[1] you keep playing until someone wins.[2] That's the general rule, to be sure, but tie games have occurred in the past, for all sorts of special reasons.[3] And the neck tie, the real subject of this essay (yes, the title is a bait and switch), has played a role in the lives of some prominent baseball guys (and others as well).

Of course, as Donald Kagan has noted, we're far removed from the time in which men routinely wore neckties for leisure activities, like going to the ballpark:

> Those who are too young to remember should look at the movies and photographs of games at Yankee Stadium in [Joe] DiMaggio's day. The men wore white shirts and ties under coats and hats, the proper attire in public, even at a ball game. People were…not insulted by the notion that another way of life might be better than their own.[4]

Indeed, in the old days a few ballplayers wouldn't have been caught alive, off the diamond, without a tie.[5] The most prominent example was DiMaggio himself. Until the end of his life (and probably beyond), Joltin' Joe was stylishly dressed. Except when he was in a baseball uniform,[6] he was seldom without a suit in public.[7]

Sad to say, that aspect of Joe DiMaggio has left and gone away, hey hey hey.[8] (And a little wo wo wo and koo-koo-ca-choo, too.) We're now in a world of "faded elegance," to borrow a phrase of Arthur Schlesinger Jr.'s.[9] In *Dinner with DiMaggio*,[10] Dr. Rock Positano described taking DiMaggio in the 1990s, long after his retirement from baseball, to the Carlyle Hotel in Manhattan, where Woody Allen would be playing in the band: "Eying the crowd, Joe had just started muttering to me, 'I don't know about this. This isn't the Carlyle that I know. Nobody in that crowd is wearing a jacket and tie. What are you getting me into, Doc?'"[11]

When it came to dress, DiMaggio's unfaded elegance resembled Charles de Gaulle's, Richard Nixon's,

and J. Robert Oppenheimer's. Those three weren't ballplayers, of course, although Nixon wanted to be commissioner of baseball, and each, in his own way, was always trying to hit a Ballantine Blast. De Gaulle was at heart a military man; DiMaggio and Oppenheimer were bombers, one of the Bronx persuasion, the other atomic; and Nixon bombed a few times too—in Cambodia, for example.

Let's take them one by one:

DE GAULLE

Author and screenwriter Frederic Raphael wrote that

> [i]n captivity [in World War I prison camps], lordly majesty led [de Gaulle] never to use the common showers, and it is reported that no one saw him naked. Philippe (later Admiral) de Gaulle says in his hagiographical memoir of his father that, even at home, the general never came out of his bedroom until fully dressed, complete with tie.[12]

Just so.

NIXON

Historian and Kennedy family gofer Arthur Schlesinger Jr., was, for a short time, a neighbor of the Nixons—an arrangement probably distasteful to both families. In his journal, Schlesinger described the Nixons "relaxing" in 1980 in what passes as a backyard in Manhattan:

> [S]prawled on a deck chair, wearing jacket and tie, was Richard Nixon. Seated near him, wearing an afternoon dress and high-heeled shoes, was one of his daughters.… The two Nixons looked as if they were dressed for a garden party: even in his own house, his own garden.[13]

Nixon wouldn't take off his coat when working alone in the Oval Office, or so he said.[14] (*The Economist* claimed in 2008 that Nixon "wore a necktie when he was in his dressing gown."[15]) In 1990, pundit Anna Quindlen spoke for Nixon detractors everywhere: "The image of him walking on the beach in a suit and lace-up shoes became a metaphor for everything we hated. He was the ultimate adult at a time when adult had become the greatest pejorative."[16] Yeah, what could be worse than being the "ultimate adult"?

Nixon's adult behavior brings to mind Robert Caro, biographer of Robert Moses and Lyndon Johnson. As reported in *The New York Times*, Caro "dresses every day in a jacket and tie, and reports to a 22nd-floor office in a nondescript building near Columbus Circle.... His office looks as if it belongs to the kind of C.P.A. who still uses ledgers and a hand-cranked adding machine."[17] Caro sees no clients there; he has none. Nor does he share the office with professional colleagues. Nixon's White House attire may have been intended to show reverence for his surroundings, but Caro's clothing must have a different justification. Impeccably dressed, reflecting the importance of his work, Caro engages, Bob Cratchit-like, in "a solitary, Dickensian occupation with long hours and few holidays."[18] It's a grown-up thing.

OPPENHEIMER

With or without a clearance, Oppenheimer wanted the security of proper dress. His biographers wrote that, at the Institute for Advanced Study in Princeton, which Oppenheimer headed for years, he relished the role history had assigned him and he tried hard to play the part well. While most of the institute's permanent scholars walked around in sport jackets—Einstein favored a rumpled sweater[19]—Oppenheimer often wore expensive English wool suits hand-tailored for him at Langrocks, the local tailor for Princeton's upper crust.[20] (And nothing, I'm told, can be crustier than Princeton.)

De Gaulle, Nixon, and Oppenheimer (Caro too) were ultimate adults, and in many respects DiMaggio wasn't. He played the field both at and away from the ballpark, and he would have been near the top in a *US News* ranking on that score.[21] Nor was DiMaggio a nice man, except with kids and best friends. Otherwise, he was often petty and rude.

But DiMaggio knew the importance of appearances, and coats and ties connote discipline and seriousness. (Joe often said he played hard regardless of a particular game's importance: "There is always some kid who may be seeing me for the first time. I owe him my best."[22]) Yes, hygienic concerns may justify not wearing ties in certain circumstances. For example, the authors of Super Freakonomics present the germ of an

David Cone recently tweeted that Joe DiMaggio schooled him on proper attire after Cone showed up at Yankee Stadium in blue jeans and a T-shirt.

idea to control hospital-based infections: "forbidding doctors to wear neckties because, as the UK Department of Health has noted, they 'are rarely laundered,' 'perform no beneficial function in patient care,'[23] and 'have been shown to be colonized by pathogens.'"[24] Yuck. But in most settings neckwear presents no health problems, and ties can be deloused. (I'll bet Joe's ties visited the dry cleaner regularly.)

DiMaggio's style was never the norm for ballplayers and baseball executives, of course; many avoided ties at all times if they could get away with it. Indeed, two baseball greats who were as compulsive in their own ways as DiMaggio was in his were famous for disdaining neckwear, with near religious conviction: Ted Williams, who wanted to be remembered as the greatest hitter who ever lived,[25] and Bill Veeck (as in wreck), Hall of Fame owner and promoter extraordinaire. (Think Eddie Gaedel, with the world's smallest strike zone.)

Williams was the consummate fisherman. As Ben Bradlee explained, "He loved the beauty and authenticity of the outdoor life. 'No stuffy characters. No formal dinners. *No tight ties around your neck.*'"[26] And Veeck was a born contrarian, or at least he wanted that image.[27] Paul Dickson wrote that Veeck "turned being tieless into an article of faith in a day when male working-class patrons showed up to watch the game in neckties, hats, and lace-up shoes."[28] For Williams and Veeck, there should have been no ties in baseball or anywhere else.

Williams admired President George H. W. Bush. Both had been fighter pilots, and Bush had played baseball at Yale.[29] In 1991, Bush wanted to award the Medal of Freedom to the once Splendid Splinter (still splendid, although no longer a splinter), but Ted declined. He didn't want to have to don a tuxedo for the ceremony. White House Chief of Staff John Sununu

Bill Veeck was infamous for his dislike of formality.

assured Ted that only a tie would be required,[30] but Ted still balked. Baseball Commissioner Fay Vincent then intervened, brokering a deal in which Ted could attend tieless. On the morning of the ceremony, Ted, wearing gray slacks and a powder-blue shirt, continued to insist that "I'm not wearing a tie."[31] But lawyer John Dowd, who would be accompanying Ted to the ceremony, laid down the law:

> "This is your commander in chief. I'm not going over there with you if you're gonna look like Joe Shit the Rag man." Then [Ted] weakened a little and said, "I don't even know how to tie the fuckin' thing." So I tied it. He's mumbling out of the side of his mouth, "This is the last time."…

> [I]n the receiving line to meet the president, [I preceded Joe]. I meet the president. Bush says, "I don't recognize this fellow with the tie on." Ted had steam coming out his ears.[32]

Ted lost his head.[33]

The contrasting styles of DiMaggio and Williams had been illustrated at the All-Star Game in Toronto earlier in 1991. DiMaggio, Williams, President Bush, Commissioner Vincent, and Williams' 22-year-old son, John Henry, were to go onto the field before the game. Doc Positano wrote that, when reminiscing about the day, DiMaggio "slapped his forehead. 'Who could forget what that kid said to the president?'"[34] John Henry apparently had told Bush "that his father didn't like to wear a jacket and tie on the field. He asked if the president would mind taking off his own jacket to accommodate his father's fashion statement and refusal to wear a jacket and tie, so he wouldn't make Ted look bad."[35] But even had Bush been inclined to honor

John Henry's request, he couldn't do so: POTUS has to wear a bulletproof coat for security. And for DiMaggio, just raising the question was a breach of decorum: "Can you imagine the balls on that kid?…Asking the president not to wear his protective jacket out on the field?"[36]

John Henry had the last laugh, for now. He made arrangements so that at his dad's death the head and body were frozen separately in a cryonics facility. The idea was that, when medicine advanced enough, Ted could be thawed and his tieless head and body repaired and reassembled, probably using more than a few replacement parts.[37]

Ted did have clout; guys who can bat .406 often get their way. And sticklers for formal dress will alter their views (and their clothing) when it's in their personal interest to do so. Bradlee said that Joe McCarthy, as manager of the New York Yankees,[38] "had always insisted that he and his Yankees wear jackets and ties off the field." But when McCarthy was hired to manage the Red Sox, "How, people wondered, would he enforce his dress code on Ted?…The manager surprised everyone in Sarasota [at spring training] with a disarming gesture: he greeted his star while wearing a shirt with an open collar."[39] A walk-off win for Williams.

Another Williams shift that shows Ted's pull occurred at the Cheeca Lodge, an upscale resort on Islamorada, in the Florida Keys, where Ted, fishing rod in hand, spent much of his retirement:

> [T]he women wore long gowns at night and the men were required to wear ties. One evening when Williams showed up in his usual khakis and T-shirt getup, he was turned away. So Ted went home, put on a tie, and returned in the same khakis and T-shirt. They let him in, and after that, the Cheeca dress code was effectively broken.[40]

Ted didn't need Alan Turing to crack that code.

As an adult, or as close as he ever came to adulthood, Veeck also refused to wear a tie, except for one period in his life. In Paul Dickson's telling:

> "I once owned a tie 15 years ago," said Veeck, addressing the issue of why he was not going to wear a tie to [a dinner hosted by Elsa Maxwell], "but I didn't like it. When I joined the Marines, they knew I didn't wear ties, but they suggested that a tie would go nicely with my uniform. I saw their point—quickly."[41]

Marine officers (guys nicknamed Mad Dog, for example) can be very persuasive. Veeck "joked that he had made the ultimate sartorial sacrifice to keep America safe,"[42] but otherwise he wore no tie, almost without exception.[43]

I'm a law professor, so let me try to tie this knotty (and occasionally naughty) subject to law. When John Roberts, now chief justice of the United States (and a man who views the judicial function as similar to umpires' calling balls and strikes) interviewed for a clerkship with Justice William Rehnquist, Roberts found Rehnquist to be quite the casual guy:

> [He] was friendly and unpretentious. He wore scuffed Hush Puppy shoes. That was my first lesson. Clothes do not make the man. The Justice sported long sideburns and Buddy Holly glasses long after they were fashionable. And he wore loud ties that I am confident were never fashionable.[44]

To his credit, Rehnquist did wear ties, grotesque though they may have been. And in the 1990s, as chief justice, he began to wear a judicial robe with four gold braid stripes on each sleeve, looking like the Lord High Chancellor.[45] He may have been making fun of convention in both cases, I suppose, but he knew that people paid attention.[46] His attire mattered.

So was Rehnquist always playful when it came to dress? Well, no, not with lawyers. As chief justice he "complained to the Justice Department that one of its female lawyers had appeared before the court in a brown dress, not the preferred black or navy blue."[47] Clothes apparently do make the woman, and Rehnquist sent a strong, albeit condescending, signal to that effect.

Had he been a lawyer, on his worst-dressed days Joe DiMaggio would have satisfied the sartorial expectations of the Supreme Court. But would Ted Williams, thawed and reconstituted as an attorney, be able to dispense with coat and tie in that setting? Maybe. A lot of baseball fans have sat on the court,[48] Ted Williams was (is?) Ted Williams, and he often got (and may still get) his way.

But maybe not. Today's court wouldn't be unanimously sympathetic to a tieless Williams. Whatever she thinks about dress codes in general—she prefers them to the tax code, I'm sure—Justice Sonia Sotomayor is unlikely to support bending the rules for someone who played (and may play again) for the Boston Red Sox. She's a Yankees fan; she's visited the Judge's Chambers ("All rise!") at Yankee Stadium.[49]

To be safe when you return, Ted, wear a tie. And may I have your autograph? ∎

Notes

1. Or whatever the appropriate number is in your setting. In Little League, games generally last only six innings. (The games just seem longer.)

2. A 1981 minor league game between the Pawtucket Red Sox and the Rochester Red Wings lasted 33 innings. It was suspended, still tied after 32 innings, at 4:07 a.m. on April 19, the morning after the game had started. (If the umpires had had an up-to-date league rulebook or had the league president been reachable, the game would have been suspended earlier.) What turned out to be the last inning was played two months later. Dan Barry, *Bottom of the 33rd: Hope, Redemption and Baseball's Longest Game* (New York: Harper Perennial, 2011).

3. In ballparks without lights, afternoon games were sometimes called on account of darkness. Even if the score was tied, the game was over. The hitting, pitching, and fielding statistics counted, but a new game was played thereafter, as soon as possible. (The called game wasn't continued, as would typically happen today. *Cf. supra* note 2.)

4. Donald Kagan, "Joe DiMaggio, Baseball's Aristocrat," Weekly Standard, March 22, 1999. http:// www.weeklystandard.com/joe-dimaggio-baseballs-aristocrat/article/11516. For that matter, we're far removed from the time when men routinely wore ties in *business* settings. I've lamented the decline in professorial dress in law schools. See Erik M. Jensen, "Law School Attire: A Call for a Uniform Uniform Code," *Oklahoma City University Law Review* 32 (2007): 419, https://papers.ssrn.com/sol3/papers.cfm?abstract_id=1020738. Although it's been written that "[l]awyers are smart professionals who wear suits," (Brian Z. Tamanaha, *Failing Law Schools* (Chicago: University of Chicago Press, 2012), 135) that statement was dated when Tamanaha wrote it. The "smart professional" part still rings true, but the rest comes from the nineteenth century: "The present-day uniform of the male professional—the coat and necktie—traces its provenance to [Beau] Brummel." Joshua Kendall, *The Man Who Made Lists* (New York: G.P. Putnam's Sons, 2008), 184. Beau may not have known diddley, but he knew style. A more up-to-date view of attorney dress is that of Mark Herrmann. Chapter 8 of *The Curmudgeon's Guide to Practicing Law* (Chicago: American Bar Association, 2006), titled "Dress for Success," reads in full: "I don't give a damn what you wear. Just make sure the brief is good." *But see* Joseph Epstein, "Hitting Eighty," *Weekly Standard*, Jan. 2/9, 2017. ("A friend in the clothing business tells me that only lawyers buy suits nowadays."). http:// www.weeklystandard.com/hitting-eighty/article/2006085.

5. The propriety of being caught dead with no tie is another question. That project would be a major undertaking.

6. Unlike other teams, the Yankees regulate hair length and facial hair—mustaches OK, but no beards. *See* Daniel Barbarisi, "No Beards—And That's Final," *Wall Street Journal*, February 23, 2013, https://www.wsj.com/articles/SB10001424127887324048904578320741510151474. Professional baseball's uniform rules are brief. *E.g., Official Baseball Rules* (2017 ed.), Rule 3.03(e) ("No player shall wear ragged, frayed or slit sleeves."); *Official Baseball Rules*, Rule 3.03(h) ("Glass buttons and polished metal shall not be used on a uniform"). It wasn't unheard of, in ancient times, for baseball managers to wear coats and ties in the dugout. (Uniform rules apply only to players.) The best-known examples are Connie Mack, manager (owner too, good for job security) of the Philadelphia Athletics from 1901 through 1950, and Burt Shotton, twice skipper of the Brooklyn Dodgers (1947, replacing the suspended Leo Durocher, and 1948–50, stepping in after Durocher's firing). Shotton supposedly wore "street clothes," but that term often meant coat and tie. The pictures I've seen show Shotton dressed to the nines. And I've seen nothing to suggest that Mr. Mack was ever tieless in the A's dugout.

7. In his memorial essay about DiMaggio, Kagan wrote: "[H]is day was not ours. America was a democracy, but of a different kind. Its people were more respectful of excellence, both of matter and manner, prepared to

follow the leadership of those they deemed superior in achievement and "class." People wanted to behave according to a higher and better code because they believed that in doing so they would themselves become better, worthier, 'classier.'" Kagan, "Joe DiMaggio." Now retired, Kagan was a Yale professor and dean, and a contemporary of Bart Giammati, who ascended to the Yale presidency and ultimately became commissioner of baseball, the highest office in the land. (A Yale connection helps only so much, however. Another Yalie, former pitcher Ron Darling, regularly says "have went" on baseball telecasts. Cornellians Strunk and White knew better.)

8. Cf. Mark Steyn, "Happy Warrior: The Mutant Present," *National Review*, December 31, 2011: "[W]hat would a visitor from Eisenhower's America make of our time?…[H]is initial reaction would be complete amazement at the people. Instead of the sober suits and hats of a 1950 Main Street, men and women crowd the sidewalks in brightly colored leisurewear that, to his mid-century eyes, gives them the air of overgrown children. https://www.nationalreview.com/nrd/articles/294066/mutant-present. Likening the scruffy to kids is common. *See, e.g.,* Joseph Epstein, "Hope I Die Before I Get Young," *Commentary*, February 2017: "I…see men I taught with [at Northwestern] who are now in their late sixties and early seventies who dress as if still students. They carry backpacks, wear baseball hats backwards, are in jeans and gym shoes…. But for their lined faces, grey hair—and the occasionally heartbreakingly sad grey ponytail—they might themselves be students. Clearly they intend to go from juvenility to senility, with no stops in between. https://www.commentarymagazine.com/articles/hope-i-die-before-i-get-young.

9. Arthur M. Schlesinger Jr., *Journals, 1952–2000* (New York: Penguin Press, 2007), 396. (Sept. 21, 1978) (complaining that Chicago's Ambassador East Hotel "has fallen on sad days. Its atmosphere is now one of faded elegance, and the lobby is filled with tieless men wearing double-knit trousers.") [Hereinafter *Schlesinger's Journals*]. The punctuation in *Jr.*,'s looks strange, with back-to-back-to-back punctuation marks, but, as far as *The New Yorker* is concerned, it's right. See Andrew Boynton, "The Correct Punctuation of Donald Trump, Jr.,'s Name," New Yorker Online, July 12, 2017, https://www.newyorker.com/news/news-desk/the-correct-punctuation-of-donald-trump-jrs-name.

10. Dr. Rock Positano & John Positano, *Dinner with DiMaggio: Memoirs of an American Hero* (New York: Simon & Schuster, 2017).

11. Positano & Positano, 229. Positano is "Foot Doctor to the Stars." In 1990, when he was treating DiMaggio for heel problems that had hobbled Joe for years, the two became friends. See Richard Ben Cramer, *Joe DiMaggio: The Hero's Life*, 474 (New York: Simon & Schuster, 2000). (Bone spurs hadn't kept Joe out of the military, however. He was in the Army Air Force, sort of, during World War II. But he just played baseball and, even so, dogged it. Reports noted a "defective attitude toward the service" and a "conscious attitude of hostility and resistance." Tom Leonard, "Joe DiMaggio made a poor soldier, military records show," *Telegraph*, Aug. 3, 2010, http://study.com/academy/lesson/the-great-joe-dimaggio-baseballin- the-old-man-and-the-sea-symbolism-use.html. The uniform probably didn't suit Joe. Nor did the salary.)

12. Frederic Raphael, "The Indomitable de Gaulle," *Wall Street Journal*, July 7-8, 2012. https:// advance.lexis.com/document/?pdmfid=1000516&crid=d0a055a4-3c08-4a9c-b929-a4e7bcff7d8a&pddocfullpath=%2Fshared%2Fdocument%2Fnews%2Furn%3Acontentitem%3A5627- XDC1-DYGY-Y41M-00000-00&pddocid=urn%3Acontentitem%3A5627-XDC1-DYGYY41M-00000-00&pdcontentcomponentid=280015&pdteaserkey=sr0&pditab=allpods&ecomp=tyffk&earg= sr0&prid=7d2b9a45-cb3c-474c-bb8b-858fbdd0df52.

13. *Schlesinger's Journals*, 438 (Aug. 16, 1980). Schlesinger was also a dress-up nerd, however ("Jerry Wiesner [science advisor to Kennedy and later MIT president] has never let me forget that once when JFK called me in [Wiesner's] office I put on the jacket before taking the call."). Oct. 16, 1989.

14. "I work in a coat and tie—and believe me, believe it or not, it's hard for people to realize, but when I'm writing a speech or working on a book or dictating or so forth, I'm always wearing a coat and tie. Even when I'm alone." Bob Greene, *Fraternity: A Journey in Search of Five Presidents* (New York: Crown Publishers, 2004), 29; see also Greene, 156 (describing discussion with former President George H. W. Bush). Bush was surprised to learn of Nixon's practice. Bush kept his suitcoat on in the Oval Office when other people were present, but not otherwise: "I would go in there to the Oval Office on a Saturday morning when nobody was there, and I wouldn't wear a jacket. At the house, the living quarters part of the White House, that's different, too. I mean, I'd walk around there in a bathrobe. I mean, you know, the bedroom? You're not going to wear a suit." *Id.* at 157. Oh yeah?! *See id.* at 28 (quoting Nixon: "[Pat and I] would not feel comfortable in [the White House] unless we were somewhat formal."); *id.* at 39 (Nixon "said that the use in newspapers of 'president,' lowercase, was very much like the idea of first families who might choose to dress casually inside the White House. He strongly disapproved of both.").

15. "The Fuel of Power," *Economist*, May 10, 2008. http://www.economist.com/node/11326268. How could they know?

16. Anna Quindlen, "Public & Private; Nixon's the One," *The New York Times*, November 11, 1990. http:// www.nytimes.com/1990/11/11/opinion/public-private-nixon-s-the-one.html. To be fair, pictures of Nixon walking in his un-beachlike clothes usually don't show a tie.

17. Charles McGrath, "Robert Caro's Big Dig," *The New York Times Magazine*, April 15, 2012. http:// www.nytimes.com/2012/04/15/magazine/robert-caros-big-dig.html.

18. McGrath.

19. The universe might be curved, but Einstein couldn't handle the breaking pitch.

20. Kai Bird & Martin J. Sherwin, *American Prometheus: The Triumph and Tragedy of J. Robert Oppenheimer* (New York: A.A. Knopf, 2005), 371.

21. He didn't necessarily approve of similar behavior in others, however. For a *Time* magazine dinner in 1998, President Clinton wanted Joe, "radiant in his bespoke Pierre Cardin tuxedo" (Cramer, *Joe DiMaggio*, 480), to be seated at the Clinton table. But "DiMaggio loathed Clinton. Hated his style. And that Monica Lewinsky! That was not up to the standard. (As Joe pointed out to some pals: 'You know, we paid for that White House. He shouldn't be doing that there.')" Joe wound up sitting between "Hank" and Nancy Kissinger, who (after prompting from Doc Positano) had asked Joe to sit with them—providing an excuse so the president wouldn't feel dissed. Across the table were Mel Brooks and Anne Bancroft, also Joe's friends. When Joe wondered how planners came up with that arrangement, Doc replied: "Joe—get it? They sat DiMaggio with Mrs. Robinson!" Cramer, 481.

22. *Quoted* at https://www.inspiringquotes.us/author/4575-joe-dimaggio. (He made the same point many times using varied language.) But see supra note 11 (noting DiMaggio's lack of enthusiasm in the military). Appearances used to matter in politics too. See Sam Knight, "The Astonishing Rise of Jeremy Corbyn: Enter Left," *The New Yorker*, May 23, 2016 (discussing Jeremy Corbyn, Labour leader and potential prime minister, at a rally: "The man next to me, a Labour councilor from Kent, whispered, 'Why the bloody hell doesn't he have a bloody tie on?'"), https://www.newyorker.com/magazine/2016/05/23/theastonishing-rise-of-jeremy-corbyn. But overdoing conservative dress can create problems. *See* Monica Langley, "Iowa Touches Off a Free-for-All: Romney's Best-Laid Plans Mugged by Political Realities," *Wall Street Journal*, January 5–6, 2008 (county co-chair "cringes when [Mitt Romney] wears his 'CEO uniform' of a suit rather than a more casual sweater. 'He comes across as cold and regimented, not warm and fuzzy.'"), https://www.wsj.com/articles/SB119949556092669169.

23. Wrong. Looking like a real doctor reassures patients.

24. Steven D. Levitt & Stephen J. Dubner, *Super Freakonomics* (New York: William Morrow, 2009), 207. But the offending garment isn't ties qua ties. Long sleeves may also be problematic. See Rachael Rettner, "Long Sleeves on Doctors' White Coats May Spread Germs," *Scientific*

American, October 14, 2017, https://www.scientificamerican.com/article/long-sleeves-on-doctors-white-coats-may-spread-germs/. The UK has adopted a "bare below the elbow policy" for hospital staff. *Id*. (I hope that means below the elbow *on the arm*.)

25. He may well have been, and may be again. *See infra* note 37 and accompanying text.

26. Ben Bradlee Jr., *The Kid: The Immortal Life of Ted Williams* (New York: Little Brown, 2013), 594 (emphasis added). In Ernest Hemingway's *The Old Man and the Sea* (New York: Scribner, 1952), Santiago, the old man, repeatedly referred to DiMaggio as the "great DiMaggio." Santiago's father had been a fisherman, "as was the father of the great DiMaggio." Unlike Williams, however, as a fisherman's son DiMaggio wasn't hooked by fishing. For one thing, fish smell.

27. Some incidents described in his autobiographical works are apocryphal, however. See Warren Corbett, "Bill Veeck," SABR Biography Project, https://sabr.org/bioproj/person/7b0b5f10. Veeck may not have been as much a maverick as he wanted people to think.

28. Paul Dickson, *Bill Veeck: Baseball's Greatest Maverick* (New York: Walker & Co., 2012), 60.

29. Leigh Montville, *Ted Williams: The Biography of an American Hero* (2004), 339; see also Herm Krabbenhoft, "The Complete Collegiate Baseball Record of President George H. W. Bush," *Baseball Research Journal* 46, no. 2 (Fall 2017).

30. Montville. The details of the story vary from telling to telling, but the basics are true.

31. Bradlee, *The Kid*, 631.

32. Bradlee. Dowd had done legal work for Ted. He later investigated Pete Rose's gambling for Major League Baseball, and, from June 2017 until March 22, 2018, was President Donald Trump's lead counsel in connection with the investigation into Russian meddling in the 2016 election. (Dowd apparently drafted a presidential tweet or two during that period.)

33. That happened later too. *See infra* note 37 and accompanying text.

34. Positano & Positano, *Dinner With DiMaggio*, 159.

35. Positano & Positano.

36. Positano & Positano.

37. Montville, *Ted Williams*, 455–56; Bradlee, *The Kid*, 750–52; see also David Hancock, "Ted Williams Frozen in Two Pieces," CBS News, December 20, 2002, https://www.cbsnews.com/news/ted-williams-frozen-in-two-pieces. It was said that Ted as a hitter had ice water in his veins. That's now close to being literally true.

38. That's the baseball guy, not the senator who was indirectly responsible for the Cincinnati Reds' being known as the Redlegs for several years in the 1950s.

39. Bradlee, *The Kid*, 295.

40. Bradley, 602.

41. Dickson, *Bill Veeck*, 169.

42. Dickson, 94.

43. Almost. In 1951, because of hotel rules, Veeck "had to put on a necktie to…close the deal to buy the St. Louis Browns." Dickson, 185 (quoting real estate developer). *He had to dress up to buy the worst team in baseball*!

44. Jeffrey Toobin, "No More Mr. Nice Guy," *The New Yorker*, May 25, 2009, https://www.newyorker.com/ magazine/2009/05/25/no-more-mr-nice-guy.

45. Robin Givhan, "Trial by Attire: Supreme Court look should go with everything we believe in," *Washington Post*, October 9, 2010, http://www.washingtonpost.com/wp-dyn/content/article/2010/10/08/AR2010100806588.html. For a stupid analysis of judicial attire, see Erik M. Jensen, "Under the Robes: A Judicial Right to Bare Arms (and Legs and…)?" *The Green Bag*, 2d 221 (2009), http://www.greenbag.org/v12n2/v12n2_jensen.pdf.

46. "[N]o [Court] rule requir[es] robes, though it is hard to recall any justice breaking from the tradition." John Eligon, "Behind the Gavel, a Sense of Style," *The New York Times*, September 6, 2008, http:// www.nytimes.com/2008/09/06/nyregion/06robes.html. Do the justices clean their robes regularly? See supra note 24 and accompanying text.

47. Tony Mauro, "Reluctant Rehnquist Chief justice in spotlight he'd just as soon avoid," *USA Today*, January 7, 1999, https://advance.lexis.com/document/?pdmfid=1000516&crid=c0fb4d9c-29ba-45a6-a708-575c38248eaa&pddocfullpath=%2Fshared%2Fdocument%2Fnews%2Furn%3AcontentItem%3A3V H0-XTF0-00C6-D4HG-00000-00&pddocid=urn%3AcontentItem%3A3VH0-XTF0-00C6- D4HG-00000-00&pdcontentcomponentid=8213&pdteaserkey=sr1&pditab=allpods&ecomp=tyffk&earg=sr 1&prid=f524e3eb-2ca4-4557-bb04-f2c49cbe6a77; see also Joan Biskupic, "Enforcing the Sartorial Code," *Washington Post*, December 6, 1999, ("Since then, women in the solicitor general's office have worn black."), http://www.washingtonpost.com/wp-srv/WPcap/1999-12/06/008r-120699-idx.html. (For the record: I think brown is okay.)

48. Adam Liptak, "This Bench Belongs in a Dugout," *The New York Times*, May 31, 2010, http:// www.nytimes.com/2010/06/01/us/01bar.html.

49. Named for Aaron Judge, who, when healthy, is seldom on the bench.

Contributors

SARA ANDRASIK is a recent graduate of Central Michigan University's Applied Statistics and Data Analytics program. During her undergraduate time at Grand Valley State University, she helped lead the softball team to two World Series appearances as a pitcher.

GARY BELLEVILLE is a retired Information Technology professional living in Victoria, British Columbia. He spent seven years as an editor and lead writer for baseball blogs devoted to local independent league and college wood-bat teams. Gary served as an official scorer in the West Coast League for two seasons, and he worked for the Asheville Tourists in the South Atlantic League. He grew up in Ottawa and graduated from the University of Waterloo with a Bachelor of Mathematics (Computer Science) degree. He patiently awaits the return of his beloved Montreal Expos.

RYAN BORGEMENKE Ryan Borgemenke is a second year medical student and holds a bachelor's degree in chemical engineering. He is a lifelong Reds fan from Mason, Ohio and has been a SABR member since 2018. His interest in WAR goes back to 2013 when he first learned of sabermetrics.

STEVE BRATKOVICH, a native of Pennsylvania, is a retired forester and wood products specialist with the US Forest Service and Dovetail Partners, Inc. He currently lives in St. Paul with his wife of 42 years. Steve is a member of the Halsey Hall Chapter of SABR. He is the author of *Bob Oldis: A Life in Baseball*, which chronicles the on-and-off-field tribulations of a major league catcher, coach, and scout. Steve's next book will focus on MLB bats. Steve roots for the Twins and Pirates and can be contacted at sbratkovich@comcast.net.

WARREN CORBETT is the author of "The Wizard of Waxahachie: Paul Richards and the End of Baseball as We Knew It" and a contributor to SABR's BioProject. He is a 2018 winner of the McFarland-SABR Baseball Research Award.

JOHN CRONIN has been a SABR member since 1985 and has previously published several articles in *The Baseball Research Journal*. He serves on the Minor League Committee and its Farm Club Subcommittee. His current research efforts are pre-1930 farm clubs. Cronin is a lifelong Yankee fan with an MBA in Accounting from St. John's University. Cronin resides in New Providence, NJ, and can be reached at jcroninjr@verizon.net.

JOHN DANIELS is an Associate Professor of Statistics at Central Michigan University. A lifelong Detroit Tigers fan, John never knew all those years spent playing Strat-o-matic in the basement would amount to something so useful or so enjoyable.

ROB EDELMAN teaches film history courses at the University at Albany. He is the author of *Great Baseball Films* and *Baseball on the Web*, and is co-author (with his wife, Audrey Kupferberg) of *Meet the Mertzes*, a double biography of *I Love Lucy*'s Vivian Vance and famed baseball fan William Frawley, and *Matthau: A Life*. He is a frequent contributor to *Base Ball: A Journal of the Early Game* and has written for *Baseball and American Culture: Across the Diamond*, *Total Baseball*, *Baseball in the Classroom*, *Memories and Dreams*, and *NINE*.

JAMES K. FLACK retired from the University of Maryland in 2004 after 37 years teaching American History and, between 1982 and 2000, being an assistant baseball coach. Prior to that he had similar high school responsibilities in Michigan where he also coached an American Legion team. Since 1966 he and his family have lived in Washington, D.C. (Bob Davids was a neighbor). In 1985, he received a SABR membership as a birthday present. That gift led in large part to his research on Deacon McGuire.

DAVID J. GORDON, is a native Chicagoan who grew up in the 1950s within earshot of Wrigley Field. After graduating from the University of Chicago, he moved to Chevy Chase, MD and spent 43 years in public health and biomedical research at the National Institutes of Health. In retirement, he has come full circle to write a historical book on major league baseball and its greatest players. Dr. Gordon is married (Susan) and has two adult children (Sam and Emily).

RICHARD HERSHBERGER writes on early baseball history. He has published in various SABR publications, and *in Base Ball: A Journal of the Early Game*. He is a paralegal in Maryland.

DAVID HOOLEY is a recent graduate of Central Michigan University's Master's in Applied Statistics and Data Analytics program. He is currently employed as a data analyst.

ERIK M. JENSEN is Coleman P. Burke Professor Emeritus of Law, Case Western Reserve University.

SARAH JOHNSON is a member of the Halsey Hall chapter of SABR and a Minnesota-based freelance writer who covers history, sports and travel for a variety of publications.

DOUGLAS JORDAN is a professor at Sonoma State University in Northern California where he teaches corporate finance and investments. He's been a SABR member since 2012. He runs marathons when not watching or writing about baseball. You can contact him at douglas.jordan@sonoma.edu.

LAURA SCHRECK is an administrator at a high school in the San Francisco Bay Area. A graduate of UC Berkeley with a degree in Rhetoric, she went on to receive Master's degrees in Education and Sport Management from Loyola Marymount University and University of San Francisco respectively. She interned with the World Champion San Francisco Giants during the 2012 season.

ERIC SICKLES is a graduate student studying Sport Management at the University of San Francisco. He completed his B.A. in History in 2016 at Purdue University Northwest where he played collegiate baseball. He currently works for the San Francisco Giants as the Special Events Intern.

DAVID W. SMITH joined SABR in 1977 and has made research presentations at 22 national SABR conventions. In 2001 at SABR31, he won the USA Today Sports Weekly Award for his presentation on the 1951 NL pennant race. In 2016 he won the Doug Pappas Award for his presentation on closers. In 2005 he received SABR's highest honor, the Bob Davids Award, and in 2012 he was honored with the Henry Chadwick award. He is founder and president of Retrosheet and an Emeritus Professor of Biology at the University of Delaware.

STEVE STEINBERG is a baseball historian of the early twentieth century. He has co-authored two award-winning books with Lyle Spatz, *1921* and *The Colonel and Hug*. His Urban Shocker biography was awarded the 2018 SABR Baseball Research Award. His latest book, *The World Series in the Deadball Era*, is a joint effort of SABR's Deadball Era Committee. Steve has also published more than 20 articles, many in SABR journals.

Society for American Baseball Research

Cronkite School at ASU
555 N. Central Ave. #416, Phoenix, AZ 85004
602.496.1460 (phone)
SABR.org

Become a SABR member today!

If you're interested in baseball — writing about it, reading about it, talking about it — there's a place for you in the Society for American Baseball Research. Our members include everyone from academics to professional sportswriters to amateur historians and statisticians to students and casual fans who enjoy reading about baseball and occasionally gathering with other members to talk baseball. What unites all SABR members is an interest in the game and joy in learning more about it.

SABR membership is open to any baseball fan; we offer 1-year and 3-year memberships. Here's a list of some of the key benefits you'll receive as a SABR member:

- Receive two editions (spring and fall) of the *Baseball Research Journal*, our flagship publication
- Receive expanded e-book edition of *The National Pastime*, our annual convention journal
- 8-10 new e-books published by the SABR Digital Library, all FREE to members
- "This Week in SABR" e-newsletter, sent to members every Friday
- Join dozens of research committees, from Statistical Analysis to Women in Baseball.
- Join one of 70+ regional chapters in the U.S., Canada, Latin America, and abroad
- Participate in online discussion groups
- Ask and answer baseball research questions on the SABR-L e-mail listserv
- Complete archives of *The Sporting News* dating back to 1886 and other research resources
- Promote your research in "This Week in SABR"
- Diamond Dollars Case Competition
- Yoseloff Scholarships

- Discounts on SABR national conferences, including the SABR National Convention, the SABR Analytics Conference, Jerry Malloy Negro League Conference, Frederick Ivor-Campbell 19th Century Conference, and the Arizona Fall League Experience
- Publish your research in peer-reviewed SABR journals
- Collaborate with SABR researchers and experts
- Contribute to Baseball Biography Project or the SABR Games Project
- List your new book in the SABR Bookshelf
- Lead a SABR research committee or chapter
- Networking opportunities at SABR Analytics Conference
- Meet baseball authors and historians at SABR events and chapter meetings
- 50% discounts on paperback versions of SABR e-books
- Discounts with other partners in the baseball community
- SABR research awards

We hope you'll join the most passionate international community of baseball fans at SABR! Check us out online at SABR.org/join.

 -

SABR MEMBERSHIP FORM

	Annual	3-year	Senior	3-yr Sr.	Under 30
Standard:	❏ $65	❏ $175	❏ $45	❏ $129	❏ $45
(International members wishing to be mailed the Baseball Research Journal should add $10/yr for Canada/Mexico or $19/yr for overseas locations.)					
Canada/Mexico:	❏ $75	❏ $205	❏ $55	❏ $159	❏ $55
Overseas:	❏ $84	❏ $232	❏ $64	❏ $186	❏ $55
Senior = 65 or older before Dec. 31 of the current year					

Participate in Our Donor Program!

Support the preservation of baseball research. Designate your gift toward:
❏ General Fund   ❏ Endowment Fund   ❏ Research Resources   ❏ _____
❏ I want to maximize the impact of my gift; do not send any donor premiums
❏ I would like this gift to remain anonymous.

Note: Any donation not designated will be placed in the General Fund.
SABR is a 501 (c) (3) not-for-profit organization & donations are tax-deductible to the extent allowed by law.

Name _____

E-mail* _____

Address _____

City _____ ST_____ ZIP_____

Phone _____ Birthday _____

* Your e-mail address on file ensures you will receive the most recent SABR news.

Dues $_____

Donation $_____

Amount Enclosed $_____

Do you work for a matching grant corporation? Call (602) 496-1460 for details.

If you wish to pay by credit card, please contact the SABR office at (602) 496-1460 or sign up securely online at SABR.org/join. We accept Visa, Mastercard & Discover.

Do you wish to receive the *Baseball Research Journal* electronically? ❏ Yes   ❏ No
Our e-books are available in PDF, Kindle, or EPUB (iBooks, iPad, Nook) formats.

Mail to: SABR, Cronkite School at ASU, 555 N. Central Ave. #416, Phoenix, AZ 85004